Dr Terry Wells is a life-long bir & Business Services having gained a Dj Imperial College, and an MBA from in Wiltshire with his two sons, Harry ..., Mary, but grew up in Tottenham, London in the 1960s. As a boy Terry was an amateur boxer, excelled at sports but was most at home exploring the wildlife of Haringey Marshes and reservoirs.

Moving to Gloucester, aged 14, Terry met new characters that would ignite and shape his passion for birds, twitching them across the country, sharing cars, sleeping rough. A successful career and overseas appointments constrained this passion until in 2017, aged 57, frustrated by work-politics and ill health, Terry quit his job to begin a new chapter. Having been inspired in the 1980s by books like Richard Millington's *A Twitcher's Diary*, and Bill Oddie and David Tomlinson's *The Big Bird Race*, Terry was in no doubt that his first retirement challenge would be to see as many birds as possible in Britain in one year! Three hundred birds was the benchmark for Britain's top birders, and so the goal was set.

A BIRDER'S JOURNEY
TO THE
BIG 300+

TERRY WELLS

SilverWood

Published in 2019 by SilverWood Books

SilverWood Books Ltd
14 Small Street, Bristol, BS1 1DE, United Kingdom
www.silverwoodbooks.co.uk

ISBN 978-1-78132-862-0

British Library Cataloguing in Publication Data
A CIP catalogue record for this book is available from the British Library

Page design and typesetting by SilverWood Books
Printed by TJ International on responsibly sourced paper

This book is dedicated foremost to my mother, Betty, who recognised the beauty of the natural world and provided love and warmth up until her passing during the writing of this book; to my father, Ken, who has always counselled and supported me whatever my chosen pursuit; to my partner, Mary, for tolerating my absences, enduring endless birding conversation and staring at bushes for long hours with me on numerous occasions. Mary proved to be a gifted bird spotter too. Finally, to my two sons, Harry and Ollie, for whom I have not been the home-maker perhaps I should have been during this past year; still they have learnt to cook at least if not yet to do a little housework!

Contents

Photographs

1   Photographs from guest photographers were taken on the date indicated in the caption beneath each. Those dates may not coincide with the date upon which the species was seen by the author but do portray the exact same bird, in the same location.

Tables

2   Bird lists comply with IOC and BOU naming conventions at the time of writing. Checklist versions used are indicated for each list.

Introduction

Am I crazy? It's the 15th of November 2017. Only a week ago I was working in the somewhat grey world of IT services. In fact, I'd only joined the company UiPath in September seeking to re-ignite lost motivation and bolster earnings in my run up to retirement. I don't think I ever truly loved IT, but it had paid me well and so at the age of 57, and considering a bout of recent ill health, retirement had become a realistic option. What does this have to do with chasing a large British Bird list? Well, for most of our lives, in the need to strive, earn, succeed and care for our loved ones, we rarely grab the chance to do what we truly love. Lying in the back of an ambulance in Amsterdam having been embarrassingly stretchered from a conference with my suit on, I vowed I would begin to live this one life while I still can. So, in short, my target retirement age of 60 was brought forward to a youthful 57…well 58 by the time my company notice period was concluded!

So, let's consider for a moment. You give up work, you regain health and now you need a project, unless, of course, you are a daytime TV fanatic! Suddenly, a long-standing hobby of seeking out and identifying rare birds looks an attractive prospect. You have the passion, the motivation, some half-decent knowledge, but why the goal of 300? How did birds become the focus of my pastime endeavours? Is it possible perhaps to flip my world on its head, turn a hobby into a fulltime sustainable activity, perhaps with a small income even? After all my financial reserves are certainly not limitless and I do have dependent offspring.

The fact is life is an uncertain journey as we all know but if you don't move yourself to a place where you might be able to enjoy it to the full then you are unlikely to achieve fulfilment.

Enough of the Philosophy! Here is my journey, *A Birder's Journey to the BIG 300+*. I hope you enjoy it whether you are a birder, birdwatcher, twitcher, photographer or none of the above.

Early Days

Being brought up in Tottenham, London, aged 10 or 11, to me excitement meant exploring local marshes, wading across the old River Lee and scrambling up the banks of the local reservoirs cautiously on the lookout for water bailiffs who regularly patrolled in a white van. Herons, grebes, kingfishers and even the thorny larder of the Red-backed Shrike could be found. It was there I became generally interested in wildlife, dragonflies, birds, butterflies, fish and, frankly, whatever we happened upon. I just got curious. How did they work? What made things alive as opposed to inanimate? I might be accompanied by a catapult, a bicycle, a bamboo stick for a fishing rod, depending on the prevailing interest and present company.

As a working-class cockney my only other engagement with the countryside were visits to my Grandad, who lived in Wannock near Eastbourne, or my uncle's farm in Chipping Norton, Cotswolds. While the family would engage in pleasant conversation and cakes with my Nan, my Grandad would take me into the garage and ask what bamboo cane I would like. After all, every adventurer needs a sword for protection, doesn't he? He, like me, was a fidget and probably welcomed the escape as much as I did. He knew I'd walk anywhere with him if I had a stick to sword-fence the large thistles that threatened to choke the local footpaths. Our mission was simple, to reach the top of the hills which made up the South Downs. "Just up this hill and we can see for miles, beautiful views," he would say. I was about 6–8 years old, so every hill was big and, as became apparent as we reached the next rise, another rose before us again and again like some foreboding mirage. In fact, I'm not certain we ever did get to the top. Along the way my Grandad would point out flowers and bugs. He was a knowledgeable gardener and kept a showcase garden. I can still picture its manicured borders, bees everywhere feasting on a banquet of nectar; wall to wall colour on all borders. That was his passion, gardening and vegetable growing.

Visits to Chipping Norton were a different affair. Armed with a small air pistol, I'd explore the barns looking for targets or accompany my cousin and father across the fields, cold and welly-wearing in search of crows/rooks, which were apparently the enemy. "They kill lambs, you know!" I was told as the rooks erupted from the rookery knowing it was time to make themselves scarce. In fact, in true West Oxfordshire accent the famed expression from my Uncle Wally was "them crows knows, you know" alluding no doubt to the guile and cunning attributed to corvids. They certainly outsmarted us as I don't remember a single kill, and, in any case, it was more the wild exploration, seek and find game that interested me.

The guilt of 1970

My keen interest in bird habits and behaviour was sparked by a school friend who, rather than looking for birds, spent time looking for birds' nests. His nickname was Robo. To be honest he was considered somewhat unreliable, a torment at school, but he was a charismatic "tale-teller" and he knew a lot more about birds than the rest of us did. He had a great instinct for nest locations and could climb like a monkey – skills no doubt honed by his need to escape those he'd tormented! Yes, like many from this era, including a few respected conservationists and TV celebrities, I am embarrassed to say egg collecting was often the focus of sunny days spent roaming Tottenham marshes. None of us knew the position of the law for sure, then set down under the Protection of Birds Act 1954. It was not as though the Headmaster of my school, Down Lane Junior School, would stand up at Assembly, clear his throat and exclaim "You boys, and we know who you are, must stop egg collecting or face the full force of the law!" Had he done so, we would have quaked in our boots and gone back to bike riding or football in the park. In short, egg collecting was hardly mainstream news. Until, that is, some years later hefty fines handed out to professional egg collectors made the six o'clock news, and a good thing too. The attraction for us juniors had rather been to sneak in to unfamiliar places: to seek, find and collect a trophy (evidence). A sort of commando raid. The mischievousness of it proved all too tempting to a bunch of oiks aged 9–11 who did not possess a pair of binoculars or camera between them. Indeed, the term conservation, the RSPB, and bird reserves would have meant nothing to us.

I am happy to say that my egging phase, as it was then referred to, was short-lived. The distress to the birds was evident to me early on. Too many eager hands scrambled for the delicate but fascinating eggs, which often did not make it home in one piece. Sometimes I would return to the nest in the hope of seeing it re-occupied, business as usual for the parent, in order to satisfy myself no damage had been done. Sadly, that was rarely the case. Nests were unoccupied; the guilt was palpable. The solution then became not to go egging but to swap various unwanted items – sweets, toys – for eggs, with an elder lad. He was something of a loner, had gathered an impressive egg collection but had seemingly lost interest in it. So, my meagre half dozen eggs shortly became a peer-impressing c.70!

Moving On

For me, eggs remained scientifically fascinating, a bird's thumbprint to diet and location, uniquely shaped to suit habitat and circumstance. By the age of 12, I'd learnt quite a bit about bird's eggs from my little *The Observer's Book of Birds' Eggs* by G. Evans, which still adorns my bookshelf to this day, but it was the book that sat alongside it, *The Observer's Book of Birds* by S Vere Benson, that really began to grab my interest!

Progressing into my teens, new friends and pastimes, music and the awakening interest in the opposite sex dominated. While dealing with a bout of glandular fever aged 13, which I was embarrassingly informed was known as "kissing disease", I found myself in a hospital isolation ward for two weeks (glandular fever is highly contagious). Using crayons, I began to copy the tiny birds of prey from Benson's book to produce large A4-sized drawings. I was a reasonable copy artist but with no real talent. As I read more about Merlin, Peregrine and Hobby I longed to track these birds down in some faraway wild place; what adventures I would have in the mountains and valleys stalking them! Those little pictures were portals to the future that I enjoy today.

Moving away from London to the fresh open countryside of Gloucestershire aged 14 in 1974, I found myself with few new friends. As such, I often wandered the fields, sometimes with an airgun, shooting posts and cans in the coursing streams close by, or simply enjoying the freedoms of the open space in what was a safer location than the marshes of London. The greenery was endless. Streams, orchards, gnarled trees frequented by water voles, badgers, foxes, little owls, woodpeckers, buzzards and, yes, the occasional angry farmer who took aversion to my trespass with an airgun. The place was alive with wildlife right on my doorstep but even then, I was acutely aware of the creeping expanse of new housing, the edge of which was embodied by our recently purchased, seemingly sizeable, four-bedroomed house. Often out till dark, I'd take an old BSA Meteor gun, roaming the fields and finding targets to shoot. I had little interest in shooting live things, having experienced the remorse of once shooting a Blue Tit. An impressive shot brought the bird still flapping with distress or nervous activity crashing to my feet. It upset me and I still recall the event vividly. It was a hugely important lesson. No, empty shotgun cartridges weighted by their brass cap and bobbing in a fast-running stream, upturned bottles, and floating cans were challenging targets enough. This presented hours of fun as I fast reloaded my air rifle sometimes shooting from the hip before the stream carried the enemy out of range and to safety. Much of the time, though, I was trying to see owls and in the twilight the airgun helped me cope with the fear of darkness. Little Owls seemed to be calling everywhere. They had a huge variety of calls, too. One lazy sunny afternoon I stumbled across 3 fluffy owlets on a branch. Startled, they fell into the wheat field below. Concerned, I began chasing the young birds around to try and set them back on the branch. It was hopeless, as soon as I caught one bird and set it back on the branch another fluttered straight back into the tall wheat. It was like a game from the TV series *It's a Knockout* with a leaky bucket with which to complete the task of filling a water tank.

And the light shone

Looking back, what happened next was a huge wakeup call for which I am eternally grateful. The English teacher at Saintbridge Boy's School had asked that we make a short presentation to the class: about a hobby/pastime, perhaps. I was by now aged 16, somewhat self-conscious and so understandably mortified by the thought of having to make a presentation to my new schoolmates (not realising of course that I would make hundreds of presentations in years to come). I floundered around for ideas as I had no hobby to speak of. Then Eureka! I dusted down my old, somewhat tired, egg collection, checked to see if I could recall what each species of egg was that I had. Yes, conveniently, eggs would be the prop for my pitch and at least divert most of the attention from me. Great plan! The day came and sure enough the English class were duly enthused with my collection but keeping the mischievous hands off the dusty eggs was something of a challenge. Except that one guy seemed put out by my moment of fame and proceeded to lambast me for my evil practice of egg collecting. While I could not disagree with him my only rebuttal was that this was something I had pursued at the young age of 10–11 and most were, well, "swapsies". Understandably perhaps, that did not seem to cut much slack. The person in question was Nigel Wheatley, now a successful world-renowned author of a series of "Where to Watch" bird books, and similarly named website providing extensive advice and guidance on where and how to see birds around the world.

At that time Nigel was one of a handful of friends I'd made at Saintbridge Boys School in Gloucester. Nigel was a quiet, somewhat charismatic guy, studious, taller than me and a pretty good cross-country runner, too, I recall. Nigel was clearly building his interest in birds and was embracing the idea of conservation at that young age. Nigel's mother managed to secure me a part-time job at WH Smiths where Nigel worked on Saturdays in the record department. As such, Nigel and I became good friends and in the months that followed it became clear that Nigel was very much into his birds. Occasionally he would point out a good-value book in the WH Smith's sale that might interest me. One such book was the *Dictionary of Birds in Colour* by Bruce Campbell that is still in pristine condition and sits on my bookshelf to this day. It has the most amazing photos but sadly was of limited use as a bird identification guide. Despite this, I still recall spending most of my Saturday earnings from WH Smiths on golf clubs from Woolworths, buying them one at a time. Sadly, most never saw more than a pitch and putt course or a field, as the cost of golfing memberships and lack of transport were somewhat prohibitive.

So, It Begins

I simply could not understand what motivated Nigel in his quest for birds. What exactly was he collecting – feathers, photos? There must be something. The presumption probably came from the fact that most hobbies entailed collecting something tangible that could be displayed as evidence of success. I began cycling to Nigel's house. He lived conveniently at the base of Robinswood Hill, Gloucester a couple of miles away. This, Nigel informed me, was his "local patch". That was a new term to me, I mean he didn't own it, did he? Armed with my father's pristine 10x50 Zenith binoculars, we rambled all over that hill on many an occasion. Nigel began alerting me to calls: "that's a Pheasant."

"How do you know?" I replied.

"It's obvious; sounds like an old car horn."

At some point we proceeded to chase a tit across open space and fallen trees: "Coal Tit!"

"Why's it not a Great Tit?" I asked.

"Paler, buff colour, white patch on back of head, *witchu* call."

"Couldn't it just be a dirty Great Tit that's good at mimicry?" I cynically replied. I was sceptical, after all there was no proof, was there?

This went on for many months. We scoured the hill finding goodies such as Grasshopper Warbler and even a Ring Ouzel on a recently laid golf course green. In fact, some days I would arrive at Nigel's house finding that he had somewhat frustratingly gone on ahead, leaving no details of his whereabouts with his mother. "He's gone up the hill... I think." "When, where?" I'd spend hours searching, torn between looking for Nigel and new birds that I needed his help to identify. Eventually, Walmore Common, Frampton-on-Severn, Witcombe reservoirs and even the further down-river Slimbridge formed part of our hunting grounds.

The bottom line is, I was hooked! The frustration of seeing what could be a rare bird but not being 100% sure, was overwhelming. At the end of the day you know how sure you are, or not, and it does help to have others present at the time of sighting to build consensus, agree/confirm the identification, as we know. Not collecting a material thing (egg, feather, photo) thus brought a whole new dimension, a level of intrigue to the hobby. It soon became apparent that jizz, calls, weather, location, accompanying species, timing, were key to identification, as well of course as the features and habits displayed by the bird. Diligence and pre-preparation were essential, or the result was plain frustration... the one that got away. In short, the more you put in, the more you got out. It was bitter sweet. Frustrations were many and often. I would describe a bird to Nigel and he would question me on key features I had not confirmed, taking my excitement of finding a new bird down to a new low. At times I felt like an underperforming apprentice. I began to learn the three or four characteristics that would combine to provide definitive identification. The challenge then became to compute that in the two-second view that birds often afford their observer, while simultaneously trying to get on target with my unwieldy Zeniths.

The list became the definitive measure of success. Garden lists, day lists, patch lists, life lists; there seemed to be no end. I recall that I was often being scolded for putting, say, Tree Sparrow down at Frampton lakes when clearly none were seen. In short, I'd conveniently assumed we must have seen some because after all sparrows are everywhere, aren't they? It became clear the list was sacrosanct, there was no room for personal doubt, or it was pointless. You had to be your own conscience and even until recently I have had to reluctantly remove birds from my life list that, looking back, I am no longer happy with. You know, the brown blob that some presumptuous birder tells you is definitely a rarity as it disappears over the hedge in fading light! I still experience such "groupthink" today on twitches. I liken it to the boardroom where a confident Director robustly spouts a conclusion and while those around ponder, silence is taken to be a vote of confidence.

Separate ways

As time passed Nigel and I went our separate ways. I went off to the University of Surrey and after a few ventures Nigel ended up at Portsmouth Polytechnic. As a biochemist the burden of scientific study, beer, girls and the lack of kindred birding spirits seemed to spell closure on this chapter for me. The extent of my birding was largely constrained to the wilds of Gloucestershire during college vacations given a lack of transport and funds, and I was no longer listing. Following the completion of final degree exams and with only a dissertation to complete in the remaining nine weeks of college, I drove to the New Forest one evening alone. Yes, I had managed to pass my driving test aged 20 and could just about afford to run an old banger, in this case a bright yellow Vauxhall Viva 1256 cc that my parents had bought me, affectionately known by all as the yellow submarine! I parked up in the forest after having a beer at a country pub by a river and promptly fell asleep in the car, exhausted from studying, only to be woken by the dawn chorus of late spring. Boy, I had missed this. There are few places better in Britain to listen to a dawn chorus than the New Forest. The wide variety of species and pure beauty of the location in late spring/early summer is mesmerising.

Suddenly, in 1982, an encounter with Nigel back in Gloucester over the summer, probably going for a beer with a few old school friends, really rekindled my interest. Now with transport, I guess I was handy transport for my birding buddy too. Ospreys at Chew Valley,

Hobbies at South Cerney, Nightingales at Lower Slaughter and the hot sites of Radipole, Lodmoor, Portland Bill, Pagham Harbour, Farlington Marshes and even the giddy reserves of Norfolk: Cley, Titchwell, Wells and Holkham fell within range. In fact, we were now really twitching: a first for Britain, a Little Whimbrel at Kenfig! Even so I confess my bird list was still no more than a couple of hundred species at this point though I'd started to pick up some half-decent ticks: Squacco Heron at Radipole; Glaucous Gull, Spotted Crake at Cley; Firecrest at Pagham Harbour; Snow Bunting at Staines; Osprey at Chew Lake.

As summer closed Nigel and I went our separate ways again and I was now at Imperial College, London, studying for a PhD in Biochemistry. Re-energised, I continued to bird alone in 1983 and Staines reservoirs became the focus of my attention. In fact, my notes showed I visited Staines reservoirs no fewer than 22 times that year, mixed in with some grey cold early spring days at Dungeness and Stodmarsh in Kent, and the odd trip to Pagham, which on one occasion rewarded me with a trio of Cirl Buntings along the shingle! Staines was within easy reach of my digs in Putney, so I could afford the fuel, just. It was here I learnt the value of patience and local knowledge. Staines could be a bland draughty watch, in part looking through iron railings. Conversation with fellow birders was highly valued in order to pass the time. I began to build a small circle of contacts and to learn from my fellow birders. Only when the reservoirs were drained, exposing a muddy basin, did the place really jump to life, yielding scarce waders, Snow Buntings, and a variety of divers and grebes. On 17th September 1983 I was rewarded with a Wilson's Phalarope, a beautiful elegant bird. My records show that a Pratincole Sp., Kentish Plover, Red-throated Pipit and Baird's Sandpiper put in brief appearances there the same year. Even as I write, there is a Horned Lark showing there on my RBA Alert Pro mobile phone application. Such is the now ever-increasing trend to denote the correct subspecies which in this case would be our better-known Shore Lark.

1984 vintage

On 27th December 1983 I birded again with Nigel at Slimbridge while on University Christmas break. It was of course the Christmas vacation and nowhere better locally to go than the now much-expanded WWT centre to freeze for a while in the draughty Holden Tower. Then in 1984 we really upped the tempo. What I learnt that year was the power of a good network, given the web and mobiles weren't around. Companionship and circumstance can make for some happy memories, too. In short, the birds were the stars, my colleagues the cast of actors, the location and habitat provided the beautiful stage and backdrop. The fact that I used three notebooks that year bears testament to my growing passion for birds and full-on entry into the world of twitching, i.e. pursuing and ticking off rare birds across the country like a man possessed. Telephone numbers of key contacts would fill the back pages of my notebook (the grapevine). Sketches and drawings of rare birds, some illustrating their anatomy, would adorn my notebooks, or, a photograph of some brightly coloured bird would be Sellotaped to the cover. It was as though I was trying to immerse myself feverishly in some addictive entity. More than 50 key locations were visited that year, some repeatedly. There were many good year ticks and my British life list started to look respectable: Red-breasted Goose; Glossy Ibis; White-tailed Eagle; Little Bittern; Ferruginous Duck; Montagu's Harrier; Rough-legged Buzzard; Lady Amherst's Pheasant; Crane; Spotted Crake; Kentish Plover; Dotterel; Stone-curlew; Semipalmated, Least, Pectoral, Broad-billed, Marsh, Solitary, Wood, Spotted Sandpipers (obviously a good year for sandpipers!); Grey Phalarope; Iceland, Glaucous, Ross's Gulls; Puffin; Long-eared Owl; Hoopoe; Wryneck; Lesser Spotted Woodpecker; Shore and Woodlarks; Olive-backed Pipit; Thrush Nightingale; Swainson's Thrush; Ring Ouzel; Blythe's Reed, Great Reed, Barred; Icterine; Melodious; Yellow-browed Warblers; Red-breasted Flycatcher; Golden Oriole; Isabelline, Red-backed and Great Grey Shrikes; Chough; Twite; Parrot Crossbill; Blackpoll Warbler; Yellowthroat; Lapland and Snow Buntings, etc.

Others had joined our collective few. One was a tallish, clean-cut lad, Nick (nicknamed Chief I recall, though I never quite worked out why) and yet another Nigel and another Nick…just to confuse things.

Crazy days. I recall on one occasion in mid-February sleeping in the bus shelter at Cley in a bitter winter north wind – not a good idea to be in a cocoon sleeping bag when you have had several beers at the local tavern before bedtime! On another occasion I recall we planned to meet at a pub in Weymouth. The aim, of course, was to catch the early spring migrants on Portland. Sadly, I arrived around 11p.m., pub closing time. Nigel and his friend "Chief" were nowhere to be seen! With no money or transport, and not certain what to do, I trudged to Portland. I can still remember crunching on hundreds of snails that traverse the poorly lit Portland Beach Road, which connects Portland to the mainland, at night. I felt desolate, let down. I was completely soaked, tired and frustrated. Oddly, to this day I am still not entirely sure why I did what I did next. Having reached the last street-lit houses of Portland, I was uncertain exactly where to head in the dark. Ahead the pavement simply disappeared in blackness. I had visions of walking straight off a cliff never to be seen by family and friends again. Would they care? I stared at a group of five fox cubs playing in the High Street and longed for the bakery to open but there was no comforting aroma drifting from its vents as it was still only about 3 a.m. So…I walked all the way back to Weymouth! That's a round trip of some 20 miles! I awoke in a bus shelter, somewhat drier, with two elderly people frowning at me. You could feel them saying "the youth of today!" I then got the double decker back to Portland, i.e. the way I'd come. As I looked out of the upper window, I spotted my two friends amongst a huddle of birders spying a Yellow-browed Warbler in a disused quarry. I had mixed feelings of relief and an urge to throttle them both for not having waited at last night's agreed rendezvous. Even so, I basked in the joy of being reunited and the excitement the day's adventures might bring. That night we slept high up in an open-sided, arched-roof barn after, of course, a few beers in the Eight Kings pub! Relieving ourselves from the top of the haystack before bedding down we homed in on a plastic-sounding object. Funny how lads always seem to need something to aim at. The next morning, we were greeted by a young couple who claimed they slept okay but the leak in the barn was dreadful!

I spent many happy days on Portland seeing Bluethroat, Great Spotted Cuckoo, Subalpine Warbler, Alpine Swift and a Hoopoe that casually flew past the toilet block to the delight of Nigel and me while Chief was in the toilet! Chief proceeded to sing a rather repetitive dip, dip, dip dippers song all day to the melody of "chick, chick, chick, chicken lay a little egg for me", a reference to dipping, of course, which is when birders miss out on a rare bird others may have seen: it drove us all nuts.

The not so big 24hr bird race

May came and, spurred on by publications such as *The Big Bird Race* by Bill Oddie and David Tomlinson, we hatched a plan to see as many species as we could in a calendar day. Norfolk was our chosen destination and the rule of thumb was that three of the four in the car had to see the bird. The trip, I recall, started at midnight, 28th May, conveniently from a local pub in Suffolk after a late coffee. At our first port of call, in the dark, I found myself stepping into a bog up to my crotch (not pleasant). I recall spending a couple of hours in the early dawn too on Kelling Heath, with the windows down, cold but excited, listening for Nightingales. Sadly, only two of us could hear the bird and the rule we had set was that three needed to hear to tick it. (Lesson 1: don't bring along a deaf birder to a 24-hr bird race where three must hear the bird!) Mid-afternoon we were losing momentum and deliberating on our next step. Sitting in the garden sun at the famed Nancy's Café at Cley (more on Nancy's later) a call came through on the grapevine phone that there had been a fall of migrants on Spurn! No, this does not refer to the plight of people making a dangerous boat crossing in a rubber dinghy but rather to the unexpected landing of rare birds on our shores in unprecedented numbers, a consequence of unusual weather interfering with bird migration. So, true to the renegade traits of a burgeoning twitcher, we abandoned the race for a mega twitch. Birds ticked included: Blythe's Reed Warbler; Great Reed Warbler; Long-eared Owl; Thrush Nightingale, and an earlier Red-backed Shrike. Somewhere en route we dipped on a Night Heron too but that turned out to be a plastic one nailed to a tree! Definitely not tickable. As for the bird total I recall we did not get past 105 species…but surely, it's the quality that counts!

New Horizons

Scillies, unforgettable

As 1984 proceeded, Nigel, Chief and I headed for a week on the Scillies in October. This was my first experience of the beautiful islands, a pure gem of a location for birders and twitchers. By this time my peers had accumulated a significant year list and were chasing the then fabled 300-a-year target. I had fallen by the wayside, succumbing to the pressures of my PhD research at Imperial College and, frankly, a lack of funds. In fact, on my very first day on St Mary's I fell even further behind as someone shouted "Rough-legged Buzzard" from the back garden of our somewhat bland overcrowded terraced accommodation. All I recall is there seemed to be bodies everywhere on the living room floor as in those days B&Bs were either full or simply too expensive for us twenty-somethings. Having opted for a hot bath after the night's long drive down from Southend, where we had painfully dipped out on a Cream-coloured Courser the day before, I'd shot into the garden in my bath towel missing the bird by seconds – much to the amusement of all. Thankfully, I caught up with it the next day on a sleet-ridden morning on one of St Mary's many rocky-sided beaches. Magnificent bird! In fact, an original hand-coloured lithograph by John Gould, from his *Birds of Great Britain* published 1832–73, of a Rough-legged Buzzard adorns my dining room wall to this day as a reminder of the occasion.

Scillies, as you can imagine, was a unique experience in the 1980s and early '90s. Those were the days of large birder numbers and low boats where experience quickly taught you where not to sit, unless you desired a good soaking. Birders slept many to a room, a bed was a luxury, and rarities were chalked on a board at the harbour end of the high street. Those exploits have been enjoyably captured by others who were also there in 1984, like Simon Davey, who published his exploits in *Scilly Birding, Joining the madding crowd*. It's a fun read for those who have yet to experience Scillies in autumn; though of course these days birder numbers are less, and two-way radios and mobiles are the norm. The chalkboard reporting the sighting of mouth-watering rarities has sadly long gone. No longer do you have to trek back and forth up the high street come rain or shine to check the latest news and trying to remember it all. In fact, often that in itself became a source of much entertainment with the gofer (often me) reciting the birds on the board. I had a terrible memory too: "Oh yes, and there is a Yellowthroat on Bryher!" For those less familiar with the species, that was then a third record for Britain, I recall, a serious mega nonchalantly reported as though merely an afterthought.

Commando raid on Bryher

After a few intakes of breath and colourful language, everyone would disbelievingly go to look at the board to confirm it really did say Yellowthroat and find out when the next boat to Bryher was leaving the following day. As you can imagine, the anticipation that evening at the log was palpable. Just getting into the log at the Mermaid Inn was a challenge with so many birders straining to hear more details of the sighting. Often log attendance would spill out onto the street and news of new sightings relayed from the inner sanctum were subject to some embellishment of the original detail recalling a "Charge of the Light Brigade" scenario. Around 06–06:30 the next morning, I recall, I was woken by the march of boots on the pavement below my window. Birders were heading for the pier to queue for boats already. No time to waste, no breakfast and limited hygiene, we joined the eager throng knowing that several boats had been laid on for an 08:00 departure. As we arrived at the quay, our shoulders sank as we saw several hundred birders ahead of us lining it end to end. It looked hopeless. I checked at the ticket box, which was just opening next to me. "Do you need to buy a ticket here to get on a boat," I asked, "or can we just pay on board?"

"You need to buy a ticket here," the ticket salesman firmly replied.

I flagged my colleagues over. We immediately bought tickets, spotting an opportunity to gain a queuing advantage. Sure enough, there was a rush for the ticket box as all in front discovered their oversight. Of course, nowadays this would not happen as most buy boat tickets in advance at their B&B. Back then, pretty much no one had a ticket, and their mistake would prove costly for some as the day unfolded.

We found ourselves at the front of the queue and excitedly on the first boat to Bryher like the head of some great naval fleet. Given the earlier time and tide there was no quay to disembark on! A double plank was hooked over the side and we were gestured to scamper off. What ensued was a commando-like disembarkation as birders jostled and slid on the increasingly wet plank, many getting a refreshing bootful of saltwater. In 10 minutes we were at the supposed shoreline location where the Yellowthroat had last been seen and within what seemed a very short time perhaps Britain's most famous twitcher (who was hotly competing to be the top year lister) decided it was in everyone's interest that he go in to flush the bird out from the extensive bracken-covered slope before us, which indeed he duly did. The Yellowthroat popped up, posed and strutted in full view, a blaze of black and yellow. Stunning! We were in awe at the bird's plumage and display. Then the heavens opened and the rain came down. Unfortunately, the twitcher doing the flushing dipped that day much to the chuckling of his fellow competitors. More and more birders were invading the island by the boatload, eagerly trotting up the shingle in the strengthening rain to the usual cries of "It's showing well". The bird, however, had other ideas and had headed for cover in the fern-clad hillside. Having decided we'd had cracking views, we headed for the only café on the island. We'd timed it perfectly. The Yellowthroat was not seen again that day and so those on the later boats missed it. Given that the return boat to St Mary's was not until the late afternoon many birders were soaked through, there being no room in the small café. Fortunately for some, the bird did put in repeat appearances in the following days but for me the events had proved as entertaining as the bird itself. The memory is as vivid to me today as it ever was.

That year, 1984, was my first visit to the Scillies and it had left me with many happy memories. I have since been there on a dozen or so occasions with my partner, Mary, who loves the islands too. It never disappoints, even when the rarities don't blow in. I have met many friends (and sadly lost one or two, like Dave Perrett) that helped cement my connection to these beautiful islands. That year I watched my birding companion Nigel deservedly get his 300. To achieve that on a low income without the aid of today's technology was indeed a triumph. In fact, it was on 22nd December while playing pool in a Gloucester tavern that Nigel talked me into travelling to Scotland to see Barnacle Goose, which he desperately needed for his 300 total. Once again only wild birds were worthy if the total was to be respected and the local flock at Slimbridge was, then at least, deemed introduced/unacceptable. Even so, Scotland is a long way to travel for such a prevalent species, I'd felt. I knew Nigel needed the bird badly, and hell it might just be an adventure too.

Four of us then shared a diesel Chrysler Sunbeam courtesy of an unknown-to-me but willing driver. The trip itself was somewhat uneventful. We duly located the Scottish Barnacles in south-west Scotland and Nigel celebrated his 300 species for the year. Upon being dropped off back in Gloucester, after a sleepless backside-numbing night in the car, we were all tired and hungry. When presented with an unexpectedly high bill for the trip I was frankly none too happy. As a postgrad I had ferried my friends around on numerous occasions in my yellow Vauxhall Viva taking little or no money for fuel but rather valuing their companionship. On this occasion it was not reciprocated. I felt like a make weight, there simply to lower fuel cost for others. That I did not mind too much, after all it was Christmas, but the driver too seemed to have been given the impression he would profit from his taxi service. After a brief exchange, I paid what I felt were fair, and probably left those remaining in the car to make up any shortfall. For me, at least, the instance left a bitter taste.

In retrospect, it was a trivial matter and now some 34 years ago, but it probably compromised my friendship with Nigel, who today somewhat ironically refers to his tours on his website as *Wheatley's Waste Not Want Not Tours*! I recall we spoke only once or twice by phone the following year, mainly to exchange gen (information) on rare birds. We were now located in different parts of the country with very different life agendas. It was the last I would see of Nigel to this day, but I look back with many fond memories.

Natural History Society to the rescue

Now at Imperial College, London I found the local Natural History Society provided the perfect vehicle through which to practise birding. As a postgraduate I was a few years older than the undergraduates who mostly made up the society's members. As such, I was able to hire Hertz rental cars more cheaply and provide information on where birds were through my now-established network of contacts. In short, I became a valued member of the team. Everyone was keen to see rarities and build their life lists and the society helped fund our ventures; shrewd move. On occasion, to get to Norfolk by dawn, I found myself trawling the college halls-of-residence press-ganging half drunken would-be birders to make up numbers and share trip costs. Off we'd set out at 1–2 a.m., usually four or five to a car, most wishing they were in bed, thinking of their latest squeeze and snoring on the back seat. As you can imagine, most could not be classed as human until we hit Nancy's café in Cley for breakfast. In fact, aside from the frozen wastes of Dungeness, grey days at Stodmarsh and Margate, and excursions to Portland, Pagham and Southsea, Norfolk was our preferred destination. With each progressive trip Hertz loaned us a worse car, I recall, having grown wise to the fact that it would come back filthy with 500+ miles clocked during the day, and in desperate need of valeting.

Sadly, the pressure of research and the final exam focus of my colleagues gradually put paid to such exploits. The final straw was having to decline a flattering invitation from my colleagues, most of them biologists of one sort or another, to join them on an expedition to Cameroon where they would be performing various wildlife studies.

"Would you like to do the bird surveys?" I was asked. Wow! What an opportunity! "Thanks, guys," I was truly flattered. The venture was linked to perhaps our greatest TV wildlife presenter David Attenborough's name, I was told. An opportunity not to be missed. Whether this was true I could not be sure but Imperial College was a wealthy institution with powerful connections, so anything was possible. The timing, however, could not be worse. Having watched a couple of close friends in tears after failing their PhD, I knew I had to give it my all. I had to submit my thesis in timely fashion while the findings remained ground-breaking and avoid wasting the financial support my family had afforded me. As such, I declined the invitation, was awarded my PhD in Biochemistry, but to this day I wonder where that venture might have carried me.

The late 1980s saw me continue birding somewhat alone, punctuated by the odd twitch. I steadily grew my list and developed a feel for habitats, best UK locations, timing and, of course, the capacity to regularly see an increasing number of those trickier scarcities, like Kentish Plover, for example which would in fact prove to be a bogey bird during my 2018 quest.

Turkish delight

Having completed my Doctorate, I shrugged off the mantle of becoming the world's oldest student and at 27 joined the ranks of the full-time employed. So, in 1988, seeing a request in a birding publication for birders to join others on a birding venture in Turkey, I duly responded and met up with the co-ordinator, Ray Moore, who lived in Bedfordshire. Ray was somewhat older than I, lightly built, highly intelligent (a Maths teacher, I recall) and had spent some years in Africa teaching and birding. Aside from being a top birder and big lister, Ray was comfortable in uncertain cultural situations, and a logical thinker. We immediately hit it off. Tony Vain, then a headmaster and somewhat less accomplished birder made up the trio. By contrast with Ray, Tony was a large, heavily built guy in his early 50s. None of us had previously met and I was certainly the spring chicken of the team.

Prior to departure, Ray and I spent some time mapping out the sites and routes across southern and central Turkey at his house in Bedfordshire. We acquired previous trip reports, for example from SM Andrews, May–June 1985; Steve Lister and Dave Gosney, August 1987. Ray himself had already birded in Turkey twice previously, in 1976 and Easter 1988, but claimed he lacked experience of the south-east region. His experience and identification skills would, however, prove invaluable. Having hired a Renault 12, about the cheapest car we could obtain from Hertz, and with no air conditioning, we met up at Antalya airport with a set of maps, a rough travel plan but no accommodation and next to no knowledge of the Turkish language between us! For those thinking Turkey is just a tourist destination and easy hop, think again. In the 1980s the country was under developed in the east. Poor folk were still living in straw-made brick houses, and many properties in the mountain villages had no windows at all. Few spoke any English and away from the main centres utilities such as running water and electricity were not guaranteed, especially if, like us, you were operating on a tight budget.

During the two-week trip, which Ray Moore meticulously documented for us between 18th August and 1st September 1988, we recorded a total of 227 species between us.

Turkey	
227 Species recorded in a two-week period from 18th August – 1st September 1988	
Attendees: Ray Moore, Terry Wells, Tony Vain	
Naming according to: Avibase, IOC World Bird Names, version 9.1	
English name	**Scientific name**
Mute Swan	*Cygnus olor*
Garganey	*Spatula querquedula*
Northern Shoveler	*Spatula clypeata*
Mallard	*Anas platyrhynchos*
Eurasian Teal	*Anas crecca*
Marbled Duck	*Marmaronetta angustirostris*
Common Pochard	*Aythya ferina*
Ferruginous Duck	*Aythya nyroca*
Tufted Duck	*Aythya fuligula*
White-headed Duck	*Oxyura leucocephala*
Chukar Partridge	*Alectoris chukar*
See-see Partridge	*Ammoperdix griseogularis*
Black Francolin	*Francolinus francolinus*
Scopoli's Shearwater	*Calonectris diomedea*
Little Grebe	*Tachybaptus ruficollis*
Red-necked Grebe	*Podiceps grisegena*
Great Crested Grebe	*Podiceps cristatus*
Greater Flamingo	*Phoenicopterus roseus*
White Stork	*Ciconia ciconia*
Northern Bald Ibis	*Geronticus eremita*
Glossy Ibis	*Plegadis falcinellus*
Eurasian Spoonbill	*Platalea leucorodia*
Little Bittern	*Ixobrychus minutus*

Black-crowned Night Heron	*Nycticorax nycticorax*
Squacco Heron	*Ardeola ralloides*
Western Cattle Egret	*Bubulcus ibis*
Grey Heron	*Ardea cinerea*
Purple Heron	*Ardea purpurea*
Great Egret	*Ardea alba*
Little Egret	*Egretta garzetta*
Great White Pelican	*Pelecanus onocrotalus*
Pygmy Cormorant	*Microcarbo pygmaeus*
Great Cormorant	*Phalacrocorax carbo*
Egyptian Vulture	*Neophron percnopterus*
European Honey Buzzard	*Pernis apivorus*
Griffon Vulture	*Gyps fulvus*
Short-toed Snake Eagle	*Circaetus gallicus*
Lesser Spotted Eagle	*Clanga pomarina*
Booted Eagle	*Hieraaetus pennatus*
Western Marsh Harrier	*Circus aeruginosus*
Pallid Harrier	*Circus macrourus*
Montagu's Harrier	*Circus pygargus*
Black Kite	*Milvus migrans*
White-tailed Eagle	*Haliaeetus albicilla*
Long-legged Buzzard	*Buteo rufinus*
Common Buzzard	*Buteo buteo*
Great Bustard	*Otis tarda*
Water Rail	*Rallus aquaticus*
Grey-headed Swamphen	*Porphyrio poliocephalus*
Common Moorhen	*Gallinula chloropus*
Eurasian Coot	*Fulica atra*
Eurasian Stone-Curlew	*Burhinus oedicnemus*
Black-winged Stilt	*Himantopus himantopus*

Pied Avocet	*Recurvirostra avosetta*
Northern Lapwing	*Vanellus vanellus*
Spur-winged Lapwing	*Vanellus spinosus*
Grey Plover	*Pluvialis squatarola*
Common Ringed Plover	*Charadrius hiaticula*
Little Ringed Plover	*Charadrius dubius*
Kentish Plover	*Charadrius alexandrinus*
Caspian Plover	*Charadrius asiaticus*
Whimbrel	*Numenius phaeopus*
Eurasian Curlew	*Numenius arquata*
Bar-tailed Godwit	*Limosa lapponica*
Black-tailed Godwit	*Limosa limosa*
Ruddy Turnstone	*Arenaria interpres*
Ruff	*Calidris pugnax*
Broad-billed Sandpiper	*Calidris falcinellus*
Curlew Sandpiper	*Calidris ferruginea*
Temminck's Stint	*Calidris temminckii*
Dunlin	*Calidris alpina*
Little Stint	*Calidris minuta*
Common Snipe	*Gallinago gallinago*
Terek Sandpiper	*Xenus cinereus*
Common Sandpiper	*Actitis hypoleucos*
Green Sandpiper	*Tringa ochropus*
Common Redshank	*Tringa totanus*
Marsh Sandpiper	*Tringa stagnatilis*
Wood Sandpiper	*Tringa glareola*
Spotted Redshank	*Tringa erythropus*
Common Greenshank	*Tringa nebularia*
Collared Pratincole	*Glareola pratincola*
Slender-billed Gull	*Chroicocephalus genei*

Black-headed Gull	*Chroicocephalus ridibundus*
Audouin's Gull	*Ichthyaetus audouinii*
Mediterranean Gull	*Ichthyaetus melanocephalus*
European Herring Gull	*Larus argentatus*
Sandwich Tern	*Thalasseus sandvicensis*
Little Tern	*Sternula albifrons*
Common Tern	*Sterna hirundo*
Whiskered Tern	*Chlidonias hybrida*
White-winged Tern	*Chlidonias leucopterus*
Black Tern	*Chlidonias niger*
Pin-tailed Sandgrouse	*Pterocles alchata*
Black-bellied Sandgrouse	*Pterocles orientalis*
Rock Dove	*Columba livia*
Stock Dove	*Columba oenas*
Common Wood Pigeon	*Columba palumbus*
European Turtle Dove	*Streptopelia turtur*
Eurasian Collared Dove	*Streptopelia decaocto*
Laughing Dove	*Streptopelia senegalensis*
Common Cuckoo	*Cuculus canorus*
Western Barn Owl	*Tyto alba*
Eurasian Scops Owl	*Otus scops*
Eurasian Eagle Owl	*Bubo bubo*
Little Owl	*Athene noctua*
Alpine Swift	*Tachymarptis melba*
Common Swift	*Apus apus*
European Roller	*Coracias garrulus*
White-throated Kingfisher	*Halcyon smyrnensis*
Common Kingfisher	*Alcedo atthis*
Pied Kingfisher	*Ceryle rudis*
European Bee-eater	*Merops apiaster*

Eurasian Hoopoe	*Upupa epops*
Eurasian Wryneck	*Jynx torquilla*
Syrian Woodpecker	*Dendrocopos syriacus*
White-backed Woodpecker	*Dendrocopos leucotos*
Common Kestrel	*Falco tinnunculus*
Eurasian Hobby	*Falco subbuteo*
Saker Falcon	*Falco cherrug*
Peregrine Falcon	*Falco peregrinus*
Red-backed Shrike	*Lanius collurio*
Lesser Grey Shrike	*Lanius minor*
Great Grey Shrike	*Lanius excubitor*
Woodchat Shrike	*Lanius senator*
Masked Shrike	*Lanius nubicus*
Eurasian Golden Oriole	*Oriolus oriolus*
Eurasian Jay	*Garrulus glandarius*
Eurasian Magpie	*Pica pica*
Red-billed Chough	*Pyrrhocorax pyrrhocorax*
Alpine Chough	*Pyrrhocorax graculus*
Western Jackdaw	*Corvus monedula*
Rook	*Corvus frugilegus*
Hooded Crow	*Corvus cornix*
Northern Raven	*Corvus corax*
Coal Tit	*Periparus ater*
Sombre Tit	*Poecile lugubris*
Eurasian Blue Tit	*Cyanistes caeruleus*
Great Tit	*Parus major*
Bearded Reedling	*Panurus biarmicus*
Eurasian Skylark	*Alauda arvensis*
Crested Lark	*Galerida cristata*
Horned Lark	*Eremophila alpestris*

Greater Short-toed Lark	*Calandrella brachydactyla*
Bimaculated Lark	*Melanocorypha bimaculata*
Calandra Lark	*Melanocorypha calandra*
Lesser Short-toed Lark	*Alaudala rufescens*
White-eared Bulbul	*Pycnonotus leucotis*
Sand Martin	*Riparia riparia*
Barn Swallow	*Hirundo rustica*
Eurasian Crag Martin	*Ptyonoprogne rupestris*
Common House Martin	*Delichon urbicum*
Red-rumped Swallow	*Cecropis daurica*
Cetti's Warbler	*Cettia cetti*
Willow Warbler	*Phylloscopus trochilus*
Common Chiffchaff	*Phylloscopus collybita*
Great Reed Warbler	*Acrocephalus arundinaceus*
Sedge Warbler	*Acrocephalus schoenobaenus*
Eurasian Reed Warbler	*Acrocephalus scirpaceus*
Eastern Olivaceous Warbler	*Iduna pallida*
Upcher's Warbler	*Hippolais languida*
Olive-tree Warbler	*Hippolais olivetorum*
Icterine Warbler	*Hippolais icterina*
Zitting Cisticola	*Cisticola juncidis*
Graceful Prinia	*Prinia gracilis*
Eurasian Blackcap	*Sylvia atricapilla*
Garden Warbler	*Sylvia borin*
Barred Warbler	*Sylvia nisoria*
Lesser Whitethroat	*Sylvia curruca*
Eastern Orphean Warbler	*Sylvia crassirostris*
Common Whitethroat	*Sylvia communis*
Subalpine Warbler	*Sylvia cantillans*
Sardinian Warbler	*Sylvia melanocephala*

Ménétries's Warbler	*Sylvia mystacea*
Rüppell's Warbler	*Sylvia ruppeli*
Goldcrest	*Regulus regulus*
Eurasian Wren	*Troglodytes troglodytes*
Krüper's Nuthatch	*Sitta krueperi*
Western Rock Nuthatch	*Sitta neumayer*
Eastern Rock Nuthatch	*Sitta tephronota*
Common Starling	*Sturnus vulgaris*
Rosy Starling	*Pastor roseus*
Ring Ouzel	*Turdus torquatus*
Common Blackbird	*Turdus merula*
Rufous-tailed Scrub Robin	*Cercotrichas galactotes*
Spotted Flycatcher	*Muscicapa striata*
White-throated Robin	*Irania gutturalis*
Black Redstart	*Phoenicurus ochruros*
Common Redstart	*Phoenicurus phoenicurus*
Common Rock Thrush	*Monticola saxatilis*
Blue Rock Thrush	*Monticola solitarius*
Whinchat	*Saxicola rubetra*
European Stonechat	*Saxicola rubicola*
Northern Wheatear	*Oenanthe oenanthe*
Isabelline Wheatear	*Oenanthe isabellina*
Black-eared Wheatear	*Oenanthe hispanica*
Pied Wheatear	*Oenanthe pleschanka*
Finsch's Wheatear	*Oenanthe finschii*
Red-tailed Wheatear	*Oenanthe chrysopygia*
House Sparrow	*Passer domesticus*
Spanish Sparrow	*Passer hispaniolensis*
Dead Sea Sparrow	*Passer moabiticus*
Eurasian Tree Sparrow	*Passer montanus*

Pale Rockfinch	*Carpospiza brachydactyla*
Rock Sparrow	*Petronia petronia*
White-winged Snowfinch	*Montifringilla nivalis*
Radde's Accentor	*Prunella ocularis*
Western Yellow Wagtail	*Motacilla flava*
Grey Wagtail	*Motacilla cinerea*
White Wagtail	*Motacilla alba*
Tawny Pipit	*Anthus campestris*
Tree Pipit	*Anthus trivialis*
Red-throated Pipit	*Anthus cervinus*
Water Pipit	*Anthus spinoletta*
Common Chaffinch	*Fringilla coelebs*
Asian Crimson-winged Finch	*Rhodopechys sanguineus*
European Greenfinch	*Chloris chloris*
Desert Finch	*Rhodospiza obsoleta*
Common Linnet	*Linaria cannabina*
European Goldfinch	*Carduelis carduelis*
Red-fronted Serin	*Serinus pusillus*
European Serin	*Serinus serinus*
Eurasian Siskin	*Spinus spinus*
Rock Bunting	*Emberiza cia*
Cinereous Bunting	*Emberiza cineracea*
Black-headed Bunting	*Granativora melanocephala*
Arctic Warbler* (unconfirmed)	*Seicercus borealis*

*Arctic Warbler does not appear on the IOC Bird List for Turkey, but it is worthy of note that records show that Ray Moore and I located a strong candidate for this species 30Km north of Manavgat on 31st Aug 1988.

To my knowledge, no record of the sighting was submitted to the relevant Turkish authority at that time. A pity as, if proven, this could have been a first Arctic Warbler for Turkey!

Turkey was frankly a blast. My first exposure to how birding without a guide could be so fulfilling. By example, whereas some sites were rendered desolate by low seasonal rainfall, other uncharted marshes proved spectacular harbours for storks, plovers and sandpipers. On one occasion we managed to find accommodation virtually on a beautiful sandy beach. It was an unfinished newly built house, and I am sure the landlord had no right to be letting it! Even so, we shook hands and immediately plunged into the cool sea with clothes on, given temperatures were in the high 30s and the car did not have aircon. The drive had been long and very dusty with many roads to the east being unsurfaced. That evening, as the landlord brought us beers, we lazed on the balcony and watched dozens of Honey Buzzards drift overhead on migration. The next day, the landlord, spotting an opportunity, suggested that a family elder take us out into the lagoon on his boat. Great, we thought, as we'd established the lagoon was impossible to watch from its shoreline owing to extensive, deep, high reed margins on all sides. The next morning, following a good breakfast, which consisted of fruit, bread and some goat cheese, we were ushered out to meet our intrepid captain and his boat. At least, I think it was a boat, or was it a punt? An elderly gentleman, old enough to be my grandfather, stood smiling, toothless, holding a long wooden barge pole. Anxiously we boarded, gauging the seaworthiness of the craft as it tilted and flexed under our weight. The elderly fellow began to punt but as we carried through to the other side of the reeds we came to a gliding halt. Silt! We were stuck! At this point our toothless captain leapt overboard and heroically began to tow us further out into the lagoon presumably gauging the silt would lessen and the boat would free up. Sadly, it didn't and so now only some 75m from the shoreline we urged the elderly fellow, somewhat concerned for his welfare, to tow us back. None of us were keen to get into the slimy mud, which was up to his thighs, and given we'd witnessed the odd snake in the reed margin. Were there poisonous snakes here? We couldn't recall. As we hastily disembarked and paid the poor fellow handsomely for his troubles his younger brother piped up, "We have another boat." At this point we held up our hands in gratitude, or was it surrender, stating we had other plans.

I can't help wondering whether we three naïve pasty-looking Englishmen were not victims of some elaborate Turkish ruse!

On one further occasion we ventured into the wadis of eastern Turkey not far from the Syrian border. Our target bird was Eagle Owl. Having checked out the location in the evening we noted that the temperature in the wadi was an eye-drying 47 degrees! It was clear we needed to conduct our search at first light to avoid the intolerable heat. On exiting the wadi, we met with a local gentleman who we suspected might be a sort of reserve warden. Either way it paid to be extra polite and welcoming in such uncertain circumstances. We greeted him warmly as he strutted towards us in authoritative manner, so we explained our quest. He did not speak English but seemed to understand, nodded and ushered us to a small unlit 4x4m hut. We cautiously stepped inside. It was almost completely dark save for the shafts of bright sunlight penetrating the poorly fitting timbers. We were immediately confronted by two Eagle Owls of some considerable size, and untethered! Backs to the wall, we were assuredly impressed with the sight before us but equally keen not to be part of a frenzy of feathers and claws as the birds hissed at us. We slid back out the door, paid the man a few Lira and headed for the hotel.

We were not sure why the gentleman had the two captive owls: breeding, entertainment or conservation but it did at least reassure us that these birds were clearly in the area. So, the next day, after two hours of trekking through wadis in the cool early morning sun, we located our wild Eagle Owl just as we were considering how to traverse a rock fall that blocked further progress. The bird eyed us, head swaying from side to side some 5m or so up in one of the many erosion cavities that peppered the sides of the wadi. Wild, free and unforgettable, the picture in my mind is as fresh as the day I was there.

Other memorable instances in Turkey saw Ray bamboozling our ever-haggling accommodation owners with a huge calculator. Ray had no doubt picked these skills up from his time teaching in Africa where for him it was everyday life. Being a Maths teacher, Ray had a calculator with the most impressive array of buttons I'd ever seen, no doubt reflecting complex algebraic formulae, you know the sort us mere mortals never use. Ray used this to great effect while lambasting the poor landlord that the price of accommodation and meals was simply too high. Frantically pressing buttons at random he would hold it up displaying the desired payment with no genuine calculation to back it up – it was all bluff. "The calculator does not lie," he would say. Clearly the locals had not witnessed such high-tech haggling and would capitulate.

Besides the fantastic birding across mountain, coastal and savannah habitats of Turkey my most memorable impressions were of the uncertainty, the anticipation, shaping the way ahead day by day, and the camaraderie that arose. Windowless hotels saw the three of us sweltering in midday temperatures of 104 degrees. One mountain campsite had a toilet literally on stilts overhanging a cliff edge with a couple of hundred metres drop that you could see beneath you as you squatted! It certainly encouraged you to speed up the process for fear of the whole structure collapsing into the ravine below. Donkeys would scream and grunt at you if you startled them in the mountains, small boys herding goats would confront you with penknives, asking for cigarettes. In the food markets people would touch my sun-bleached fair hair – a bit disconcerting. Many shop owners would insist you had tea with them as part of the elaborate sales process. Chairs would be set out, the family would be introduced, including daughters for whom the parents were keen to find a British husband. If you claimed, as a means of escape, that you were seeking an object they clearly did not have in the shop they always had a brother with a shop next door that did. It was a cartel, no escape. Even so it was all very friendly and engaging. I am sure society in Eastern Turkey is now much advanced but back then it was bordering on the biblical.

US nomad

The 1990s saw large gaps in my UK birding. Work took me overseas frequently and much time was spent visiting hospitals, medical centres, and universities, where I would discuss design requirements for MRI scanners with leading professors and consultants. In fact, I visited 26 states of the USA on business. Every weekend presented an opportunity to hop in a rented Buick or Chevy to go exploring the local habitat. If only the US were not so damn big and I had a telescope to accompany my under-powered Pentax 7x30 binoculars! It was in New Jersey where one evening following a visit to Princeton University that, while in search of birds and a suitable place to eat, I learnt the lesson of distraction. A nasty collision resulted with a huge, good old American pick-up truck hurtling towards me on a country lane. The force of the impact was so hard I snapped the steering wheel of my red Buick. The ambulance arrived in good time and proceeded to administer oxygen while firing questions about my medical cover and getting me to sign forms at the same time as they scissored through my clothes from trouser bottom to collar! I felt a bit like I was being mugged. The hospital, while suspecting my ribs were broken, discharged me somewhat ironically claiming their scanner was broken! (I think I missed a business opportunity here.) As I stood rigidly at the taxi stop outside the hospital, one arm strapped high at right angles, chest bandaged, shredded clothes flapping in the midnight breeze, I could not help wondering how the experience might have compared with that under the NHS.

Aside from that, and one other adrenalin-filled occasion when I was pinned to the fence bordering a private property by two Doberman Pinschers, most birding was literally a walk in the park. In North Carolina I recall relaxing in the pool of my Days Inn Hotel. In an air-filled floating armchair with beer in hand I watched my first Northern Cardinals drinking from puddles on the recently washed tiled pool surround. Tick! Work, you can't beat it!

The birds seen on my US ventures were a tiny sliver of what is possible, of course, given the vast area traversed. I had to be opportunistic, limited maps, poor optics, no internet or birding network. I'd find parks, beaches, forests, when and where I could within reach of the hotel. The table below summarises species I recorded:

USA	
Species recorded while travelling with work across 26 states during the early 1990s	
Naming according to: Avibase, IOC World Bird Names, version 8.2	
English name	Scientific name
Brant Goose	*Branta bernicla*
Canada Goose	*Branta canadensis*
Cinnamon Teal	*Spatula cyanoptera*
Mallard	*Anas platyrhynchos*
Common Merganser	*Mergus merganser*
Common Loon	*Gavia immer*
Horned Grebe	*Podiceps auritus*
Great Blue Heron	*Ardea herodias*
Great Egret	*Ardea alba*
Snowy Egret	*Egretta thula*
American White Pelican	*Pelecanus erythrorhynchos*
Brown Pelican	*Pelecanus occidentalis*
Pelagic Cormorant	*Phalacrocorax pelagicus*
Great Cormorant	*Phalacrocorax carbo*
Turkey Vulture	*Cathartes aura*
Black Vulture	*Coragyps atratus*
Western Osprey	*Pandion haliaetus*
Cooper's Hawk	*Accipiter cooperii*
Northern Harrier	*Circus hudsonius*

Red-tailed Hawk	*Buteo jamaicensis*
American Coot	*Fulica americana*
American Oystercatcher	*Haematopus palliatus*
Grey Plover	*Pluvialis squatarola*
Killdeer	*Charadrius vociferus*
Long-billed Curlew	*Numenius americanus*
Surfbird	*Calidris virgata*
Rock Sandpiper	*Calidris ptilocnemis*
Greater Yellowlegs	*Tringa melanoleuca*
Laughing Gull	*Leucophaeus atricilla*
Heermann's Gull	*Larus heermanni*
Ring-billed Gull	*Larus delawarensis*
European Herring Gull	*Larus argentatus*
Lesser Black-backed Gull	*Larus fuscus*
Rock Dove	*Columba livia*
Mourning Dove	*Zenaida macroura*
Chimney Swift	*Chaetura pelagica*
Belted Kingfisher	*Megaceryle alcyon*
Acorn Woodpecker	*Melanerpes formicivorus*
Downy Woodpecker	*Dryobates pubescens*
Hairy Woodpecker	*Leuconotopicus villosus*
Northern Flicker	*Colaptes auratus*
American Kestrel	*Falco sparverius*
Peregrine Falcon	*Falco peregrinus*
Red-eyed Vireo	*Vireo olivaceus*
Blue Jay	*Cyanocitta cristata*
Florida Scrub Jay	*Aphelocoma coerulescens*
Western Jackdaw	*Coloeus monedula*
American Crow	*Corvus brachyrhynchos*
Fish Crow	*Corvus ossifragus*

Tufted Titmouse	*Baeolophus bicolor*
Carolina Chickadee	*Poecile carolinensis*
Black-capped Chickadee	*Poecile atricapillus*
Eurasian Skylark	*Alauda arvensis*
Barn Swallow	*Hirundo rustica*
Golden-crowned Kinglet	*Regulus satrapa*
Brown-headed Nuthatch	*Sitta pusilla*
White-breasted Nuthatch	*Sitta carolinensis*
Grey Catbird	*Dumetella carolinensis*
Common Starling	*Sturnus vulgaris*
Eastern Bluebird	*Sialia sialis*
American Robin	*Turdus migratorius*
Purple Finch	*Haemorhous purpureus*
House Finch	*Haemorhous mexicanus*
White-crowned Sparrow	*Zonotrichia leucophrys*
White-throated Sparrow	*Zonotrichia albicollis*
Dark-eyed Junco	*Junco hyemalis*
Eastern Towhee	*Pipilo erythrophthalmus*
Yellow-headed Blackbird	*Xanthocephalus xanthocephalus*
Orchard Oriole	*Icterus spurius*
Red-winged Blackbird	*Agelaius phoeniceus*
Brewer's Blackbird	*Euphagus cyanocephalus*
Rose-breasted Grosbeak	*Pheucticus ludovicianus*
Northern Cardinal	*Cardinalis cardinalis*

To me the USA really brought home one appeal of birding. Here I was a lone birder in a vast unknown country, unfamiliar locations and species, a pair of bins, a field guide and some of the cheapest motoring on the planet...all courtesy of my employer! Surely the way to go! Birding is an anytime, anywhere hobby.

Majorca – short hop sensation

During the 1990s every family holiday became a potential birding venture with multiple visits to Majorca, southern Spain and the Dominican Republic dominating. On every occasion I would seek to persuade family, subliminally of course, of a location that I secretly knew was a birding hotspot so that I could go walkabout.

Majorca had gained something of a reputation amongst birders. It was a short two-and-a-half-hour hop by plane, reasonably cheap, super climate, breath taking mountain scenery and great for migrants. It also had great beach coves for the younger members of the family to enjoy. So, what's not to like? SOLD! When it comes to birds Majorca has some outright winners too, for it harbours one of the largest and rarest birds in the world: the spectacular Black Vulture often referred to as "the flying door". Stealthy Eleanora's Falcons, too, can be found in abundance, having likely migrated up from Madagascar. These Hobby-like birds of prey are adept at taking dragonflies and small birds on the wing and are a joy to watch in action. Somewhat startling is their reputation for pulling the wings from the birds they catch and hiding them in crevices to eat later!

I found one of the best ways to get about in Majorca was by moped, because you could simply pull to the side of the road almost anywhere, raise the bins and just start looking. So, I'd duly hired a 50cc stallion and, armed with my copy of *A Guide to Bird-Watching in Mallorca* by Eddie Watkinson, spluttered off, sporting my Optolyth 10x50 bins. And what a fantastic little guide book it proved to be. Eddie's hand-drawn maps and detailed descriptions often led me to a tree, a bush, a gate where the birds were to be found true to form. As I followed Eddie's guide to the letter, birds kept coming. By example: Bee-eater; Little Bittern; Cirl Bunting; Turtle Dove; Booted Eagle; Eleanora's Falcon; Firecrest; Purple Heron; Hoopoe; Short-toed Lark; Crag Martin; Nightingale; Osprey; Scops Owl; Kentish Plover; Serin; Cory's Shearwater; Woodchat Shrike; Black-winged Stilt; Pallid Swift; Blue Rock Thrush; Blue-headed Wagtail; Fan-tailed, Great Reed, Marmora's, Moustached and Sardinian

Warblers; and nesting Wrynecks in a nearby orchard – all ticked in the glorious summer sun. However, there were two birds I especially wanted: Rock Thrush, because of its spectacular colour and reputation as a mega in the UK, and Black Vulture for its size and increasing scarcity.

One dawn I set off on the moped in tee shirt, baseball hat and shorts to head for a certain military base in the mountains, topped up with fuel to the brim. Garages were few and far between in the north of Majorca and often barely recognisable then, consisting of just one pump and no sign to advertise they were open. The moped, I knew, would be hard-pushed to make it up the mountains and I recall three racing cyclists overtaking me on the way towards Puig Magor! After several pull offs, collecting Cirl Bunting, Nightingale and Osprey on the way along the winding mountain roads, I eventually came to a quarry where I'd received a report that Rock Thrush could be seen. What I had not expected was that the quarry was within the confines of a military base! By now I was cold in the early morning air with only a tee shirt on and so climbed a rocky sunlit slope to warm up, take in the views and contemplate my next move. The skull-and-crossbones signs on the gates certainly looked foreboding. At that moment I looked up for inspiration and a single Black Vulture cruised low overhead as if contemplating whether I might be its next meal. What a thrill! The length and breadth of wing certainly deserved the 'door-like' comparison. So, full of elation and bravado, I clambered down the rocky outcrop, crossed the road and hopped over the military gates. The military zone was flat; the quarry lay some 400m ahead off to the left-hand side. Trying to keep out of sight, I moved through the sunken area of ground to the left of the elevated gravel road that traversed the centre of the military zone. I found myself in the quarry, scope raised, scanning the crags before me. To my alarm, just then a military convoy came around a dusty track to the base of the mountain and halted some 100m behind me! The thought of spending time in a Spanish gaol flashed before me. My scope, a very portable Opticron Piccolo 15–45x60, was on its Velbon tripod and looked something like a theodolite used by surveyors assessing the lie of the land.

As the leader of the convoy halted his vehicle, flipping open his turret, I could feel him staring at the back of my head. I immediately picked up a small stick and held it vertically in front of the scope to imitate a surveyor gauging line and distance. I then confidently turned, waved and just carried on. The military officer pondered for 30 seconds, lowered his turret and the convoy trundled on and eventually out through the forbidding gates of the military zone. Once the convoy was out of site, I scarpered, not knowing if the officer had sent for someone to remove and arrest me. I headed back to my moped, keeping low in a nearby ditch, praying I'd got away with it.

No doubt the soldiers were saying "did you see that daft Englishman pretending he was a surveyor" and enjoying a good laugh! In short, I dipped the magnificent Rock Thrush and did not brave another attempt at this location.

Majorca	
Species recorded during a 2-week family vacation 7th to 21st August 1991	
Naming according to: Avibase, IOC World Bird Names, version 8.2	
English name	**Scientific name**
Mallard	*Anas platyrhynchos*
Cory's Shearwater	*Calonectris borealis*
Little Grebe	*Tachybaptus ruficollis*
Little Bittern	*Ixobrychus minutus*
Purple Heron	*Ardea purpurea*
Little Egret	*Egretta garzetta*
European Shag	*Phalacrocorax aristotelis*
Western Osprey	*Pandion haliaetus*
Cinereous Vulture	*Aegypius monachus*
Booted Eagle	*Hieraaetus pennatus*
Western Marsh Harrier	*Circus aeruginosus*

Water Rail	*Rallus aquaticus*
Common Moorhen	*Gallinula chloropus*
Eurasian Coot	*Fulica atra*
Eurasian Stone-curlew	*Burhinus oedicnemus*
Black-winged Stilt	*Himantopus himantopus*
Northern Lapwing	*Vanellus vanellus*
Little Ringed Plover	*Charadrius dubius*
Kentish Plover	*Charadrius alexandrinus*
Audouin's Gull	*Ichthyaetus audouinii*
European Herring Gull	*Larus argentatus*
Rock Dove	*Columba livia*
Common Wood Pigeon	*Columba palumbus*
European Turtle Dove	*Streptopelia turtur*
Eurasian Scops Owl	*Otus scops*
Long-eared Owl	*Asio otus*
Common Swift	*Apus apus*
Pallid Swift	*Apus pallidus*
European Bee-eater	*Merops apiaster*
Eurasian Hoopoe	*Upupa epops*
Eurasian Wryneck	*Jynx torquilla*
Common Kestrel	*Falco tinnunculus*
Eleonora's Falcon	*Falco eleonorae*
Peregrine Falcon	*Falco peregrinus*
Woodchat Shrike	*Lanius senator*
Northern Raven	*Corvus corax*
Great Tit	*Parus major*
Greater Short-toed Lark	*Calandrella brachydactyla*
Sand Martin	*Riparia riparia*
Barn Swallow	*Hirundo rustica*
Eurasian Crag Martin	*Ptyonoprogne rupestris*

Common House Martin	*Delichon urbicum*
Cetti's Warbler	*Cettia cetti*
Great Reed Warbler	*Acrocephalus arundinaceus*
Moustached Warbler	*Acrocephalus melanopogon*
Eurasian Reed Warbler	*Acrocephalus scirpaceus*
Zitting Cisticola	*Cisticola juncidis*
Eurasian Blackcap	*Sylvia atricapilla*
Dartford Warbler	*Sylvia undata*
Balearic Warbler	*Sylvia balearica*
Sardinian Warbler	*Sylvia melanocephala*
Common Firecrest	*Regulus ignicapilla*
Eurasian Wren	*Troglodytes troglodytes*
Common Blackbird	*Turdus merula*
Spotted Flycatcher	*Muscicapa striata*
European Robin	*Erithacus rubecula*
Common Nightingale	*Luscinia megarhynchos*
Blue Rock Thrush	*Monticola solitarius*
Whinchat	*Saxicola rubetra*
European Stonechat	*Saxicola rubicola*
House Sparrow	*Passer domesticus*
Western Yellow Wagtail	*Motacilla flava*
White Wagtail	*Motacilla alba*
Common Chaffinch	*Fringilla coelebs*
European Greenfinch	*Chloris chloris*
Common Linnet	*Linaria cannabina*
European Goldfinch	*Carduelis carduelis*
European Serin	*Serinus serinus*
Corn Bunting	*Emberiza calandra*
Cirl Bunting	*Emberiza cirlus*
Common Reed Bunting	*Emberiza schoeniclus*

Going tropical

As with many birders, for me remote exotic rain forests seemed to represent the pinnacle of birding. Places like Papua New Guinea, Thailand and Costa Rica have long been popular destinations where a birder could be confronted by a multitude of species in a blink, but the habitat could fast become the enemy, harbouring things that bite and the odd hostile native. Organised tours were becoming increasingly available post 1990 but still felt comparatively expensive and often spanned beyond the maximum two-week holiday I could realistically expect my employer to permit. For me, the soft option then was Dominican Republic! Part tropical, part holiday resort, cheap flights, package deals, comfortable hotels, reasonably safe (providing you did not stray into Haiti I was warned). In fact, I was to visit the island three times, in 1991, 2013 and 2015, and St Lucia in 1993 where I classically dipped on the famed St Lucian Parrot despite hiring a guide to locate them! Then again, these were not formal birding trips, rather a bird, bathe, babe and beer mix combined.

Arriving in Dominican Republic in the 1990s saw one confronted with shanty towns where roofs were made of corrugated metal, houses were windowless and old car parts and tyres were often found on the roofs of these shacks, no doubt to prevent them from being blown away in a hurricane. Locals would be selling nuts/fruit by the side of the road. Trees were painted with horizontal coloured bands, which, I was reliably informed, reflected the political party that town had voted for.

My hotel was pleasant enough, a three-star with a machine-gun toting guard at the entrance. Definitely reassuring…not. Clearly this was not a place to go wandering alone so of course that is exactly what I did the very next morning: into the secondary rain forest across the road at dawn with scope and bins, sunglasses and hat. Within minutes I was confronted by: Hispaniolan Lizard Cuckoo; Stolid Flycatcher; Broad-billed Tody; Common Ground Dove; 2 Common Nighthawks displaying; Black-crowned Palm Tanager; Snowy Egret; Yellow-crowned Night Heron; Zenaida Dove and Grey Kingbird. It was hard to keep up. An

58

hour in and I heard chopping and voices. I'd stumbled across a coppicing team who were keen to see what I was up to. All were wearing shorts or leather front and back flapped equivalents but no shirts. They looked like a lost South American tribe and, yes, each carried a machete, which added to my anxiety. I had no idea whether I was trespassing, what they were saying, and I definitely wanted to stay in one piece and keep my optics. It was a "beam me up, Scotty" moment so I decided to take the initiative and offered them a look through my binoculars and telescope, which they were now passing round and eyeing enthusiastically.

Now hold on a minute, this is 1991 not 1901, isn't it! These guys surprisingly could not grasp how optics worked. They jumped back at seeing the magnified image, and laughed and pointed when their colleagues appeared to be miles away when they looked through the bins the wrong way around. In fact, it became quite a party! Surprisingly, they eventually returned my optics, all shook my hand and left smiling.

Great! I now felt a whole lot safer with my new-found friends to hand, so I waved goodbye and continued to bird at will as though I'd gained some rite of passage.

I've never had a subsequent encounter quite like that and it was clear that upon my return to the islands 12 years later the place had advanced immeasurably. Improved roads and many more hotels starkly contrasted with the scene I'd previously witnessed, which was more akin to the "lost tribes of the Amazon". Even so, the island still has masses to offer. The table below illustrates species seen during my three two-week vacations to Dominican Republic:

Dominican Republic	
Species recorded during three 2-week vacations in 1991, 2013 and 2015	
Naming according to: Avibase, IOC World Bird Names, version 8.2	
English name	Scientific name
White-faced Whistling Duck	*Dendrocygna viduata*
White-cheeked Pintail	*Anas bahamensis*

Least Grebe	*Tachybaptus dominicus*
Pied-billed Grebe	*Podilymbus podiceps*
White-tailed Tropicbird	*Phaethon lepturus*
American White Ibis	*Eudocimus albus*
Least Bittern	*Ixobrychus exilis*
Black-crowned Night Heron	*Nycticorax nycticorax*
Yellow-crowned Night Heron	*Nyctanassa violacea*
Green Heron	*Butorides virescens*
Western Cattle Egret	*Bubulcus ibis*
Great Egret	*Ardea alba*
Tricolored Heron	*Egretta tricolor*
Little Blue Heron	*Egretta caerulea*
Snowy Egret	*Egretta thula*
Brown Pelican	*Pelecanus occidentalis*
Magnificent Frigatebird	*Fregata magnificens*
Red-footed Booby	*Sula sula*
Brown Booby	*Sula leucogaster*
Anhinga	*Anhinga anhinga*
Turkey Vulture	*Cathartes aura*
Western Osprey	*Pandion haliaetus*
Purple Gallinule	*Porphyrio martinica*
Common Gallinule	*Gallinula galeata*
American Coot	*Fulica americana*
Killdeer	*Charadrius vociferus*
Ruddy Turnstone	*Arenaria interpres*
Least Sandpiper	*Calidris minutilla*
Semipalmated Sandpiper	*Calidris pusilla*
Western Sandpiper	*Calidris mauri*
Wilson's Snipe	*Gallinago delicata*
Spotted Sandpiper	*Actitis macularius*

Laughing Gull	*Leucophaeus atricilla*
Royal Tern	*Thalasseus maximus*
Least Tern	*Sternula antillarum*
Rock Dove	*Columba livia*
White-crowned Pigeon	*Patagioenas leucocephala*
Scaly-naped Pigeon	*Patagioenas squamosa*
Plain Pigeon	*Patagioenas inornata*
Common Ground Dove	*Columbina passerina*
Mourning Dove	*Zenaida macroura*
Zenaida Dove	*Zenaida aurita*
White-winged Dove	*Zenaida asiatica*
Smooth-billed Ani	*Crotophaga ani*
Mangrove Cuckoo	*Coccyzus minor*
Hispaniolan Lizard Cuckoo	*Coccyzus longirostris*
Common Nighthawk	*Chordeiles minor*
American Black Swift	*Cypseloides niger*
Chimney Swift	*Chaetura pelagica*
Antillean Palm Swift	*Tachornis phoenicobia*
Antillean Mango	*Anthracothorax dominicus*
Hispaniolan Emerald	*Chlorostilbon swainsonii*
Vervain Hummingbird	*Mellisuga minima*
Ruby-throated Hummingbird	*Archilochus colubris*
Broad-billed Tody	*Todus subulatus*
Narrow-billed Tody	*Todus angustirostris*
Hispaniolan Woodpecker	*Melanerpes striatus*
American Kestrel	*Falco sparverius*
Hispaniolan Amazon	*Amazona ventralis*
Olive-throated Parakeet	*Eupsittula nana*
Greater Antillean Elaenia	*Elaenia fallax*
Grey Kingbird	*Tyrannus dominicensis*

Stolid Flycatcher	*Myiarchus stolidus*
Hispaniolan Palm Crow	*Corvus palmarum*
Palmchat	*Dulus dominicus*
Purple Martin	*Progne subis*
Caribbean Martin	*Progne dominicensis*
Northern Mockingbird	*Mimus polyglottos*
La Selle Thrush	*Turdus swalesi*
Red-legged Thrush	*Turdus plumbeus*
House Sparrow	*Passer domesticus*
Village Weaver	*Ploceus cucullatus*
Scaly-breasted Munia	*Lonchura punctulata*
Antillean Euphonia	*Euphonia musica*
Black-crowned Tanager	*Phaenicophilus palmarum*
Hispaniolan Oriole	*Icterus dominicensis*
Shiny Cowbird	*Molothrus bonariensis*
Greater Antillean Grackle	*Quiscalus niger*
American Redstart	*Setophaga ruticilla*
Mangrove Warbler	*Setophaga petechia*
Prairie Warbler	*Setophaga discolor*
Bananaquit	*Coereba flaveola*
Yellow-faced Grassquit	*Tiaris olivaceus*
Greater Antillean Bullfinch	*Loxigilla violacea*

Scillies reignition

Such ventures I have enjoyed but none have quite filled the void of 1984, the year of what might have been had I pressed on for a 300+ total. The truth is that during the 2000s my birding had been patchy as children, divorce, re-location and career took precedence. Even when I met my partner, Mary, in 2003, nothing immediately changed until 2007, when she declared she would like to go to the Scillies! Having started to do some local birding again that year, I immediately scheduled a trip for

19th October. Mary was somewhat perplexed as to the choice of date so I began explaining to her my past exploits on Scillies and how that timing was everything if you were to catch the autumn migrants. I don't think she had any idea of the fanatic that lies within me. The night before our departure for Penzance at around 3 a.m. to catch the ferry to St Mary's I could not sleep. I was buzzing and lay awake like a schoolboy on Christmas Eve wanting a sneak peek at his toys. Now in my late 50s I still get the same feeling every time we go!

Revisiting Scillies, seeing old familiar faces, feeling the buzz of the chase and envying the big lists of previously known birders there that had shared my earlier exploits during the 80s was the spark I needed. Since that day Mary and I have returned most years to the Scillies and as I type, we are due to return in 2018 yet again. Aside from the uncertainty of what birds might turn up, the Scillies is a beautiful place, a compact diversity of accessible habitats and hospitality unlike anywhere else. It never fails to deliver on many fronts, making new and greeting old acquaintances year after year. The only stain here is the loss of my good friend and local birding partner, David Perrett, a superb bird photographer who would join us there with his wife, Sue, and Mary's keen birding school friend Karen. David sadly passed away a few years ago but I have no doubt he would have been my birding companion in life's next chapter. David's ashes are scattered in the Cairngorms, another fantastic location he, like me, regularly visited to see Ptarmigan and Dotterel before his untimely death from cancer.

Starting Block

So, there you have it. Having previously forsaken the opportunity to apply sustained effort and achieve 300+ birds in Britain in a year along with my peers, I felt that some things just could not be put off any longer. Although I cannot claim to be a celebrity nor an acclaimed author or artist, hopefully the average birder will derive something from the following exploits and feel inspired to do something similar. As you can tell from my simple reflections too, for me it's not just about the birds but about the uncertain circumstance, the unique places visited, the characters met along the way, and adventure that unfolds. Also, knowing that you are seeing something that has overcome great challenges and distance to reach our shores, and that most people will probably not even notice is there, makes you feel genuinely privileged.

As for me, I am not really a fanatic but rather a determined birder of moderate patience. In line with previous authors I concur that it's possible to achieve 250 birds a year attending the right locations (habitats) at the right time. That leaves a minimum of 50 scarcities/rarities to bag on top, e.g. one a week.

Perhaps one of the most inspiring publications, which demonstrates how 300 can be achieved, is Richard Millington's *A Twitcher's Diary*, published in 1981. Seeing Richard in those early days in Norfolk and his fantastic drawings in the log book at Nancy's café was an absolute pleasure. His Diary has served as an inspiration to me and remains a valuable guide. Since then I believe others have gone way beyond this threshold with one multimillionaire, I was informed, claiming a record 417 species in 2016 spending £89,768 covering some 82,000 miles. I do not know if that's true but one renowned twitcher, Lee Evans (LGRE), is reported in Wikipedia to have seen 386 species in 1996 in Britain and Ireland and, perhaps even more remarkably, claims to have surpassed 300 in Britain year on year since. Often, and usefully so, such big listers display their lists, locations and dates on the BUBO website for all to see. Clearly dedication and deep pockets are essential given the amount of travel involved. The question then, aside from satisfying my personal ambition, is what is there left to do? Is the target number of 300 too low, perhaps? Should I not be aiming higher? Hopefully, I will achieve more than 300 birds but for me the value is in the journey and the telling, the choices made, and not just the number of species or ornithological exactness. And in any case only a handful of birders break 300 in a year according to BUBO, a tiny proportion of the many hundreds of keen twitchers out there.

This, then, is very much the personal journey of an enthusiastic birder wanting to see more than half the birds ever recorded in Britain in just one year. From its telling I hope others will gain a little inspiration so as to embark on their own unique adventure. Either way, don't put off indefinitely that which you desire most. Life's journey may be shorter than you think and, indeed, rarely goes to plan.

JANUARY

It's *1st January* and as any birder will tell you if you are year listing it is a very special day. I was like a small excited boy once again: up at 06:30 sharp, coffee and snacks pre-prepared, waterproofs, woolly hat and gloves on, a plan with target birds in mind. Gloucestershire was my destination as it gets good coverage by the local birders, who are very active on Twitter. I'd started my birding there in my early teens and have family there today, so I know it well.

It was cold and clear and my first key bird was to be a beautiful **Penduline Tit** at Plock Court in Gloucester at 08:30. I had seen these before, for example at Stodmarsh in Kent, but that was some years back. This bird would obligingly stay around for many weeks to come, delighting hundreds of birders.

I then headed to Ashleworth Ham to locate a reported Green-winged Teal. I thought I knew the place well enough despite the gen on the bird being somewhat poor, but the area was flooded, and the birds widely dispersed. Some small roads were becoming impassable and I was confined largely to birding from a half-open car window due to a steady downpour. (I guess I'll just have to get used to this...) After an hour or so, I decided to cut my losses and head to Sharpness where I added an obliging **Black Redstart** at 11:00, flitting between a small building on a grassy green in front of houses on Dock Road and the rails of a nearby boat. That was followed by a juvenile **Great Northern**

01 Penduline Tit, Plock Court, Gloucester, 18th December 2017.
(Courtesy of Ian Bollen)

Diver 11:20 not more than half a mile away from the same location, viewed as close as 8m showing off its fabulous spangled back. This was almost certainly the closest I'd been to a GND ever.

A great start, and by now I was beginning to buzz as I headed to Frampton Lake. Immediately, I saw a couple of birders focused on a large, dying tree. **Tawny Owl** 11:45 roosting! A peep through their scope revealed the beauty, snoozing in the sun-facing hole of the tree. Normally I'd pick these up at my partner's farm, but this was a cracking and unexpected daytime view on what used to be my local patch! On the Frampton Court lake, a lone **Whooper Swan** 12:15 unexpectedly presented itself. These birds often turn up at Slimbridge WWT along with the many Bewick's for which the place is well renowned, but they can be easily overlooked, and sightings seem to be decreasing there. A flash of brilliant blue – **Kingfisher** 12:30 – tore across the Frampton Court lake adding icing to the cake.

Given Slimbridge was around the corner it was the logical next step, and is in any case, a must for winter birding. Light is short too at this time of year, so I needed to make the best of the few remaining hours. The only issue with Slimbridge is that counting selected species here as part of my list might be dubious, and so it was to prove. Slimbridge quickly offered up a **Red-breasted Goose** 14:20 from the Holden Tower but word was out that this ringed bird was probably an escape, so I decided it would not count towards my total. These days it seems almost by default that if something is ringed it can't possibly be wild, yet we are increasingly ringing and tagging everything! I recall an earlier Red-breasted Goose some 30+ years ago, also at Slimbridge, deemed wild at the time, heavily twitched and ticked by many birders. I wonder if that was ringed? Much the same could be said perhaps of the 50+ Barnacle Geese and perhaps the three **Common Cranes** 14:20 simultaneously viewed, and which have become a feature (most tagged with trackers). The Barnacle flock was originally feral but has increased year on year, a few wild birds I dare say bolstering their numbers each winter, though it is frankly near impossible to separate them from the feral ones in the field. Again, the Common Cranes have been released by the dozen in the south-west these past years. They continue to breed successfully, frequently moving between the Somerset Levels and Slimbridge. Given their breeding success then, I decided that while I'd pass on the Barnacle and Red-breasted Geese I would tick the south-west Common Cranes for the first time, though I'd bump into others, given a couple of these birds were not ringed! It had been a great first day.

2nd January saw me heading down to Chew Lake in Somerset, another frequent haunt. It was a wet grey day but a £5 permit from the Fishing Lodge ensured I could find shelter in the Moreton Hide where, it seemed, half a dozen or so birders had the same idea. Reports of the Lesser Scaup suggested it was likely to be way off in the gloom. After some eye-watering searching, I decided to head off to the Stratford Hide. Again, no sign. Returning to the Moreton Hide I quickly latched on to a couple of **Greater Scaup** 12:30 (male and female). All the ducks had drifted closer in now and so I began trawling the flock once again until I came across a third bird that stood out and fitted the characteristics of Lesser Scaup. Pretty certain that this was the bird, I alerted others as we squinted to get confirmatory views of the essential white inner wing. Fortunately, the photographer next to me, Gareth Jones, managed just that, capturing the bird mid-flap. **Lesser Scaup** 13:05, a somewhat tricky rarity in the bag.

I managed to top up my list with a few further common species during that morning, including: Goosander; Goldeneye; Green Woodpecker; Jay and an obliging **Green Sandpiper** 10:00, but frustratingly missed a Bearded Tit that flew in front of Moreton Hide whilst I was fiddling with my bulky scope.

I decided to head to Barrow tanks in the drizzle to try to locate the reported Long-tailed Duck. Not knowing the location well, I needed to find tank No.1 where the bird had been reported. Arriving at a suitable parking point opposite the tanks, I noticed three or four birders clambering the steep bank to the reservoir. I decided to follow and 10 minutes later was viewing a superb male **Long-tailed Duck** 14:20.

The Somerset Levels have increasingly turned up some very tricky birds. With the carve up into reserves: Ham Wall, Shapwick Heath and Greylake all in close proximity and, with good access, the area is now one of the country's top birding destinations. So, on *4th January*

02 Lesser Scaup, Chew Lake
Moreton Hide, 2nd January.
(Courtesy Gareth Jones)

I found myself there in the drizzle on a wet and windy day locating an adult male **Ring-necked Duck** 12:39 on Noah's Lake, after some two hours of searching. Again, gen is so important. I'd unwittingly been searching the wrong quadrant of the lake (I needed the north-west quadrant but was in a wind-whistling hide to the east) with more than 1,000 wildfowl to sift through. Even so, the interim birding had turned up 4 **Marsh Harriers** 09:45, 2 **Great White Egrets** 10:00 in the nearby channel and a **Lesser Redpoll** 10:05 in the woodland adjacent to Noah's Lake. Perhaps the greatest pleasure, though, was watching an approaching wet and bedraggled birder traipsing up the long path towards me. He seemed to be drained of all hope of seeing the Ring-necked Duck in the deteriorating wind and rain, but I was able to give him the uplifting news of not only having seen the bird but then relocating it with him! Definitely a halo moment.

On *6th January* I left the county of Gloucestershire to hit the Dorset coast and one of my favourite birding locations, Portland Bill. Another early start saw me at the coast around 09:00 on a cold breezy morning, searching the harbour where I quickly located 11 **Red-breasted Mergansers**, 2 **Black-necked Grebes** 09:25 and 2 Great Northern Divers. With a little input from the locals, Pulpit Rock on the bill pleasingly yielded 6 **Purple Sandpipers** 11:09. That was a bonus – I usually dip Purple Sands. here. The cold cutting wind signalled time for a coffee. Reinvigorated, I then saw a host of common species, including an obliging **Fulmar** 11:12 close in to the bill. Sadly, the steep descent into Church Ope Cove, which followed an interesting 15 minutes of my trying to reverse uphill through a narrow stone-sided dead-end street, much to the amusement of onlookers, did not yield the reported Yellow-browed Warbler. My first dip. Still, I'd unearthed a new spot I'd never visited before, that's the beauty of birding. Frustratingly, the Yellow-browed continued to show itself to just about every birder that visited this site in coming weeks! Still, I would be bound to catch up with these smart little fellows on the Scillies.

03 Steep descent to Church Ope Cove, Portland Bill, 6th January, but no sign of the enduring Yellow-browed Warbler. (Terry Wells)

Despite this minor setback Ferrybridge yielded 44 **Brent Geese** 12:30 and 30+ **Mediterranean Gulls** 13:00. A surprising flock of a dozen or so Skylarks in front of the café no more than 5m away entertained me and a fellow birder for half an hour as we tried to turn them into something more evocative. Woodlark perhaps? At Old Castle, further Black-necked Grebes, Razorbills and Mergansers were located, and at Lodmoor a female Marsh Harrier floated past the Ruff, Dunlin and Snipe feeding on the scrape. A further 5 Med Gulls flew by the beach in front of Lodmoor, gleaming in the setting sun as I headed home.

Before I travelled to Norfolk, where a few rarities had been unearthed, the mass influx of Hawfinches spreading across the country had finally reached Corsham Court churchyard, a few miles from my home. On *7th January* I managed to locate 4 **Hawfinches** 13:15 at the rear of the churchyard, much to the delight of the photographers camped the other side of the church; they then had a nightmare trying to photograph the flighty few. A quick visit to close by Box Mill saw me dip the Dippers, which I'd thought were a certainty. The water was just too high, but the evening yielded a consolation **Barn Owl** 18:09 in trees by the entrance of Townlease Farm. I was to see this obliging bird four times in the following hour!

In my first week of birding my records reveal I'd hit 102 species excluding Barnacle Goose and Red-breasted Goose and had reached my first minor milestone, i.e. to break 100.

Norfolk jaunt...first of many

True to form, Norfolk was beginning to show its colours and so I'd booked a couple of nights in Hunstanton from *9th January*. Given I live in land-locked Wiltshire, it is always a pleasure to visit this coastal county, which holds such great memories for me.

My first stop was Santon Warren where sadly I could not locate the Parrot Crossbills that continued to show themselves for some weeks to come. Surprisingly, aside from a **Treecreeper** 10:30, my only year tick at this pretty spot was 2 **Egyptian Geese** 10:26, not exactly the woodland species I'd anticipated. After a couple of hours trekking in the forest, I headed off to find the Hume's Warbler reported at Waxham near Sea Palling an hour or so away. Despite good gen it took me some time to locate Shangri-La Chalet garden, which borders the beach, where the bird had been last reported. After hearing the bird give out its wispy call several times, I decided to leave the few birders I'd been chatting with and to explore the bushes on the seaward side of the garden. Scrabbling along a small obscured track that ran parallel to the bushes, I quickly located two frenetic birders chasing something in the undergrowth with a camera. "There!" "No, there!" "Over there!" All I could see was leaf movement until suddenly **Hume's Leaf Warbler** 13:35 bagged. This was a Lifer for me as I'd decided not to add the species to my list a few years back on St Mary's, Scillies, given two birders emerged from the bushes ahead of me playing a recording, creating some doubt! Very frustrating… This time, despite the bird's agile movement through the leafy ground vegetation, good views were had of the bird calling, too. In truth, it looked somewhat like a washed out Yellow-browed Warbler, but the call is very distinctive, so homework proved key. I certainly began to appreciate why this was referred to as a "Leaf Warbler", too: photos, even as good as the one below, just cannot

04 Hume's Warbler, Waxham, Norfolk, 12th January.
(Courtesy Steve Gantlett)

do justice to the habit and jizz that make this bird so much fun to seek.

Thinking that I'd made up for the missed Parrot Crossbills, I decided to head over to Happisburgh a few miles along the coast to see if I could locate the Snow Bunting and Shore Lark reported to be in a field south by the lighthouse. The gen was good but the field was huge. As I fed the car park meter, made use of the toilet facilities and took a much-needed coffee break, I contemplated my approach. Fortunately, after 20 minutes of walking, the 31-strong **Snow Bunting** flock 14:20 was making itself blatantly obvious close to the coastal path. The Shore Lark, however, was nowhere to be seen and the parking meter was running out. I headed back, fed the meter once more, fearing an over-zealous coastal parking attendant, and headed to the higher parts of the field where earlier I'd seen a birder scoping something. As I was just about to resign myself to getting better views of the Snow Bunting, I disturbed a lone **Shore Lark** 14:50. I pursued the bird for 15–20 minutes to achieve frankly average views but was satisfied with my endeavour and first day's tally for Norfolk.

On *10th January*, my second day in Norfolk, I visited Holme but saw the reserve did not open until 10:00 so I diverted for Thornham to locate the reported Twite! 17 **Twite** 09:05. Wow! I first watched them in the grey and drizzle from the car with the birds 16m from my open window – amazing views milling about the thistle area of the harbour. A van of birders on a tour promptly arrived to join the spectacle.

"Did you see the Spotted Redshank in the creek?" the tour guide asked. I had not really looked. Ten minutes later, and after some heart-stopping slipping on a mud-covered boardwalk, I located a single **Spotted Redshank** 09:30. As is so often the case, the good synergy amongst keen birders leads to, well, more birds for all. In fact, it turned out this birding group was staying in the B&B next door to me in Hunstanton! Organised birding tours are becoming increasingly numerous in Norfolk. Rounding off the day with a visit to Titchwell in the continuing grey, wet and cold weather produced 1 **Bar-tailed Godwit**

10:11; 1 **Sanderling** 11:10 and a **Whimbrel** 11:04. I was picking up decent birds all right but could do with another rarity, I felt.

On my final day in Norfolk, *11th January*, I decided to traverse the top of Norfolk to try to locate both Coue's Arctic Redpoll and Iceland Gull near Cromer. The weather was appalling again: grey, drizzle and just a couple of degrees above freezing. A trek across the golf course as directed by several birders revealed nothing at all so I decided to head up to the reported Coue's Arctic Redpoll location in a commercial yard near The Royal Cromer Golf Club. Surprisingly, the very first bird I saw was the juvenile **Iceland Gull** 13:35, which now was on a putting green close to the commercial yard! Juveniles, I find, always display a subtly more interesting plumage than their respective adults.

Fellow birders then directed me to the Coue's. The redpoll flock spilled and splintered in bushes around the yard with poor visibility through drizzle and mist. Both adult male and first winter **Coue's Arctic Redpolls** 14:00 birds were finally identified with no shortage

05 Juvenile Iceland Gull, Cromer, Norfolk, 3rd January.
(Courtesy Steve Gantlett)

of help from local birders and one gentleman who claimed to have first found the birds on this his local patch. I spent a further hour or more checking the flock to be confident in picking out both the adult and first-winter males from the Mealy Redpolls. Sadly, photographing the birds was proving near impossible in the swirling afternoon mist.

A visit to Snettisham and Holkham on my last day in Norfolk produced little aside from a flock of c.30 **Pink-footed Geese** 09:04 in a field to the right of the approach road to Snettisham reserve; **Grey Plover** 09:30; a single **Barnacle Goose** 10:00 flying over the reserve; 8 **Red-legged Partridges** 12:15 at Holkham. I confess I was rather hoping them to be Grey Partridge as these are becoming increasingly scarce where I live in Wiltshire.

Closer to home

The following week Gloucestershire and Somerset were again throwing up some good birds. On *13th January* a **Richard's Pipit** 11:00 was located in the fields by the river at Arlingham, after much squelching in familiar Gloucestershire clay that plagued former school rugby pitches in my youth when showers were rarely working and in any case butt-clenchingly cold. I'd normally expect to pick up a Richard's in Scillies but given it's not a certainty this early bird was a nice bonus. A brief visit to Crabtree hill, Forest of Dean, also on 13th January, to locate a Great Grey Shrike whilst visiting my parents in Gloucester resulted in a dip. The gen was poor, and I simply did not know this location well enough. I cursed myself for not having prepared better and vowed to return later in the month if the bird remained. After all, shrikes, particularly adult males, are sharp-looking fascinating birds, renowned for impaling their prey, often small birds, on thorns. The Great Grey is the largest of the family we are likely to see in the UK.

15th January saw an early start to arrive at a rainy Greylake reserve in Somerset. This was my first visit to the reserve, which hosted hundreds if not thousands of Teal and Wigeon. After half an hour of systematically searching the sea of Teal, I located the single **Green-winged Teal** 10:20 from the lower of the two reserve hides. It was a joy to personally locate the bird and I congratulated myself on my diligence, pointing out the bird to arriving birders, who were equally pleased by their good fortune. As I looked up from the hide, a flyby probable Jack Snipe became a missed opportunity but the single **Water Rail** 10:45 beneath the hide was nevertheless welcome.

Buoyed by my success with the Green-winged Teal, I headed on to Matford Marsh in Devon where an American Wigeon had been putting in a regular appearance. The Marsh was small, and the only parking point seemed to be a layby on the opposite side of a busy dual carriage-way! At least the weather had improved. After scouting a small flock of Wigeon from the viewing platform I felt sure the bird was not among them. But wait: a further flock bobbing above the lumpy grass on the opposite side of the lake materialised from nowhere. Eventually the new flock emptied onto the water giving excellent views of, yes, the Yank. **American Wigeon** 12:38. This definitely was not a banker for my year list, so a great bird to find.

A brief visit to Topsham failed to produce the Water Pipit reported on the jetties by the recreation ground but I would catch up with this not uncommon species in abundance somewhat later.

On *17th January* I determined that Dawlish Warren may be worth a shot. At this time of year grebes and divers are prevalent there and sea watching on a stormy day can throw up some interesting birds – scoters, divers, etc. My first stop was the Life Boat Station where I quickly scoped a **Red-throated Diver** 13:30 close in, its upturned bill, grey-white contrasting throat and somewhat lithesome demeanour clearly evident: perhaps the sharpest of the divers in winter plumage. My second Long-tailed Duck, this one a female, was in the channel and then, pleasingly, a **Slavonian Grebe** 15:40 was located in the harbour from the reserve hide, though somewhat distant. Amongst the many waders on the sands of the estuary 4 **Greenshank** 15:30 provided another easy-to-find year tick.

19th January saw me back on familiar grounds in the Forest of Dean but first a brief stop at Highnam Woods provided excellent views of **Marsh Tit** 10:12 on the feeders in front of the hide. This is a great spot for this species, but on this occasion I was blessed with only a single bird, which I studied for some time, keen to remind myself of the bird's profile, jizz and call to aid me in discerning it from Willow Tit, which had become increasingly scarce. On to Crabtree Hill then, yet again, to locate the **Great Grey Shrike** 12:06 that I'd previously missed. This time I had better gen/maps – and I'd done my homework. Fantastic views were had of the bird hovering extensively 5m above the ground and hunting the hillside. Only one other birder was present to witness a superb display at close range. Having had my fill, I put the bird out on RBA and others quickly began to arrive despite the fact the bird had now been around for some weeks. Shrikes are always a great draw, the Weasels of the bird world, predators that punch above their weight. A single female **Common Crossbill** 12:00 on the walk up to the shrike site was a bonus, but I aspired to get much better views of these birds that demonstrate fascinating and entertaining bonding behaviour when in small family groups. The day was rounded off with a meagre count of 5 **Mandarin Duck** 13:25 at Cannop Ponds. I say meagre because this is one of the best sites in the country for this species, where more than 20 birds are regularly reported.

The need to pick up a few more of these introduced ducks reminded me to stop in at the Cotswold Water Park on *21st January*, where a short drive-round yielded 26 **Red-crested Pochard** 10:20 on Pit 44. These birds have made the western section of the park their home for some years, creating an abundant and self-sustaining population. Given the wet weather, I stayed local and a stop in Slimbridge at last gave up the **Little Stint** 11:38, which I'd missed previously. Several had been there for some months and my notebooks show I'd in fact seen two on the

Rushy Pen on 25th November 2017 along with the remaining (presumed escape) Red-breasted Goose. It brought back memories from Cley in the 1980s, where my first ever Little Stints were watched running beneath the legs of the tripod belonging to an overly keen birder attempting to photograph them. I'm sure they were saying "Silly man, now try and photograph us with that big lens!"

I'd been tracking the status of a Stilt Sandpiper that for some weeks now had been frequenting Brownsea Island. The island was off limits it seemed: no boats running, so no access to the general public during the winter months. By *22nd January*, however, it was putting in a regular showing at Coward's Marsh, Christchurch, hopping back and forth across to Stanpit Marsh in the company of Redshank. Encouraged by a last report of it being seen at Coward's Marsh around 10:17, I staked out the site that morning but no luck. Again, a later wander around Stanpit Marsh in the cold showery weather produced a no show, just a welcome **Spoonbill** 12:00. On this occasion the Stilt Sandpiper had evaded me. I berated myself for not making an earlier start, which might have met with success. Still, the day was not over, and Blashford Lakes was a stone's throw away. A visit to the Tern Hide at Ibsley Water produced an adult **Ring-billed Gull** and at least 2 adult **Yellow-legged Gulls** 15:00. Although at this time of year light can be challenging, mid-afternoon had given way to a short break of sun picking out the gulls well in the late daylight hours. By 16:10 I had to give up the quest for the first-winter Caspian Gull reported there, for despite claims and shouts "that's it, there!" from various birders around me, I was unconvinced, though not an expert in identifying this tricky species. Still, Ibsley is an excellent place for gull roosts and I had a feeling I'd be back soon. A shout out for a zoom-by Merlin missed just before my departure reminded me of another bird I needed to catch up with.

While I waited for the next twitchable rarity to ping to my mobile on Rare Bird Alert Pro, I again resolved to clean up locally, maximising use of the short daylight hours. On *24th January* 3 **Short-eared Owls**

14:19 at Aust Wharf put on a dazzling display at what must surely be Gloucestershire's best site for these birds. The only blight was the dog walker who opted to walk straight through the middle of them with three large untethered dogs! Just thoughtless. To add to the annoyance a dog walker later shouted at me for not keeping my dog under control as a large Rottweiler, minus its owner, bounded by me to dally with her three dogs. Her language was somewhat colourful to say the least, to which I simply replied, "I don't have a dog!" She disappeared smartly behind a hedge, no doubt embarrassed by her mistake.

Wiltshire being land-locked offers up a limited feast of birds compared with coastal counties but given I was compiling quarterly updates on my progress to WOS (Wiltshire Ornithological Society), I felt I should make use of local habitat and skills. A tweet exchange with a well-known local ringer, Matt Prior, revealed a site near Avery good for Tree Sparrows. He was right, as on *26th January* I was greeted by a flock of some 100+ **Tree Sparrows** 11:18 with c.20 **Corn Buntings** 11:30 and c.50 **Yellowhammers** 11:24. Fabulous to see all three species thriving on my doorstep and a reminder too of the power of local network. A lonesome **Red Kite** 12:24 circled the field nearby as I slipped and stumbled on the muddy track back to the car. I could not believe I had not seen a single Kite to date given I'd previously seen them daily near Reading on the M4 on my way to work. A visit to Salisbury Plain in the afternoon failed to produce much-needed Hen Harrier: despite multiple reports of this species in the coming weeks, this fantastic bird would rather unexpectedly continue to elude me.

27th January – looking across the map of colourful blobs that RBA Bird Pro uses to show reports of Rarities and Scarcities, there was little going on locally and in neighbouring Gloucestershire by way of further ticks, aside from a Smew at the Cotswold Water Park, which I managed to dip. A local duck shoot at the CWP location had temporarily scared the bird off for sure. Slimbridge WWT was quiet too, the eagerly anticipated Bean Goose had yet to arrive and all I found were the ever-present Cranes, this time 5 in all and a **Peregrine Falcon** 16:35 pursuing Lapwings with impressive dive speeds and agility, viewable from the Rushy pen in the fading light.

By contrast, Somerset was stumping up good ticks. On the *29th January* a **Glossy Ibis** 09:40 Ham Wall Platform 1; **Ferruginous Duck** 09:45 Walton Heath Hide (always a tricky bird to see) and c.20 **Cattle Egret** 12:20 with another 2 Great White Egrets on the road connecting Westhay to Burtle, near peat works. Who'd have thought Cattle Egrets would conquer Britain in such numbers with roosts of 30 or more becoming common. I should have known, too, from my experiences in the Caribbean that these birds are somewhat lazy, scavenging, apt to congregate where man was actively turning the soil, in this case peat harvesting. I even managed to catch up with the previously dipped **Smew** 15:25 at Pit 28 in CWP on the way home. Happily, the shooters were nowhere to be seen.

There was one final throw of the dice before January was done. Having missed Parrot Crossbills at Santon Warren in Norfolk on 9th January, I found that an alternative location, Wishmoor Bottom in Surrey, was yielding consistent sightings of these birds. On *31st January* I went in search of the birds on what was a cool rainy day: not ideal. More unfortunate was the brush clearing operation underway at the very spot the birds were last seen! After scouring the area without luck and talking to the local warden in charge of the clearing operation, I decided to head to Staines Reservoir where the female North American Horned Lark (nominate *Alpestris/Hoyti/Praticola*) had consistently been reported for some weeks. For some strange reason I had resisted the pull of this splendid bird, partly because I'd seen Shore Lark in Norfolk and this bird was essentially another subspecies of the same (so not deemed a further year tick). As such, it does not yet appear on the current BOU list. Staines was formerly a local patch for me while studying for my Doctorate at Imperial College in the 1980s. While delivering some great birds it is an extremely bland location, unless of course the reservoirs are drained, which they were not. Even so, on a cold sunny afternoon the **Horned Lark** 12:30 was duly located. Who knows, perhaps by the time I publish it will be an armchair tick! Species splits are becoming increasingly common. Either way it was a beautiful bird and provided excellent views for me and the three other birders present. It even made me feel nostalgic about the reservoirs, though I had no regrets of leaving behind the dog mess ridden causeway – disgusting – 28 piles in all peppered the sloping part of the causeway from the main road. I have to say by this point in my travels I was becoming increasingly exasperated with dog owners' blatant disregard both for their fellow members of the public and for wildlife.

As January closed I was 154 ticks in. I had surpassed my first month's target of 150 birds, managing to bird on 20 separate days, a luxury, I know. February, however, would be a very different matter. With no spring migrants yet, of course, I would need to travel more widely. I was targeting 200 species, but I knew that was probably stretching it. A milestone of 180+ was, however, a must if I was to remain on track. Turbulent winter weather would play a vital part.

FEBRUARY

The month kicked off with some local and, frankly, fruitless birding. Visits to New Passage, on the Severn on *1st February* for Water Pipit; Harnhill, Gloucestershire *2nd February* for Grey Partridge; and Ladbrook Lane Cemetery for Brambling did not produce a single tick! In fact, the only gift was 2 **Little Owls** 19:00 at my partner's Townlease Farm, Wiltshire, a regular for this location along with Barn Owl, Tawny Owl and the occasional Long-eared Owl. Perseverance, however, paid off with **Grey Partridge** 08:40 at Harnhill on *3rd February*. I'd returned, armed with a little more gen but in persistent rain, and three birds were located at the centre of a large barren field, no doubt boldly offering themselves for sacrifice to the circling Red Kite. It's no wonder these birds are becoming scarce!

To provide focus to the month's birding, I'd decided another trip was due but this time to Cornwall. My partner Mary and I frequently visit the county given the family has an apartment in Looe but on this occasion Mousehole was our chosen destination. In fact, I'm sure the trip was part of my Christmas gift to Mary: "A holiday in Cornwall, February, sea watching. What do you say?" How could she resist! Well, my timing was perfect, Cornwall was having more than its fair share of top birds and the county did not disappoint. The Ship Inn, too, proved perfect given its proximity to the sea front, good beer and food, though for some reason they have the miserly habit of not switching the central heating on before 6 p.m. There were problems with the toilet plumbing too, which resulted in a couple of room changes and multiple apologies from the somewhat embarrassed youthful Inn Manager. Clearly, this was a cheap Christmas gift from me!

Our first port of call on *4th February* was Pendower Beach on the south coast. After the usual trauma of negotiating tight Cornish lanes, we parked up. Half a dozen birders were in the car park; I hopped out to get the gen while Mary remained in the comparative warmth of the car, nursing a cold. I had never seen so many divers and in the cold sunshine. I notched up 2 **Red-necked Grebe** 16:39; 5 **Common Scoter** 16:50; at least 6 **Black-throated Divers** 16.15 in a tight group (but I am sure there were many more present) along with numerous Great Northern Divers and c.30 Med Gulls on the sea (both previously seen species). A fab start but then the real fun began as we began to sort out the reported rarity, a Pacific Diver! Eventually we homed in on a bird with the Black-throated Divers: no white on the flanks, moderate bill, clean lines unlike Great Northern, faint broken neck line emphasising cheek, and generally browner tone. We had all independently picked out the same individual and agreed we had our bird: my first UK **Pacific Diver** 17:00.

Our second day in Cornwall, *5th February*, continued to be fruitful. As we strolled along Penzance seafront where, incredibly, yet another Pacific Diver had been reported, an elderly lady volunteered, "You must be looking for the sandpipers." We indicated that we were indeed looking for birds but not sandpipers especially. She pointed downwards. "They are down there," she said, "on the sea wall. They are always there." And she walked off. I politely thanked her, silently thinking she might be a little crazy. I then looked over the wall to count no fewer than 39 Purple Sandpipers roosting in the crevices 5–6m below us, between Penzance quay and Jubilee Pool. It was poignant reminder to listen always to the locals as you pick up some useful birding insights. While Purple Sandpipers were not a year tick, and the views of the Pacific Diver in the harbour were comparatively poor, a subsequent juvenile

06 An obliging juvenile Glaucous Gull. Newlyn Harbour, Cornwall, 5th February. (Terry Wells)

Glaucous Gull 11:30 at Newlyn Harbour most certainly was a tick.

Once again, it was friendly input that helped us. On the Penzance sea front, two visiting birders, Ian Hayes and his partner, ensured we had no trouble locating the Glaucous.

A subsequent visit to Long Rock produced 11 Common Scoter but a visit to Cape Cornwall and Pendeen Watch failed to produce Chough, only Guillemots, Shags, Gannets and Raven were seen. As we circuited the birding hotspots of Cornwall, we again bumped into Ian and partner at Cot Valley. Climbing the coastal path, Mary and I found 2 **Choughs** 14:20 and a nicely perched male **Merlin** 14:30. Sadly, Ian and his partner had departed before we could give them the good news and return the earlier favour. Amazingly, I would see them both again at Speech House car park in the Forest of Dean, Gloucestershire where they were looking for Great Grey Shrike. Small world indeed!

Unfortunately, we missed 3 reported Eider Ducks at Sennen Cove but had good views again of the Glaucous Gull that evening while searching for, but failing to locate, the reported American Herring Gull in Newlyn Harbour.

Scoter day

Reports that there were Surf Scoters at Porthpean made for our next quest. So, on **6th February**, we headed off to arrive at a small cove in the sleet and snow to search for the birds. At first, sightings of a Scoter flock of 8 strong were too distant and I feared the worst. On the beach Mary spotted a **Common Sandpiper** 11:53, which offered a useful distraction and then a Rock Pipit that I'd hoped would somehow miraculously turn into a Water Pipit, a tick I still required.

As the weather moved in, hands froze and eyes watered and the snow fell, but the birds, fortunately, sought shelter in the cove. Closer now, the Scoters all looked to be Common (a mix of male and female) but, wait a minute, a Long-tailed Duck (my third for the year) emerged from the right with a smaller group of 4 Scoters that must have been just around the corner out of sight. As they came ever closer in the worsening conditions, what looked to be a first-winter **Velvet Scoter** 12:00 was first identified, as subsequent white wing flapping would confirm. Then, yes, 2 **Surf Scoters** 12:00, a female and juvenile, were confirmed. The fourth bird was less clear but as 3 Surf Scoters were posted on RBA this, I assumed, must have been the third Surf Scoter. By now, Mary and I felt absolutely frozen but I, at least, was elated.

Surprisingly, discerning scoters with half-decent views is not so difficult as it may first appear but usually views are distant, so time is required between their simultaneous dives to capture all the key features. I wondered how many times I may have simply recorded Common Scoter by default while squinting at bobbing distant scoters on a cold morning sea watch when there could have been a Surf Scoter tucked amongst them. Patience and homework certainly paid off in this instance.

7th February saw us rounding off time on Cornwall with a visit to Drift Reservoir where the only bird of interest was a huge Muscovy Duck (sadly, not a tick). A visit to Chapel Amble produced an impressive 8 **Water Pipits** 13:20 on a flooded field with 3 Ruff and 1 Green Sandpiper. It was about a 70-mile drive for Water Pipit but back home I'd just kept missing this bird and frustration was setting in. The day was rounded off with yet another Black Redstart, this time an immature on the boat ropes in Mousehole quay, spotted by Mary in the fading light. Is it me or does she spot everything before I do?

I was sad to leave Cornwall but while viewing the Smew at Cotswold Water Park on 29th January I'd learnt that my good friend Kevan Smith aged 62 had died of cancer, leaving his wife, Carol, and three sons. We decided to return a day early in time for Kevan's funeral. It was a stark reminder of just why, at the comparatively youthful age of 58, I was doing something I enjoy most in life. Postponement was not an option.

Following the yellow dots

Every time I consulted my RBA Word Pro app. on my mobile, I would be confronted by a cluster of yellow spots showing rarities around the southern part of the Dorset/Hampshire border. I immediately knew what they were, of course, by their precise location and having picked up the Ring-billed Gull and Yellow-legged Gulls there previously. The missed Stilt Sandpiper on 22nd January was still showing, too, and was now becoming a bad itch that required scratching. The report of a Thayer's Gull was enough to spark my return to the region on ***11th February***. Now, Thayer's Gull is widely considered to be a subspecies of Iceland Gull, which I'd already seen at Cromer in Norfolk 10th January, but it is a rarity and, of course, with advances in genomics who could say that one day it would not be a separate species? Species splits are increasingly common and big listers pay close attention to updates on such developments by bodies like the British Birds Rarities Committee (BBRC), in the hope of gaining an armchair tick.

07 Chilly birders searching for the Thayer's Gull at
a pig farm near Tidpit, Hants., 11th February.
(Terry Wells)

My first stop, then, was Stanpit Marsh, which was becoming the preferred location for the Stilt Sandpiper. After a quick check with a helpful volunteer in the reserve's centre, I located the bird from Fisherman's Bank feeding with Dunlin. **Stilt Sandpiper** 11:05 at last! Long-legged, buff-grey underparts, elegant, the bird was remaining close to the channels that cut into the edge of the marsh.

My next stop was a pig farm between Tidpit and Cranborne where the Thayer's Gull had last been seen and there were continuing reports of young Caspian Gulls, too. Pig farms are not the first place you might think of for gull watching but this place was crammed with gulls and I reminded myself that something like 4 Caspian Gulls were previously reported on a pig farm in Norfolk earlier in January. The light was good but the temperature icy cold.

Eventually I located the Thayer's Gull – or did I? Within probably 20 seconds and with only one other viewer using my scope to get onto the bird, the large gull flock took flight, and it was gone. Left with that gnawing uncertainty I knew I could not tick the bird. I continued to search and with the help of a fellow birder located a second-winter **Caspian Gull** 14:35 providing a little consolation. Since missing the earlier Caspian at Ibsley, and the 4 birds in Norfolk, I'd adone my identification homework, and it had paid off.

I decided to depart the pig farm, feet frozen, after some good views of my second Merlin and a flock of a dozen or so Lesser Redpoll in a nearby hedgerow. To my mind a significant number of larger gulls had departed, presumably to roost at Ibsley lake. I suspected the Thayer's might be amongst them. As I reached the car my mobile bleeped: the Thayer's was indeed showing at Ibsley. A mad dash through narrow back lanes, with my Korean Satnav intent on wrecking my car, found me in the Tern Hide at 16:20 viewing the bird along with a dozen or more other birders many of whom had been at the pig farm earlier. Juvenile **Thayer's Gull** 16:20, a nice pale bird with pale-chocolate coloured as opposed to dark primaries and a dark bill. Once seen, it was not too difficult to pick out from the numerous immature Herring Gulls and, pleasingly too, I felt sure my earlier spot at the pig farm was the very same bird.

Following my exploits in Hampshire, I decided to regroup and bird close to home. There were several more common species I still needed and when I looked at the rarities reported that I might chase, options seemed to be limited to Long-billed Dowitcher at Oare Marshes in Kent, a King Eider at Ceredigion in North Wales or a long-staying Spotted Sandpiper at Holme Pierrepont, Nottinghamshire – all a very long drive for a single bird with few proximate scarcities as potential backup. So, with my economic head on, I stepped back from twitching and returned to birding mode.

08 Juvenile Thayer's Gull, in a field near Tidpit, Hants., 9th February.
(Courtesy Gareth Rees)

My first port of call on *12th February* was St Anne's Church at Oldland Common, Bristol, where at last Ring-necked Parakeets seemed to be taking hold, though not to everyone's liking. Parakeets have a reputation for being noisy and brash and perhaps something of a bully. On the plus side they are bright, beautiful and we have little else like them in the UK. Up to 4 birds were regularly being reported on Twitter and while I'd seen as many as 400 heading to roost in the Staines area of London some years ago on my way home from work; I for one was pleased a local colony had taken hold. A single **Ring-necked Parakeet** 15:50 was seen twice, once upstream from the church and then in the churchyard itself. Unmistakable call, spectacular green, streamlined flight profile.

On *13th February* I visited Great Barrington where a female Hen Harrier had been regularly seen from a local trig point. Aside from a chance view on the Somerset Levels or Salisbury Plain, I knew of no other locations within say a 70-mile radius where I might see this magnificent bird. On arrival at the trig point I could see why the birds were attracted to the area: as I looked down into the valley I could see feeder bins and pheasants everywhere. Three Buzzards and a Red Kite were hunting, too. Sadly, four hours later the Hen Harrier was still eluding me. With the temperature feeling about −3° in the sleet and breeze, I surrendered, wet and cold, to the warmth of my car. I don't believe the Hen Harrier was further reported for this location, but a bird was occasionally being seen at Otmoor – the same bird, perhaps!

On **15th February** I was to have better luck in my search for scarce birds of prey: 2 **Goshawks** 10:00 at New Fancy in the Forest of Dean displaying and a further sighting at Nagshead of a single bird, and then again two from the Cyril Hart Arboretum (possibly the same birds). In fact, New Fancy view point was the location at which I'd seen my first ever UK Goshawk powering down the valley just below me, uttering its distinct, almost Green Woodpecker-like chatter call. Unforgettable! Sadly, the feeders at New Fancy are no more, a shame as I'd hoped to pick up Brambling here: it continued to elude me, despite just about everyone posting great pictures of this species on their garden feeders!

Great Berry Quarry, Lydbrook, Gloucestershire was cited as a good spot for the increasingly difficult Willow Tit with Dipper as a possibility. This was my first visit to the site where a local gent informed me Beavers were being reintroduced to help stop flooding. Clearly the site was being prepared for this and, despite the evident disruption caused by heavy-tracked machinery, a **Dipper** 15:30 put in a good display on Greathough Brook. It was turning into a good day in the forest but, sadly, only Coal Tits were in good song and the elusive Willow Tit would have to wait till another day. Further brief visits to Speech House car park and Crabtree Hill in the afternoon produced no new ticks. Neither did a visit to Oldbury on Severn on **17th February** looking for Little Gull nor Stinchcombe Hill for Woodcock.

All this comparatively local birding was very nice, but I was beginning to feel twitchy again, so on **18th February** I began to look further afield. I'd been going for general, nice-to-see birds, and dipping a few too many. Pulborough Brooks, Sussex, had been consistently showing a Temminck's Stint for some weeks and a Bluethroat and Black Guillemot were showing on and off in the Eastbourne area. I opted to head for Pulborough Brooks, my first visit to this RSPB reserve and what a popular place it proved to be, with a swish-looking information centre and café packed full of people. Retirees trouped round the reserve in tour groups. Heathland, mature woodland and open flooded area all within close proximity.

As I do on my ventures, I greet everyone and talk freely to birders just as I find them. The first guy I bump into, Graham, has a Walkie Talkie. I am not certain if he is a warden or a keen volunteer, but he is very polite and walks me to the West Mead Hide where I enjoy reasonable views of the **Temminck's Stint** 10:20. He promptly introduces me to half a dozen or so birders in the hide. What a nice thing to do. When I state my quest, unsurprisingly, discussion turns to what birds I've seen, need to see, and where.

They were clearly having a great time birding and so it should be. For me the reserve was a reminder of how far the RSPB has come. Still, I needed fresh ticks. A quick skirt of the reserve failed to produce the Woodlark reported in the log book, nor the Hawfinches at the churchyard. As I lunched, sat on the boot of my hatchback in the reserve car park, on lemon curd sandwiches, which reminded me of my London childhood, I contemplated my next step. On RBA the Bluethroat and Black Guillemot near Eastbourne were not showing so I decided to head for Pagham Harbour. There, in the late afternoon sun, aside from the 5 Velvet Scoters and a couple of Mergansers on the sea, I located first 4 **Knot** 14:10 and a single female **Eider Duck** 14:55. As the daylight faded, with a cup of warm coffee in hand at Church Norton car park, I watched 30 Goldfinches swilling around, hoping a Siskin might appear from somewhere, or a lone Firecrest might call from the churchyard where they were occasionally seen. Sadly, it was not to be but the hundreds of Brent Geese milling above me were putting on a spectacular display. As the sun sank towards the horizon in the cool late afternoon air, I felt privileged to enjoy such freedom when so many could not.

Scanning tweets on Twitter that evening, I saw that one birder reported how two Woodlarks were singing in competition at a Norfolk location. For me, Woodlarks meant a visit to the New Forest where I had a decent site for them, though I was a touch doubtful I would be so lucky as to find them singing this early in the year. I contemplated that I might be able to pick up Lesser Spotted Woodpecker, Brambling and Siskin there. too: all birds I somewhat surprisingly still needed. So, on **21st February**, an early start for the New Forest rewarded me with two **Dartford Warblers** 09:40 near Slufters Inclosure. Sadly, a nearby site for Woodlark produced not a tweet and there was no drumming from the reported Lesser Spotted Woodpecker at Mark Ash Wood. Despite what looked to be great habitat and strong evidence of the bird's presence. A couple of Tawny Owls exchanged unusual calls from their secret roosting sites. Then I noticed many dead leaves being flicked up almost aggressively beneath some Beech trees to my right – **Brambling** 12:30. Yes, a flock of around 20 and proving to be a little skittish as I crunched my way across the leaf-strewn forest floor to grab a closer look. I find this a beautifully marked little bird and one I'd so far hoped in vain to see on my garden bird feeders. By contrast, here, with the Chaffinches present, they fed frenetically, causing greater disturbance to the leaves, almost like a small child excitedly ripping open a Christmas gift. It's a simple reminder that so often habit and jizz are better than a photo in providing that key first indicator of a bird's presence.

Sub- zero, pink evasion

Although January had provided a feast of white wingers (a term broadly used to describe scarce and rare white-winged gulls), there was still room for more, and February did not disappoint.

09 & 10 Birders at Ferrybridge (above) and Lodmoor (opposite), 23rd February, searching for adult Ross's Gull. (Terry Wells)

A Ross's Gull had been reported in the Weymouth area on 21st February, frequenting Ferrybridge and Lodmoor. This surprisingly pretty pink-washed gull seemed to be mobile and the weather was turning bitterly cold and breezy. I figured, taking into account the high/low tide times and gen on RBA and Twitter, that the bird was best seen early in the morning and would probably move on about 09:15–09:30 to Lodmoor. As I set off from my home in Wiltshire on *23rd February*, aiming to arrive around 09:00, news came through that the bird was showing at Ferrybridge at 07:51. Great, but I cursed myself for not making an

earlier start. However, I was not counting on the lorries and roadworks, so I did not arrive until 10:00 to find half a dozen or so birders in the cold, hoping for the bird's return, it having last allegedly been seen at 09:45. It did not return! Hope was not lost, given that the bird had favoured Lodmoor's west side scrapes on the 21st and 22nd. I hopped across to Lodmoor then to find 60–70 birders, and many familiar faces, like Lee Evans of fame from TV twitching programmes and radio interviews, evidencing the revered status given to Ross's Gull. As we talked and milled around in the biting cold, the hours passed. A short walk along the reserve's west path revealed two **Bearded Tits**

12:14 calling to my left, then another flitting and calling to the right. Not bad, I thought, given the breezy conditions, which can make catching these birds difficult. Lodmoor produced a no show but after several hours news broke at 15:45 of the Ross's Gull showing at Bowleaze Cove. A stampede ensued, and a crowd amassed on the sea front's walk-way to the west side of the cove but only those on the cove's jetty to the east would have had a decent view. Most of us were left scanning a thousand distant gulls bobbing on a turbulent sea, knowing it was in there somewhere but impossible to find.

After my expensive dip at Weymouth and despite the Ross's Gull still frequenting Radipole on the 24th, I decided I needed to chance my arm elsewhere. A visit to East Budleigh in Devon on **25th February** produced a putative **Italian Sparrow** (*Passer italiae*) at 11:00 at Cadbury Gardens. It did not disappoint and although there were questions over the bird being a hybrid it clearly seemed to fit the bill (a pun there somewhere). It was shyer than the House Sparrows, one particular male of which would repeatedly boss the Italian bird from the nut feeder, while the tolerant occupant of the property whose garden the bird occupied lowered her blinds, no doubt by now fed up with birder intrusions.

The only other birder there told me there were in fact two sites, Wynards Road and Cadbury Gardens, that the bird frequented. As I wandered between both sites an elderly local gentleman chatted to me, confirmed Cadbury was the better viewpoint, that the bird was shy, and told me exactly where I should stand to see it. He was right, the bird favoured a certain feeder largely screened from the main road and took longer than the accompanying House Sparrows to feel comfortable in my presence. Once again, listening to local knowledge had proved vital. However, I did not feel justified in adding the bird to my year list as it is not BOU listed (though present on the 2018 BUBO listing). DNA testing would probably be required to support a case for its identity.

Next stop Teignmouth for a Bonaparte's Gull reported from The Point car park. Here I complicated life by first parking at the wrong end of the bay. Once again, my Korean Satnav was having the last laugh. Having found the correct location, I scanned the cycling Black-headed Gulls, confident I could pick the bird out as I had seen a Bonaparte's in Cornwall late last year. The sea was red-brown, thrashing against the sea wall, the wind making viewing unpleasant through lens-spattered binoculars. No luck. I could see a bunch more gulls to the right of me on a spit. Walking down through the somewhat concealed Lower Point car park beach huts, I emerged onto the exposed spit and quickly met two birders (new acquaintances), Steph Murphy and Rob, looking for the bird and armed with camera. Time was running out on the parking meter and, knowing how zealous some seaside parking attendants can be, I left them vowing to return as soon as I'd moved my car to a closer location. On my return, Steph, despite previously confessing her inexperience in identifying Bonaparte's, produced some snaps that confirmed she had indeed captured the gull. Within 10 minutes or so, sure enough we were all seeing the gull again quite close, cycling back and forth with Black-headed Gulls along the shore in strong wind. Smaller than Black-headed, pink legs, dark bill, characteristic eye spot, more buoyant flight – **Bonaparte's Gull** 13:30. There would be several further opportunities to see one of these birds later in the year, but it was good to get this one under my belt.

The day ended with a trawl of the fields around Powderham, which failed to produce 2 reported white morph Snow Geese. A good day but the previously dipped Ross's Gull was, frankly, still raw and the bird was brazenly showing yet again now from the warmth of the RSPB Radipole reception centre!

Time was running out in February. I risked being short of my targeted bird total of 180 species. Unfortunately, the very next day I'd put my back out lifting a basket of fire wood. I could barely walk and getting in and out of chairs/cars was a Herculean challenge. My body was somewhat amusingly zigzag shaped! Even so, I needed to finish the month strongly. So, after a day of exercising, Deep Heat, Ibuprofen, my

11 & 12 (above) Angry seas at Teignmouth Point car park (Terry Wells); adult Bonaparte's Gull (below), Teignmouth spit, Devon, 25th February. (Courtesy Steph Murphy)

back seemingly clicked back into place during the night while simply turning over in bed. Although my back was still painful, the next morning, 28th February, found me at Radipole looking for the Ross's Gull once more. It was –6° on the way down, and only –3° on the coast; the cold wind was ferocious, producing a feels-like –9° according to the Met. forecast! No sign at Radipole so off to Lodmoor: 3 Spoonbill here, the scrapes were frozen. Only a few birders here at Lodmoor viewpoint, watching the antics of Black-tailed Godwit as they shouted and chased each other close in. Walking was a struggle, but I felt humbled by an elderly lady birder with bins and walking stick who overtook me. "I've had a hip operation," she told me, as I whined to her about my incapacity somewhat embarrassed by my shuffling. "I've got to catch my bus now," she said. It was time to man up, so I headed off to freezing Ferrybridge. Only large gulls here by the bridge; too cold, exposed, dangerously low temperatures here, and no sign of Ross's. The final option then was to camp in the warmth of the Radipole centre following a stolen 10 minutes in the car with flask and snacks.

At Radipole everyone had the same idea. The biting cold wind was intolerable. A dozen or more largely middle-aged birders scanned the gulls through the window, bolstered by the occasional coffee and genial hospitality the centre offered. Included were several birders from Gloucestershire, Mike King of "Glosterbirder" website fame, and Duncan Dine, a Gloucester birder and photographer I follow on Twitter. After a few hours, with myself largely seated to minimise my back discomfort, a shout went up. "I've got it, I've got it; the Ross's!" Duncan had spotted the bird quite close in to the left of the small island right in front of the RSPB centre. **Ross's Gull** 15:27.

To me, Ross's Gulls are special. While not sporting the attractive pink wash its name would suggest, it was petite, dove-like, ghostly pale, and elegant-looking with a fluted tail. As photographers ducked out the back of the centre to avoid the window interfering with image quality, the bird suddenly shot over the centre and alighted in the car park

13 Adult Ross's Gull, car park at Radipole RSPB reserve,
28th February. (Courtesy Duncan Dine)

behind. Birders and photographers tucked behind cars, crouched and lay on the ground to get photos of our welcome guest. It looked like SWAT at a stakeout. Good views were had by all in the bitter cold; birders high-fiving in jubilation. What an end to a tough week and month! I'd just beaten my targeted 180 species to reach 181. Could it get any better?

MARCH

March is perhaps the most difficult month to find birds. The weather can be wet and cold, and our winter visitors begin to disperse, making birds missed in January/February difficult to locate. On the upside, mild temperatures in late March can bring early spring migrants and indeed the odd scarcity. It is not a month for high ticks but often a time for winter clean-up of those trickier birds missed.

Snow stopped play on *1st* and *2nd March* as icy drifts made it frustratingly impossible to travel by car. The *4th* saw me visit Portbury Wharf, North Somerset, only to get a good soaking and dip on a reported Little Gull. I then spent three hours in the afternoon attempting to see a Lesser Spotted Woodpecker at Highnam Wood that a local birder had put out on Twitter. I arrived to catch the spotter, in the familiar Marsh Tit Hide, elated at having seen the bird and keen to offer directions. Three hours later, soaked once more, cold and muddy I'd seen several Marsh Tits and Great Spotted Woodpeckers…but no LSW! Not a good start.

Commitments on *5th March* saw me surveying farmland with a local landowner keen to monitor birds across his large estate. Although we witnessed impressive flocks of hundreds of Yellowhammers, Linnets and Reed Buntings from a small petrol golf-like buggy we used to tour the estate (in part due to the many feed bins for Pheasant rearing) the tour did not throw up any new year ticks.

Things seemed to go from bad to worse when on **6th March** I'd decided the long-staying Little Bunting at Walthamstow deserved my attention. Given the reserve was situated in the heart of London I did not relish the journey, though in part I was curious to see how the reserve had shaped up, especially given this formed part of the area I had mischievously frequented as a youngster. Six hours in the car; I'd been held up in the M4 traffic then overshot the entrance. Stuck in more one-way traffic; it was becoming infuriating. I found myself in some M1 services having a coffee, fed up, and frustrated. I decided to head home! I'd reached a low point and the success of January and February was fast waning.

With the weather improving on **8th March** and a lack of new birds appearing on Twitter and on RBA, I headed to Labrador Bay, Devon. I traversed the steep slopes in the warming sun and experienced breath taking views of the sea and coastline, **Cirl Bunting** 10:29 was added

14 Glorious views over Labrador Bay, home of the Devon Cirl Buntings, 8th March. (Terry Wells)

to my list – incredibly, only my first tick of the month! Two birds seen, both males in scrub 200m just below the main car park; the song always reminds me of Yellowhammer without the "*no cheese*" sounding ending. I was heartened. A stop at Dawlish Warren upon my return home sadly did not produce hoped for skuas from the coastguard watch. The sea was too calm.

News of a male Garganey at Saul Warth, Gloucestershire on *9th March* saw me park at Cadbury Bridge, squelch hastily down a track to the shoreline in the failing afternoon light, to scope the huge flocks of wildfowl before me. Despite a lot of birding in this part of Gloucestershire, this was my first visit to Saul Warth, and I was duly impressed. Sadly, a large group of somewhat noisy walkers emerged around the corner of woodland on the shoreline between me and the birds. Everything flushed and yes, I dipped.

11th March saw me get my male **Garganey** 09:50, but it had taken a lengthy drive to Farlington Marshes near Southsea where the bird was obligingly in the open on water in front of the information centre. The only other bird of interest on the reserve was a distant Bearded Tit calling and a Spoonbill, both already on my list. A wander on the beachfront at Elmer Rocks failed to produce a reported Black Guillemot and the only early migrants at Selsey Bill were two **Chiffchaffs** 15:44 by the recreational area.

A visit to Shorncote in the Cotswold Water Park on *13th March* failed to produce new birds and on *14th March* I knew I would be unable to venture out due to attendance at the Royal Agricultural College, Cirencester, where an event was being hosted by "Redlist Revival". What is this, you may well ask. Essentially it is a charity set up to restore Red-listed species (Birds of Conservation Concern list produced in 2016 by the UK's leading bird conservation organisations). It is directed at large landowners/farmers who, let's face it, are responsible for managing the largest rural areas of our country but who often have the competing although occasionally complementary challenge of producing food for us all. Getting landowners to operate sympathetically in support of conservation is, of course, most likely to work if government payments/farm subsidies reflect improvements made. My role in this affair, along with many BTO recorders around the country, would be to monitor lands owned by farmers close to the M4 junction, including the farm belonging to my partner. It was a worthy cause and the bird surveys I would enjoy immensely but the clock was ticking, and I'd added only three ticks so far this month! Could I really afford the time? That evening I pondered my position, wondering how much time Redlist Revival surveys might take across c.600ha of land. I decided to amble through 5.5ha of land I own and had planted with mixed woodland a dozen years ago simply to gather my thoughts. To my utter delight I flushed 5 **Woodcock** 16:55 as well as 3 Roe Deer and a Raven. Woodcock has been something of a bogey bird for me and to realise I had afforded them a new home in what was once a barren field was immensely satisfying.

I resolved to just keep grinding out the ticks. March was not going to kill off my chances so early of reaching my 300+ target. Back at the Cotswold Water Park again on *15th March* but nothing to show except an encouraging 69 Red Crested Pochard at the Waterhay. Then at RSPB Nagshead again, my first **Siskin** 14:55, while still on the trail of Lesser Spotted Woodpecker, which had once again been seen that morning on the reserve's short walk by two elderly gentlemen lunching, sat on a log. If only it were that easy for me. This was now the fourth location I had site visited to find LSW! Two Goshawks diving above Nagshead woodland, a single squawking Brambling at Park End and c.20 Mandarin at Cannop Ponds were, however, pleasing.

Blue is the colour

With spring still struggling to reveal itself, and snow again on *18th March* making travel somewhat difficult, my frustration continued. Experience told me I needed to be south and east on the coast to catch scarce migrants at this time, and that, thankfully, was where the recent snows had fallen least, so minimising travel disruption. So, on ***19th March*** I booked a B&B (Hayes Bank) in Ashford with Kent in my sights.

A brief stop at Dungeness RSPB information centre on 19th March gave me the gen I needed on the two reported Bluethroats. My first encounter, however, was with a friendly **Firecrest** 11:54 frantically feeding in the long grass by Denge Marsh Road. I would come across a couple more of these delightful little birds later in the day. Moving on swiftly to the few birders a couple of hundred metres ahead of me, I soon located the first **White-spotted Bluethroat** 12:08 in the dry part of a man-made channel. This looked to be a female/juvenile bird. Returning the way I'd come to enjoy the more elusive male, which was not on show when I first passed the spot and "Bingo"! I'd bagged my second Bluethroat at 12:40. A magnificent male with the white spot almost invisible amongst the iridescent blue. I then saw Lee Evans eyeing my first bird, which I again picked up. But then, what else? Lee had dropped down into the channel straddled by concrete structures and begun viewing something else: a Wheatear perhaps as one had been

15 White-spotted Bluethroat, Denge Marsh, Kent, 19th March.
(Courtesy Terry Laws)

reported. I followed Lee to see two Bluethroats together, again females/juveniles, I was not entirely certain. "So, there are three Bluethroats!" I exclaimed.

"No, four," Lee Evans replied. He was right, I turned and could still see my first bird and birders were still watching the adult male further back down the ditch. I backtracked to do a recount, there were indeed four Bluethroats here. Awesome! As birders passed by upon my long walk back to the car in the bitter sub-zero temperatures most, understandably, thought I must be the village idiot when I declared there were four Bluethroats on show, and not two, it being extremely rare to see that many together in Britain.

After coffee and a warm up I decided to brave the Dungeness shingle heading for "The Patch" by Dungeness power station. There a single adult **Little Gull** 15:11 spiralled back and forth amid a large flock of mainly Black-headed Gulls, its dark underwing, smaller size and buoyant flight evident. The hide was locked, and with limited shelter in such an exposed location I called it a day, confident I would never again find 4 Bluethroats in one UK location.

After a comfortable night's stopover in what was essentially a loft conversion at the Hayes Bank B&B in Ashford, followed by a hearty full-English, I decided to visit Rye Reserve where 100+ **Sandwich Terns** 11:00 were spied from the John Gooders Hide. Fresh visitors were arriving continuously as though signalling the imminence of spring as I delighted in the swirling cacophony. Even so, a few Chiffchaffs aside, cold temperatures were holding the bird migration at bay and so I opted for a drop-in visit to Eastbourne Harbour along the coast where I duly located the reported first-winter **Black Guillemot** 15:00 in Sovereign Harbour. The bird was skulking and, I confess, somewhat scraggy looking, presumably being mid-way between summer and winter plumage.

On *24th March*, somewhat frustrated by the sustained cold and slow-to-arrive migrants, I opted for a trip to Arne RSPB in the hope of picking up an early Osprey, or perhaps one of several Hen Harriers that were reported in the area. Alas, aside from enjoying views of no fewer than 5 Dartford Warblers on the reserve, all I could manage were 3 male **Northern Wheatears** 14:09, the latter only after an afternoon jaunt across to Portland Bill. I was still struggling to find a good Hen Harrier site and the birds were now clearly on the move from their winter grounds to their preferred breeding locations. This was an uncommon bird I now feared I could miss.

Returning to economy-first mode, I decided to stay local for a few days, but March was to continue to frustrate. A fellow birder, Graham Lawler, had been kind enough to point out the location of up to 6 **Little Ringed Plovers** 12:42 inhabiting Pit 305 of the Cotswold Water Park, though I saw only three on *26th March*. On *27th March* a **Jack Snipe** 09:52 reluctantly offered itself up at Slimbridge's Willow Hide, doing what Jack Snipes often do, nothing but sit! A pity – their bobbing action I find comic to witness. A visit to Liddington Hill, Wiltshire, in the afternoon failed to produce the reported Ring Ouzel, though this had proved to be a reliable stop off point for the birds in the past. A visit to the Cotswold Water Park on a showery cold *28th March* with temperatures still failing to climb above 8° produced 3 intrepid **Sand Martins** 16:56 at Kent End Quarry and I was to witness a further 50+ on a murky afternoon at Chew Lake on *30th March*, during a desperate attempt to close out the month with an Osprey that had been frequenting the area. The fact is March felt like something of a disaster. I'd added only 14 ticks to my year list and was short of my target of 200 birds. If only I knew how bad things could really get! It had been a cold, hard slog and, frankly, I began to question why I was doing this at all. I needed to recheck my strategy and remain determined.

APRIL

Sometimes logic says just move on, look for new prospects to chase, but still there were few migrants arriving and the cold single-figure temperatures continued mixed with heavy and uncertain rainfall. Lesser Spotted Woodpecker (LSW) was a bird beginning to irritate. Every year I struggled with it despite often receiving details of some new location of which those famous words were uttered "You cannot fail!". Or, indeed be permitted no site details at all owing to some well-intentioned birder seeking to safeguard the species. Despite that I decided I'd look around Savernake Forest on *1st April* where LSWs had been reported, though I had virtually no details and the forest is, well, sizeable. This was my fifth site visit for LSW in 2018 and on this occasion my keen-eared partner, Mary, joined me. As we walked blind, gauging the suitability of the habitat, we happened across a suitable spot. Here we immediately picked out prolonged drumming distinct from that of the Great Spotted Woodpeckers we'd become attuned to. Was this an April fool! Then came the unique LSW chattering followed by fleeting views to our right in an area of dead birch and oak. **Lesser Spotted Woodpecker** 15:45. My bogey bird had been conquered and, for me at least, a new Wiltshire site located for this species.

With migrants still few on the ground, a report of 2 Ring Ouzels reported in the early morning on *2nd April* at Sand Point near Bristol presented a reasonable opportunity. I'd missed the bird twice now at Liddington Hill and sadly I did again at Sand Point. One at Crook Peak in Somerset also seemed difficult to get a bearing on and in parking by a church to take a steep path up the slopes I nearly rendered my car un-roadworthy. I was not even certain it was the right path either, once again owing to poor gen, so I abandoned the attempt. My one consolation was an early **Tree Pipit** 14:00 on the slopes of Middle Hope, Sand Point. I'd first noticed the bird by its single and peculiar buzzy call, then streaky appearance and size compared with nearby Meadow Pipits before it launched into full aerial song. As the day faded, I decided to cut back through Blagdon Lake where Ospreys had frequented in past years including two in recent days. To my utter delight, after an hour or so wait, a single bird glided over from the east end of the lake (**Osprey** 19:16) just 10 minutes after a Somerset birder left me to chance his arm at Chew Lake. I immediately put it out on Twitter and RBA, hoping he might still intercept the news, as I knew how disappointed the fellow might have been. I watched the Osprey fishing for a full half hour, moving ever more to the shallows of the lake in the fading light and finally gliding over local woodland no doubt seeking a suitable roost.

Sometimes it's not the rarity that counts but simply enjoying a bird's magnificence, doing naturally what it does best, in beautiful surroundings.

Still hot on the trail of Ring Ouzels, on *4th April* I found myself again knocked back by torrential rain and high wind and the disappointment of a yet another dip at Coombe Gibbet in Berkshire. It did not help that I had not realised either that Coombe Gibbet was not a place but rather a gibbet on Gallows Down in Berkshire. It's only when I googled it that I realised why my Satnav was sending me in circles. A lone **Swallow** 14:10 at Hungerford Reserve also provided little solace and left me short of options for the remainder of the day but I knew the weather would brighten. As such, I decided to head up to Ashton Rowant, Oxfordshire where 4 male Ring Ouzels had been reported. Surely, I could find just one! Unfamiliar with the location, I spent the best part of an hour circumventing the site seemingly not able to park close to where the grid reference was pointing me to. Eventually, parking at Cowleaze Wood,

I found a sign with a map of the reserve, photographed it so I could refer back to it and headed off to look for some local birders. Observing a lone guy with binoculars focused intently on some distant object, I decided he would be my first port of call. The gentleman had a male **Redstart** 16:56 in sight, not what I expected but most welcome and my 200th bird of the year. I had hit my March target of 200 birds four days behind schedule. A couple more birders arrived and while dialoguing 3 **Ring Ouzels** 17:15 appeared on Linky Down, one sharp male bird the others likely females. At last perseverance and close weather monitoring had afforded me the opportunity I needed. As is one of the joys of birding too, I had discovered what for me was yet another new reserve for Oxfordshire.

White ghost returns to haunt

After a long day and a check of my Twitter feeds, I saw that a Snowy Owl had been showing at St David's Head, Pembrokeshire. I had a chance of going for the bird should it still be there the next day, *5th April*, and to somewhat redeem myself for not twitching the earlier Norfolk bird that showed at Scolt Head, Thornham then Snettisham from 9th to the 11th March. The forecast looked great for St David's too. Sadly, when I awoke on the 5th I felt lethargic and tired. I was not certain whether this was due to the previous day's exploits or a virus. I had to content myself with my first **Willow Warbler** 11:15 in the garden, but content was not what I felt as the tweets came rolling in, revealing how well the Snowy was performing. I may yet again have missed my chance. I resigned to going to bed for a few hours and awoke in the evening to check the gen, resolved to make an early start the following morning. The weather was due to close in at St David's late morning, so I'd need to be there in good time. So, on *6th April*, I was up at 05:30 and soon heading across the bridge to Wales. As expected, traffic at this time was light. Unexpectedly, however, my first obstacle was to get through the Severn Bridge toll. Yes, for some reason it took three attempts, first entering an unmanned gate and then a second for wide loads. A lot of embarrassing reversing accompanied by horn beeping from lorry drivers ensued. Despite my Mr Bean moment, I arrived at St David's shortly before 09:00 where I was duly accosted by an eager, grinning parking attendant for a £5 parking fee (a day ticket being the only option). I had the distinct impression that he'd worked out that megas meant ticket sales and so worth braving the elements. A quick change into some waterproofs (this is Pembrokeshire after all), a brief stop at the toilets but no change (it will have to wait) and I was hoofing up St David's Head in search of quarry…aaaaargh! Minus my bins! Jeez, I was just not thinking straight. Other birders were now climbing St David's.

"Have you seen the bird?" they repeatedly asked as I hoofed back down the slope.

"Forgot my bins," I replied in embarrassment, much to their amusement. Okay, second attempt; let's catch them up! I panted my way up the path and into the somewhat squidgy valley.

"It's on the rocks to the right!" an approaching birder exclaimed as I squelched across open bog, nearly losing my footing. I could just see the bird in my bins and, like many twitchers, wanted to hurriedly bag my tick before enjoying proper views. **Snowy Owl** 09:40. Regaining my breath, I smartly walked up the valley where I could see the bird was huddled behind a gorse bush out of the wind at Carn Llidi rocks. The Snowy, evidently a female, was well marked with banding and sat majestically preening and dozing, eyelids drooping, seemingly oblivious to the biting wind and green-clad brigade below. As others arrived, a large family with young children eager to see the owl, even the baby, wanted a view through my scope. It was a privilege to show them and explain (though I am no expert) a little about Snowy Owls and their

16 Female Snowy Owl, St David's Head, Pembrokeshire, 6th April. (Courtesy Mike Watson)

movements. I watched the bird until 11:30 as the rain steadily began to fall and my stomach demanded breakfast. The Met Office had got it spot on. I'd timed my visit to perfection. In the next hour birders began to pour into St David's beach café all elated with success though soaked to the bone. Perhaps the only tinge of disappointment for me was that I did not get to see this magnificent creature perform its ghostly flight.

The encounter with the Snowy Owl was a tonic: it lifted my spirits. I'd got back a lost bird. It was a sober reminder to rise early, make the long journey, and go get these big ticks where possible. The commoner species will be picked up along the way. Seems obvious, I know, but when you are birding daily it's easy to lose sight of the obvious. With that philosophy at the top of mind my next venture was to Rye Harbour on *9th April* (my second visit) where 2 **Black-winged Stilts** 12:36 were duly located in a shallow scrape at the west end of the reserve. One was a sharp adult male, the other looked to be a younger male going by the dark on the back of its neck. The reserve also offered up no fewer than 7 singing **Sedge Warblers** 12:20, signalling the arrival of yet more migrants as the sun warmed my back for the first time this year.

A quick hop along the coast to West Rise Marsh failed to produce a reported Savi's Warbler despite a 2.5-hour vigil. With torrential rain forecast any moment by the Met Office, I headed home but not before collecting **Reed Warbler** 15:30, 2 **House Martins** among 50+ Swallows**, 3 Yellow Wagtails** 16:27 by the lakeside, before departing at 16:45. Deciding to make the most of the light, I stopped by the Kittiwake roost at Splash Point on the way home. **Kittiwake** 18:38. This was my first visit to the location, and I estimated there were at least 800+ birds present on the cliffs and sea, an amazing sight. I can't think why I had not been there before!

On the way home, I felt reasonably content with my day's efforts, until, that is, I saw that the West Rise Savi's Warbler had been singing from 17:30! You can't win them all and there was time enough during spring for another shot at this species.

On *11th* and *12th April* migrants were continuing to arrive, and this

17 Black-winged Stilt, Rye Harbour, Sussex, 9th April.
(Courtesy Mark Dawson)

presented great fun trying to list the birds as early as possible. Somehow, I'd missed overwintering Blackcaps but duly located 4 at Kingsgate Park Yate on the 11th. **Blackcap** 15:06; two male and two female followed by a half dozen or more at the Cotswold Water Park on the 12th where hundreds of House Martins, Swallows and Sand Martins were gathering. Even so, it took me a second visit on the 12th to Kingsgate Park Yate to locate the reported lone male **Pied Flycatcher** 11:15 in the Willows overhanging the main lake. I'd forgotten just how smart these birds are. Strangely, just about every warbler seemed to be fly catching that afternoon, perhaps mimicking the evident success of the flycatcher. A wander round Shorncote in the late afternoon failed to produce Cuckoo, Whitethroat, Lesser Whitethroat or Garden Warbler in a cold grey 7°.

With temperatures remaining depressed in the following days, few new birds were on offer that were not, well, more than 250 miles away. Two visits to Sand Point near Weston Supermare on *13th April* failed to produce the reported Wryneck and Grasshopper Warbler; so did a visit to Chew Lake where a male Hen Harrier had been frequenting the area. I can't help thinking how I miss the flocks of Ruddy Duck that used to frequent Chew before the cull.

Time something a bit more entertaining showed up...and it did! Portland Bill is within comfortable twitching distance for me, and with migrant potential in April, so the **Hoopoe** 09:25 behind Portland Observatory on *15th April* was a welcome injection. With little information, I'd arrived in drizzle to find a few birders wandering around the huts and bushes just beyond the observatory. Once again, good nature and polite conversation paid off as a mature couple I'd been talking to five minutes earlier whistled and pointed to a bush some 25m away. There it was, a dashing display of orange, black and brown, somewhat nervously looking over its shoulder at us by the side of a bramble bush. Hoopoes usually make me think of castanets, fans and flamenco dancers but this bird was behaving somewhat cautiously rather than strutting its stuff, not in the sharpest plumage perhaps given its long journey. Still... it's a Hoopoe! I remembered seeing my first ever on Portland some 30+ years earlier not a few hundred metres from where I was standing.

The only other ticks to be found were 3 **Manx Shearwaters** 10:45 from the main lighthouse, a Fulmar, Med Gull and 3 Wheatears (3 males, same location number as per my earlier visit on 24th March). Ferrybridge revealed 11 Sandwich Terns but the eagerly anticipated Little Terns once again did a no show and, aside from a single Spoonbill at Lodmoor, the only new development was a count of 5 Reed Warblers singing as I circuited the reserve, signalling their numbers were rising. A Serin, reported earlier that day on RBA to have last been seen flying towards the Rugby Football club near Lodmoor, failed to appear despite an hour-long search.

To be or not to be – the Hinksey experience

On the *17th April* news of an Iberian Chiffchaff at Hinksey Heights Golf Club in Oxfordshire got me scuttling out the door with some haste.

18 Hoopoe, Portland Bill, Dorset, 15th April.
(Courtesy Cliff Smith)

I'd seen one the previous year in Yate on 23rd March and recalled that the call was highly distinctive despite similar appearance to Chiffchaff. I was confident I could pick out the bird, especially after a quick refresh using "xeno-canto", a useful website affording access to a vast catalogue of bird sounds. The bird took no time at all for me to locate, 09:12, despite being the only birder present. It began to make its way from the far Willows to one close to the car park. As expected, the appearance of the bird was, well, much like Chiffchaff. Job done…errrr…or was it?

On 19th April I noticed, to my disappointment, that RBA was posting a question mark against reports of the Iberian Chiffchaff. Why? Will Soar (RBA Bird News Operator) kindly informed me that recordings and sonograms confirmed this was in fact a Chiffchaff: critically, it had lacked the "*wheet*" call of the usual 3-part song of the Iberian and had uttered notes associated with common Chiffchaff. The lack of "*wheet*" had been picked out by Mick Cunningham who, along with Dave Pennington, was credited with providing the online sonograms I was now frantically listening to and comparing to every Iberian recording I could find on xeno-canto and YouTube. They were right; no "*wheet wheet*". Could a species really be determined by such a small factor?

Ian Lewington (Oxfordshire's County Bird Recorder) followed up with an excellent balanced article on the Oxon Birding Blog pulling together visual, biometric and audio recordings of the bird, the summary of which was that the bird did not tick all the boxes for Iberian nor for Chiffchaff and could perhaps be a hybrid! I could not argue with the analysis nor conclusion so disappointingly Iberian Chiffchaff had to come off the list, but I'd learnt a lot and, importantly, to try to record some of these tricky warblers if at all possible.

The Hinksey experience had left me feeling that I needed desperately to find a cluster of scarce migrants of which one or more was perhaps a mega. (Trips of more than 150 miles for complete dips were uneconomical as miles and expense were ratcheting up quickly.) As luck would have it, an American Bittern at Carlton Marshes in Norfolk presented such an opportunity. I had not seen one of these in the UK since the 1980s, and the last reported record was 2010, I believe. After a three-hour wait in the marshes on *18th April*, predominantly watching a beautiful Blue-headed Wagtail, an elderly gentleman to my right spotted the Yank momentarily in open ground but no one else saw it. Then it was visible 100m to my left. Could it really move through the reeds that fast? I remembered again what running with a tripod felt like as I scampered up the track with a dozen or so others. Missed it!

Another 20 or so minutes go by then a bird flaps across an open ditch…that is almost certainly it. Now the Lapwings are going nuts to my left and I spot a bittern-like creature running in the long grass, and yes, they can certainly move at speed. Jeez, this bird knows how to tease!

It is baking hot and I have been without breakfast, lunch and water after a four-hour drive and three and half-hour wait but I am hanging in there. "It's up!" A beautiful fly past, neck streaks, darkening of wings, etc. all clear as can be. What an absolute beauty! **American Bittern** 16:56 – a genuine mega. The mix of exuberance and relief among the 20 or more birders present is palpable.

A quick snack back at the car was followed by a **Grasshopper Warbler** 18:13 in the beautiful evening sun. Two Barnacle Geese, a handful of Marsh Harriers and a lone Snipe provided main cast support.

I don't think I've ever visited Suffolk without a drop in at Minsmere and, buoyed by my exploits with the American, I decided I just had enough time and light to head to the Island Mere Hide where a Savi's Warbler had been reported. The weather was perfect. As I came across Westleton Heath, stopping but failing to hear calling of Stone-curlew, I got a little disorientated. I had pulled over to check the maps on my

19 Male American Bittern, Carlton Marshes, Suffolk, 10th April.
(Courtesy Steve Gantlett)

mobile when **Nightingale** 19:00 burst through my open car window. It was atmospheric, my first of the year. At Island Mere I strained to hear the Savi's despite help from a younger birder with keener hearing. Still, a **Cuckoo** 21:00 to round off the evening reinforced the enchantment of this location. I'd first experienced Minsmere in my 20s, camping within walking distance of the reserve. I will never forget my first ever dawn walk down those back lanes with the full expanse of the reserve opening up before me in the morning sun. I knew I'd be back again and again.

19th April **Savi's Warbler** 09:57 Island Mere Hide (You see? I said I'd be back!) Now it was clearly reeling on and off for a good half an hour. I listened to the highly distinctive calls of unprecedented numbers of Med Gulls circling the mere in full summer plumage. Bearded Tits were uttering their characteristic pinging call from the reed tops, while Red-legged Partridges wandered close to the tracks behind the hide. **Lesser Whitethroat** 16:25 – one, possibly two, birds near the North Wall. I recall it favoured this area, and the species can easily be picked out by the end rattle to its song. A flock of 8 Barnacle Geese from the Shore Hide served as a reminder to just how prevalent this species had become since the 1980s. The Sand Martin colony too was thriving with more than 100+ birds diving and reeling much to the entertainment of the café garden dwellers. Sadly, the 29 or so Arctic Terns reported to be heading north from Languard on my RBA Pro App. failed to appear as I searched among the few **Common Terns** 11:00 and Sandwich Terns on the shoreline, lazily floating past the reserve.

The weather, still roasting for April, saw me trek around nearby Westleton Heath in the afternoon. Two **Woodlarks** 16:40 were affording close views while perched. A couple of Nightingales singing, and an impressive number (9) Dartford Warblers! They were singing and popping up above the gorse like yoyos, each appearing to be protecting territory when another approached. It was at that point that I suddenly felt like a peeping tom as by an old quarry I caught an elderly couple re-living the joys of nature, but in a different way. A huge bare backside filled my binocular lens and, at first, I could not tell what I was seeing. After a few glances (just curious of course) it became all too evident and so I beat a hasty retreat down the dusty track to the car. I reminded myself I was deeply missing my partner, Mary, who normally accompanied me on such trips. Not to suggest, of course, that there was any similarity in backsides here!

I'd already clocked up eight ticks for the trip and while Stone-curlew had arrived in the Minsmere area, according to one reserve representative, they were difficult to see, and it was too early for Hobby and Nightjar. As such, I decided I'd spend *20th April* at Weeting Heath for an early shot at Stone-curlew. I was in luck. I was told there were up to six birds present and four on show. I managed only 3 **Stone-curlew** 10:32 from the West Hide, which was affording good views, though the hot sun was beginning to introduce shimmer through my scope as the morning wore on. Spotted Flycatchers and Wood Warblers were not yet present it seemed, so I contented myself whiling away an hour at the Forest Hide watching Marsh Tits at the feeders and Goldcrest bathing in the small pond where Grass Snakes can frequently be seen.

Before I headed home, news was out of a White Stork at Sutton Gault in Cambridgeshire. Upon my arrival, the reporter of the sighting pulled his car over to convey through his side window where the bird was last seen and the territory it favoured. He also added, "The bird is ringed!" Much as there can, of course, be all sorts of reasons for ringing a bird, my experience told me that ringed White Storks were usually deemed escapes, unless of course the ring details offered proof of the bird's wild credentials. After an hour's stroll yielding yet another Egyptian Goose and Lesser Whitethroat, I consigned myself to the hot five-and-a-half hour journey home, enduring the M25 clogged with Friday getaway traffic! Still, East Anglia had, as usual, surpassed expectation.

By now I determined I was on 222 species, but I felt Portland still had more migrants to offer as it had been unusually quiet of late. The report of Pomarine Skua and Puffin and the possibility of an early Little

Tern saw me heading down on the morning of *24th April*. It was cold, grey and foggy; a poor impersonation of spring. Aside from a pleasing 30+ Manx Shearwaters seen from the bill in 30 minutes, the only tick of the day was my first two **Swifts** 16:29 over Lodmoor. Having enjoyed warm days in East Anglia I'd come back down to earth with a bang; 200 miles of motoring for two Swifts and still no skuas! I needed to schedule time for some serious sea watching.

A visit to Ham Wall reserve in Somerset on *26th April* saw the return of better weather. A couple of hundred metres along the main track I picked up a singing **Garden Warbler** 11:07; then a **Hobby** 11:10. In fact, I then saw 4 Hobbies and 2 Great White Egrets in the same binocular view from the Tor View Hide! Magic! (Ham Wall has come of age during this past decade: the Bittern booming chorus there for me tops any UK site I've visited for those intriguing birds, affording regular in-flight views, too.) Then, on the main track, **Whitethroat** 11:20 – could it really be this late in the year to see my first Whitethroat? However, I was still picking up ticks, albeit commoner species, and was determined to remain reasonably local for a day or two considering budget and commitments.

On Twitter, welcome news came through of an Arctic Tern, or possibly two at Frampton boating lake. A photographer taking a shot of what he thought was a Common Tern, appeared to have captured an Arctic Tern! A Twitter debate ensued. I decided that Frampton was too local to pass up so, I hopped across from Ham Wall. It was sunny, warm and after a scan for 20 minutes or so, I determined there were no terns of any sort in view. The boat yard keeper reminded me there was a path around the perimeter of the lake that could be accessed from the boat yard, so I decided to wander round it and the wider Frampton Court estate. Still no terns: just a single Whitethroat, 30+ Swifts and 100+ Sand Martins signalling a large migrant movement was in progress. One last look in the boat club yard upon my return to the car revealed a birder cross-legged on the jetty focusing on two terns floating over the far side of the lake. How could I have missed them? As usual with these birds, at a distance they display buoyant flight, translucent wings and thin dark trailing edge. The features pointed to Arctic…but was I genuinely certain? How many times had I been in this situation only to conclude "Comic Tern" was the only acceptable conclusion? Just then, as if to check us out, the two birds skirted overhead and alighted on a nearby pontoon. Short red legs, dark red bill, grey underside contrasting with the white cheek below the dark cap were now clearly visible. Two exquisite **Arctic Terns** 17:39. gleamed in the afternoon sun. Who knows what tales these super globe trekkers could tell?

On *27th April* a Wood Sandpiper at Northwick Wharf presented a somewhat local opportunity. As with the Arctic Terns I'd learnt by bitter experience how these birds could come and go in a day so, although a relatively frequent visitor, it can be an easy bird to dip. And yes, I did just that dipped! Having spent the afternoon watching c.30 Yellow Wagtails, including a splendid velvety grey-blue-headed Channel Wagtail, I departed only to learn that the Wood Sandpiper had reappeared 30 minutes or so after I'd left! Uuuugh! Oh well, it is not often you see 30 Yellow Wagtails in this part of the world, I concluded. This was not the only time I would dip Wood Sandpiper. On *28th April* a visit to Goldcliff Pools, Newport, but again I dipped this species. Compounding my frustration that day, a Green Heron was reported to be showing near Narbeth about 100 miles in the opposite direction as I was heading home. It was 16:30, I was tired and hungry; I decided not to turn the car round and head for Narbeth, praying my hesitancy would not have cost me the chance of this magnificent rare visitor. Goldcliff had, though, afforded some decent birds: Spotted Redshank; 3 Yellow Wagtails; 3 Knot; Greenshank; numerous Avocet and Black-tailed Godwit; Ruff. Although there were no year ticks here it's a surprising little hot spot for migrants and I had a feeling I would be back for that reason.

Green is the colour, twitching is the game

Awaking on *29th April*, I had no dilemma: the Green Heron had contin-ued to show the previous evening and, yes, I was on my way to Narbeth,

Pembrokeshire, as soon as the first early morning bleep on my mobile confirmed the bird's continued presence. The local crematorium was the designated parking spot as there was no parking at Llan Mill, where the bird was showing. The property itself belonged to Carmarthen West and South Pembrokeshire MP Simon Hart, who had obligingly put a notice for visiting birders at the end of his access track telling them where to head. Definitely a vote winner! The property and grounds offered up a superb setting as birders crowded the garden to take in the idyllic scene looking across the fast-flowing stream into the sunlit wood and reedy pools beyond. You could not imagine a more beautiful spot, though I confess my previous sighting of a Green Heron in the UK had also been at an idyllic place – the Lost Gardens of Heligan in 2010. A coffee pot and cups were laid on, no doubt made good use of by the first twitchers arriving in the cool morning air. It was truly gratifying to see the openness and receptiveness of the

20 Birders spying Green Heron, Llan Mill, Narberth, Pembrokeshire, 29th April. (Terry Wells)

Mill's owners to the green-booted lens-clad army that, understandably, are not always a welcome intrusion.

The bird readily made itself noticed. **Green Heron** 11:54. It proved to be quite a performer, pulling fish and newts from the pond opposite, using various vantage points afforded by the dead tree branches at the pond's borders. Occasionally, the iridescent green, blue and purple of the bird's plumage would gleam, and the bird would cock its head to one side perhaps spying its quarry or wary of overhead predators. This was twitching at its best, a wholly positive experience complemented by the chatter and banter of relieved, satiated birders from all over the country.

21 Green Heron, Llan Mill, Narberth, Pembrokeshire, 28th April. (Courtesy Arfon Williams)

MAY

April then was completed with 228 birds on the list, two short of my 230 target. Even so, I felt I was roughly on track for my 250 birds by May's end. That target I had to make. Spring had proved slow to awaken, with untypically low temperatures. As such, compact windows of sun and warmth were seeing sudden bursts of migrants unloading onto UK shores. For example, the large Hirundine arrival I'd witnessed at Frampton upon Severn in late April. Following a brief stop at Nagshead then on *1st May* to bag **Wood Warbler** 16:00, at a familiar spot in the woods, along with the expected Pied Flycatchers, it was no surprise to find me yet again at Portland Bill on *2nd May*. A Golden Oriole had been reported there by the large barn in the upper fields. Despite the possibility of catching up with these birds in Norfolk later in May at Lakenheath, this species is struggling to breed successfully, so sightings are certainly not guaranteed. As I hoofed up the slope from a one-hour timed parking slot near the "Old Boat House" I spotted two birders seemingly looking my way. I engaged them as they were getting into their car on Sweet Hill Road to learn they'd been watching the male Oriole from the opposite side of the field to me. They were surprised that I'd missed the bird. Encouraged, I spent the next hour or so patiently watching the fields and bushes from two gates with half a dozen or more birders, knowing that I needed to move the car at some point or receive a parking ticket. You guessed it, my urge to remain lawful cost me dearly. Ten minutes after my departure for the car to renew the ticket, the male bird reappeared for a few lucky birders. Frustrated but determined, I decided to stake out the bird, which I bagged after three hours of patient waiting. **Golden Oriole** 14:00. The Oriole had made a brief flyby above bushes at 70m distance in my binocular view while I was talking to fellow birders. Myself and a lady were the only two birders to get views of what was a female/first-summer bird: olive to pale yellow underside with contrasting grey outer wing distinctly visible as the bird arced across my field-of-view at surprising speed, wings held to the shape of an attacking Spitfire. Despite a further hour or two to secure better views, the bird did not reappear though it repeatedly called. What a contrast this was to when I first saw these birds in the 1980s. At that time, I'd park up near Lakenheath before it became an RSPB reserve and see several males and females dancing through the poplars just metres in front of me. I was then informed by fellow birders, and I assume it still holds true, that the original poplars were planted for the purpose of making matches by Bryant and May. Well, strike-a-light!

A quick stop at Ferrybridge on what was a gloriously sunny afternoon finally rewarded me with Little Terns on a sand bar, some displaying high above their likely nesting ground with deep but delicate wing flaps in a sort of aerial caress. **Little Tern** 17:47. The birds were distant so, parking near Crab House Café, I had taken the coastal path for 200m to gain excellent, albeit slightly silhouetted, views of the birds. I'd forgotten just how tiny these birds are by comparison with

22 Female/first-winter male Golden Oriole, Portland Bill, Dorset, 30 April. (Courtesy Peter Alan Coe)

the accompanying Sandwich Terns that had arrived some weeks earlier. As the rush hour traffic from Portland built up on Portland Beach Road I took pleasure in the thought that normally, on a mid-week evening such as this, I would be anxiously prepping for some stressful morning presentation or readying for an overseas business trip. Aaaaaaaaah… the bliss!

While migrants continued to stream onto our shores, most within a reasonable day's travel from home, they were scarcities/rarities I'd already seen. As such, I remained closer to home. A visit to Chipping Sodbury Common on *4th May* revealed a pair of Whinchats of which the male was breathtakingly beautiful. **Whinchat** 15:10. A pair of Wheatears and a few Reed Buntings but sadly no shrikes, which occasionally pass through this area. On the *5th May*, three Wood Sandpipers were put out on Twitter at Coombe Hill Meadows, Gloucestershire! Having dipped these birds a couple of times already in 2018, I just had to go. I knew the reserve well enough, having visited recently, and stomped off to the Grundon Hide where the birds were reported. Taking the shortest track, I had stupidly not allowed for the extensive mud despite the day's warming sun, but once committed you just press on, don't you? This was no doubt much to the amusement of Mike King (of Gloster Birder fame) who sat on the walkway with his grandson grinning as I squelched through the mud not in wellies. None the less, 2 **Wood Sandpiper** 11:50. Three Whimbrel, Little Ringed Plover, Cuckoo and a Glossy Ibis (of which there seemed to be an abundance this year) provided an impressive supporting cast.

7th May saw me at Otmoor RSPB reserve. I'd made the mistake perhaps of not pursuing Hen Harrier here earlier in the year and in fact that was one species I still had to get! However, when a Turtle Dove was reported I knew exactly where it would be: in the tall trees by the T junction in the reserve tracks. **Turtle Dove** 12:48. The bird was calling and readily picked up in a large tree before display-flying to and back from a nearby telegraph pole. The distinctive purring call was an easy give away. The bird was again heard from the main reserve car park as I returned to my car late afternoon. Aside from the usual Sedge, Reed and Cetti's Warblers and Whitethroats, Marsh Harriers lazed over the marsh and Hobbies tumbled in pursuit of dragonflies; a Yellow Wagtail called briefly. Yes, it was yet another shorts and tee shirt day in May so what on earth were those blue geese doing there? I'd located two dark morph Snow Geese to the west of the reserve and mused at whether they could be wild. Both were very wary and unringed but, come on, it's too late for Snow Geese this far south, isn't it? A quick check of the Oxon Bird Blog revealed that Snow Geese had been reported before on Otmoor as late as 8th May 2014! The closest shout on RBA for Snow Geese I'd seen that day was Lancashire. I'd also missed two birds earlier in the year at Devon. A quick mail to Ian Lewington, the Oxon Bird Recorder, soon killed any slim hope I might have of the Otmoor birds being wild, stating they are regarded as feral, probably from a resident breeding population found at Blenheim or Linch Hill/Standlake. Ian indicated there was also currently a visiting flock of c.95 birds in the county, often frequenting Farmoor and Dix Pit. This roaming group is seen across the Midlands and the birds spend much of their time in Cheshire. He also mentioned there had been a feral Ross's Goose visiting Otmoor, which I'd in fact seen but immediately discounted.

To be honest I felt a little embarrassed. Was I getting desperate for ticks or simply challenging assumptions? I confess Oxfordshire is not a county I know at all well for birds. Still, it had been good to see "Blue" variety and I had avoided the unwanted fame of posting a feral Snow Goose on RBA. The great thing about spring is that there are lots of new birds to chase and the weather is, well, usually much improved. However, blink and a species has passed you by and already I was mentally writing off Alpine Swift and Red-rumped Swallow as east coast sightings thinned and the birds pushed northwards. It's risky, too, twitching such mobile birds more than 200 miles away, though one or two of the Red-rumped Swallows did contest that view by lingering in Essex for some days. I was also conscious of the need to see some skuas. Dawlish

Warren NNR had proved successful in the past at this time of year and was only a two-hour drive for me but I was in Gloucestershire on *8th May*, taking my mother who has terminal cancer to hospital in Cheltenham for assessment, and for whom treatment was sadly not working. In fact, balancing the needs of family and home remains key within this quest. It is certainly not all birds first. With that in mind I'd returned to my parents' home in Gloucester after the hospital visit to cook lunch and spend valued time with them. Regularly checking RBA, I suddenly noticed that a male Red-backed Shrike was on view at Dawlish Warren. I got the itch! The weather was warm and sunny, and I knew searching for skuas was likely to be hopeless mid-afternoon, but I just had to go! After all, it's a male bird and one of the sharpest looking birds you'll find!

Red-backed Shrike 15:33, performing by the end of Greenland Lake in scrub close to the beach side of the main track. An absolute cracker! You just cannot help but admire shrikes for their fearsome

23 Red-backed Shrike, Dawlish Warren, Devon, 9th May.
(Courtesy Steph Murphy)

reputation and predatory prowess, albeit their habit of using thorns as barbs by which to larder their prey is gruesome to behold. The sighting reminded me of the first time I had witnessed that on Tottenham Marshes, aged 11, believing it to be some sort of cruel joke when a friend known for his mischievousness first pointed out a skewered House Sparrow.

As expected, a 30-minute sea watch at Dawlish Warren had little to offer given calm seas and cool, light afternoon breeze. A couple of immature male Eiders, which afforded me some speculation at least, was all I could muster. So still not a single skua on my list!

On *11th May* I was back at Portbury Wharf reserve viewing a beautiful, very spotty **Spotted Sandpiper** 18:23 on the shore of an island in front of the North Pool Hide. The bird moved with fast short bursts through the weedy shoreline: take your eye off the scope and you lost it. Dark flecking on the back was also a characteristic that I had rarely noted on previous UK visitors of this species. Here I was to bump into a fellow Somerset birder, Julian Thomas, who was clearly active in the field from his tweets on Twitter. Strangely, I felt sure we'd meet again.

13th May saw me back on Portland Bill after a 4.30 a.m. get up! Yes, I was after those skuas again, principally Pomarine Skua. It was sunny and as calm as I'd ever seen the Bill. **Arctic Skua** 07:15, my first of 3 birds, all of which looked to be dark phase birds. Then…was that a Pom.? At 08:55. a pale phase bird, somewhat bulkier, flew past the Bill, but distant. As I inspected the photos of David the sharp-eyed, quick-snapping birder next to me, I could not see the tail spoons due to the bird's angle of trajectory, but the bird did have a protruding chest and the indicative (not conclusive) complete neck band. We stopped by the Portland Bird Observatory and I noted that they had recorded in their log 4 Arctic Skuas that morning! Martin Cade, the Warden, looked at David's photo and felt uncertain about our Pom. Skua, declaring it to be "somewhat spikey". I'm not exactly certain what that meant but I felt enormous disappointment as I knew Martin by reputation to be skilled in identification. However, later I noted that the Portland Observatory report showed 4 Arctics and a Pom. Skua! A tweet exchange with Martin confirmed the Pom. had indeed been seen in the morning when we were doing our sea watch, too! So, faced with something of a dilemma, I decided that Pom. Skua would, sadly, just have to remain *the one that got away*…for the time being.

There was little else on Portland that day. The three-hour sea watch had produced: 17 Manx Shearwaters; 4 Common Scoters; 6 Kittiwakes and a similar number of Fulmars but surprisingly not a single Bonxie. I decided to head to Pennington Marshes in the afternoon and after several hours traipsing the wrong part of the reserve in hot sun I duly located the reported **Curlew Sandpiper** 17:15 on Fishtail Lagoon among c.30 Dunlin. I was pleased that tenacity had paid off, especially as only minutes earlier a fellow birder had assured me he'd checked the Dunlin flock and there was no Curlew Sandpiper among them.

14th and ***15th May*** saw migration in full swing. Black Kites and White Storks continued to pepper my RBA Pro map of reported birds but often these were fly-overs or short stays, making twitching virtually impossible. My notes recall that a Crag Martin, Black-faced Bunting and Marmora's Warbler were being reported on Shetland; a Song Sparrow on Fair Isle; a Rustic Bunting on the Farne Islands; a Bee-eater at Spurn; a Laughing Gull on St Martin's and a Semipalmated Sandpiper on North Uist! I was beginning to feel I had not been bold enough in booking a trip to the Scottish Isles or Scilly sooner. These birds would certainly separate me from the top life-listers, who would no doubt be chartering planes while I deliberated.

A purple patch

Surely at this point in the year a Little Bittern or Night Heron would appear closer to home, on the Somerset Levels perhaps. Just as I was contemplating it "Purple Heron" came on the radar on the morning of ***15th May***, but it was unconfirmed and there were no further sightings as the day wore on. I decided to chance the two-hour drive to Noah's Hide, Shapwick Heath, where the bird had last been reported. I passed a few depressed-looking birders on the track to the hide – it did not seem promising. Only Julian Thomas, whom I'd met at the earlier Spotted Sandpiper twitch, remained in the hide. As we chatted, I began to scan the far side of the lake and, by chance, while cleaning my telescope lens, noticed that the reeds were moving. I could just make out the shape of a heron. "I think I've got it!" **Purple Heron** 16:10. Julian confirmed the view; we put out the news through the usual channels and birders began to fill the hide. For the next couple of hours our purple friend was to prove difficult: "there, its head"; "you can just see the orange bill, and a leg". As the silhouetting got worse everybody was squinting through each other's scopes and in some cases not entirely certain whether they were looking at a bird at all! Suddenly, just as all were chatting and interest seemed to be waning, I saw it take flight. "It's flying!" I shouted, and the purple wonder careered towards the hide in the blinding sun, eventually to give a last-minute aerial salute in front of the hide to the delight of all. The sense of fulfilment on everyone's faces was an absolute delight. That long snake-like, striated neck and disproportionately large orange bill conjured up an almost prehistoric image. I dare say Purple Heron is a bogey bird for many good birders, often staying well hidden in dense reeds and not relocating till dusk.

As the middle of the month passed, prevailing winds continued to favour the east and north-east coastline. In desperation, on *19th May* I decided to head towards Staines reservoir, an old local patch of mine

24 Purple Heron, Noah's Hide, Shapwick Heath, 15th May. (Courtesy Penny Wills)

where Black Terns had been reported. Perhaps something rarer would turn up *en route*. Well, it did as I hurried towards London; and just before the M25 turn off. Literally a split-second decision sent me heading towards Rye Harbour, Sussex, to tick the **Terek Sandpiper** 12:32. The bird remained on the opposite side of the pool and in the growing heat haze presented some difficulty for the slowly growing army of photographers. As compared with a nearby Common Sandpiper, the upturned bill and noticeably darker, somewhat grey plumage and bright orange legs were evident. The bird held a more horizontal pose than I'd associate with most sandpipers and, as witnessed with Spotted Sandpiper, had the ability to cover a lot of ground very fast.

As luck would have it, on *21st May* Black Terns were at last making their presence felt locally. Six **Black Terns** 14:05 at Pit 74 of the Cotswold Water Park was pleasing. Equally so was bumping into a keen birder from my own village, Brian Piercey. To think I'd lived in the village for 18 years and we'd never met!

25 Terek Sandpiper,
Rye Harbour Nature Reserve,
Sussex, 19th May.
(Courtesy Cliff Smith)

132

Norfolk – where else in spring?

Having planned ahead, I'd booked three nights at Stable Court, Langham, Norfolk, a reasonably priced B&B near Holt from **22nd** to **25th May**. Although my accommodation was not up to much (in part due to my opting for one of the cheapest rooms) the village has the all-important pub, the Blue Bell, which serves an excellent pint to round off those long spring days birding. Pure heaven! The only problem was "where were the birds?" – mainly in Lincolnshire and Northumberland, it seemed. I decided to stop at Lakenheath on the way to contemplate my next move. While taking a coffee and talking to the Lakenheath staff I had superb views of a Kingfisher feeding in front of the information centre. I was loath to leave this superb reserve so quickly, given its breadth of wildlife on such a beautiful sunny day, but I could not contemplate seeing new birds here. As if to reinforce the travesty of my pending departure, a Stoat appeared right by my feet as I leant against the car scouring the latest rarity reports on my mobile for inspiration. He was completely unaware of my presence, sat there contemplating his options 60cm from my shoe before slinking off under the adjacent cars! My next stop in the afternoon of **22nd May** was Eyebrook Reservoir, which straddles the border between Leicestershire and Rutland where 2 White-winged Black Terns had been reported. As I pulled up in the dusty car park on this hot afternoon, the first birds I laid eyes on were 2 **White-winged Black Terns** 14:15, circling back and forth near a buoy some 150m away. Stunning! The white coverts flashed in the sun contrasting with the jet-black underbelly and back. These looked to be clean full-summer birds and the sharpest I'd seen, my first ever sighting having been at Dungeness in the 1980s. Just then 2 Ospreys careered overhead, making their presence felt, exposing their characteristic barred and banded underwing and purposeful eye stripe.

The day had already been a long one with several hundred miles covered by the time I reached my B&B in Langham in the late evening. I was staggered at how many Red Kites I'd seen – 16 during my trip from

Lakenheath to Eyebrook then Langham. Clearly, they were doing well.

Just time for a last gasp stop at Kelling Heath where true to form the Nightjars were calling. **Nightjar** 21:12. Not content with just hearing the birds calling from the car park, I ventured onto the heath's tracks with torch past the lone camper van (occupants must have thought me a prowler) to get views. Startled, one bird close by proceeded to circle within 5–6m, clapping its wings and uttering the distinctive call which my Collins guide aptly describes as "*fior, fior, fior*"! I have seen many Nightjars, of course, but never this close. Two Muntjac, one small as a Jack Russell, presented a pleasing sight in the darkness of a nearby lane, helping to complete that inner feeling of contentment and being at one with nature.

Day 2 in Norfolk, *23rd May*, first stop Cley. I sat in the reserve's main car park in the early morning considering my options as a lone Spoonbill flew over and Marsh Harriers patrolled the marshes. I decided I could use a Norfolk Crane, given I had some lingering concern over whether I could truly count birds seen in the West Country. A visit to Hickling Broad drew a blank. No Cranes only Marsh Harriers, Hobbies and Egyptian Geese. As I grabbed an afternoon coffee at the smart Hickling reception centre, RBA was reporting a mega, Little Crake at Ouse Fen, Cambridgeshire! Apparently, the bird had been singing around 21.30 Monday 21st. Why had it taken so long for news to get out? Either way, I decided I needed to give it a shot and could conveniently take in Weeting Heath on the way for another view of Stone-curlew and, perhaps, pick up Spotted Flycatcher that must surely by now be frequenting the woods behind the hides. Indeed, 2 Stone-curlews performed nicely in the late afternoon heat in front of the West Hide. They appeared to have at least one small chick, very encouraging. Sadly, after a couple of hours I gave up on Spotted Flycatcher, which I was assured was around. I would surely pick up this species elsewhere. I managed to kill some time chatting to staff and other birders at Weeting while I waited for the evening to draw in, as Little Crakes are best seen and heard after dark.

Arriving at Ouse Fen around 20:00, a new location for me, it was immediately evident that I had not done my homework. News that the bird had not been seen the previous day was disappointing. Two cars occupied the reserve's unlit car park and they did not look like they belonged to birders but rather to party revellers. I was loth to leave my optical equipment in the car in this darkened place unattended. Also, the pin on the map indicating the bird's location did not look right, i.e. the habitat was not as I would expect, and I could not get a phone signal there to re-check the location details I had saved. Tired and hungry and not knowing the reserve layout, I decided to abandon the venture and headed back to Langham and the warmth of the Blue Bell pub for a late beer and snack. It had been a somewhat fruitless day and once again a keen reminder that good preparation/gen is vital. Tomorrow I would need to step up!

Around 07:30 on ***24th May*** I was contemplating the day ahead from my room when a mega was called at Titchwell! A Greenish Warbler. By 08:00 I was washed, dressed and out of the door, picking up a majestic Barn Owl en route. It did not take long to hear the somewhat mobile **Greenish Warbler** 08:48. The bird was providing fleeting views and

26 Greenish Warbler, Titchwell, Norfolk, 24th May.
(Courtesy Andy Hayle)

leading the growing throng of birders on a merry-go-round between the reserve's car park, Meadow Trail and West Path, the rapid high-pitched calls providing a constant reminder as to the bird's location. To be honest, the bird was rather nondescript in appearance – brownish with a tidy eye stripe and short wing bar. The bird's stay was comparatively brief (two days) but long enough for photographers to get a few decent photos.

Sadly, the rest of the day was something of a disappointment. No sign of the Montagu's Harrier that had been reported the previous day at Burnham Overy Staithe. And as I watched the Marsh Harriers, Avocets, Comic Terns, Brent and Egyptian Geese over the marshes I could see birders on a distant sea wall scoping a White-winged Black Tern, somewhat taking the sparkle off my earlier success at Eyebrook on the 22nd. Late that afternoon a further opportunity appeared: a Blythe's Reed Warbler, singing at Holkham by a pill box. Unfortunately, the bird did a no show despite a couple of hours watching and several trips to the parking meter to ensure the prowling parking attendant did not spoil my day. Stops at Blakeney produced nothing new, and all Weybourne Camp could offer was a couple of Sandwich Terns patrolling the beach in search of quarry as the wind got up and drizzle set in.
Back to the Blue Bell pub, I guess.

25th May, my final day in Norfolk was cut short. I just had time to look for a Serin in Hunstanton. The bird had appeared in a garden in a property near a camp site; I was confused as to whether I was in the right location. Consulting newly arriving birders, I found out that the bird had, disappointingly, flown. Too late! As I took a coffee in Tesco's, yet another Blythe's Reed Warbler was reported on a Hunstanton camp site. I must be close. The gen was poor and there seemed to be three camp sites showing on my phone and I had only about 30 minutes before I had to depart for a lunchtime appointment at Royston, Hertfordshire. It was a Friday before bank holiday, so I knew traffic would be hell, too. Given my dip the previous day, I was loth to let this opportunity slip but I simply had no choice. My trip to Royston was at least in a worthy cause, being given a chance first hand to see how "Redlist Revival" were attempting to transform farming practices to improve the prospects of our more endangered birds. I'd offered my field support to the organisation so could not let them down.

By my reckoning my few days in Norfolk had brought me to a total of 244 species to date…still well short of my stretch target of 250 by May's end. Even so, I was not too downhearted: after all, I did have seven months to go to find the remaining 56 birds.

Rounding May off with some local birding, I duly picked up **Spotted Flycatcher** 16:30 at Nagshead on *27th May*. Three individuals on the reserve's short trail, noisily giving their whereabouts away but still difficult to locate as they perched motionless for minutes on end in the high dead branches of this mature woodland. A visit to Kingston Seymour in Somerset on *28th May* failed to produce the reported Kentish Plover, which had ventured into a coastal reserve unbeknown to me that is administered by the Avon Wildlife Trust. There were no trust signs and no mention of restricted access on the RBA location report. In fact, given uncertainty over whether I needed to cross private land to see the bird, I'd already called in at one farm house to okay access, but no one answered the doorbell. I decided to go for it. Three birders, myself included, were confronted an hour or two later by a local farmer with an Alsatian and a Doberman, somewhat disgruntled and keen to see our permits, explaining he kept a rare breed of cattle and so wanted to keep trespassers out, particularly dog walkers, for fear of spreading infection. It was an uncomfortable moment to say the least. Fortunately, reason prevailed, and we were permitted to stay, and in my case on the understanding that next time I would have a permit. (It's a reminder to us all to be careful where we walk and to always be polite and diplomatic.) Somewhat frustratingly the Kentish Plover remained for the following day and, though distant, could be seen from the reserve boundary gate (permit not required here). Still not in possession of my permit, I decided not to return for fear that the bird might hop to the wrong side of the gate with the changing tide and so present further temptation/ frustration. Fortunately, the day was not entirely lost as a Red-necked Phalarope was still showing well at Slimbridge at Middle Point, having been there since 25th May along with a Gull-billed Tern while I had been in Norfolk. Quick-footing it from a crowded Slimbridge reception (it being a bank holiday weekend) I headed out through the Holden Tower Hide to the coastal path and on to Middle Point. Just one birder present with no scope! Although distant, the bird was sitting on the mud some 300m away in the sun, occasionally making small rapid forays to feed. **Red-necked Phalarope** 13:25. It seemed extremely vulnerable out there. Sadly, there was no sign of the Gull-billed Tern, a mega tick that looked to have moved on the day before. Two Cranes and a single Bar-tailed Godwit on South Lake complemented the day's total.

On *30th May*. I ventured to see a Red-footed Falcon at Isle Brewers, Somerset. The bird was a female and previously reported to be showing well. When I arrived, the morning air was somewhat cooler than of recent days and the Mayflies were not in abundance. After two hours I opted for coffee and scones at Hambridge Post Office, noting that the Met. forecast favoured increased warmth and sun in the afternoon. Upon my return to the site, the signs, however, did not look good. The photographers I had left there were gathered in the layby about to depart, which meant I'd either missed the bird or it had not shown. They quickly confirmed a no show but as I stepped out of the car I spotted the falcon above a poplar stand by the river where the bird had apparently been roosting. Having got everyone's attention it immediately disappeared, casting doubts as to my observation. (Don't you just hate it when someone says there was a crow in there as though you could be devoid of any observational skills!) Fortunately, after a chase round the back of the poplars, the bird reappeared over the river to provide spectacular displays akin to the Fairford Air Show. Who says female birds are dull? This bird was a beautiful orange-buff colour and was quite content to hunt with us close by. **Red-footed Falcon** 13:25.

27 First-summer female Red-footed Falcon, Isle Brewers, Somerset, 31st May. (Courtesy Steph Murphy)

Following on from my success with the Red-foot., I decided to hop across for a Rose-coloured Starling at Portland Bill. The bird had been obliging birders at the Qinetiq compound and, sure enough, upon my arrival two birders confirmed the bird had been showing well on and off the past few hours. I had decided to walk round the compound when a birder approached, confirming the bird was on the fence by the cliffs at the back of the compound; he briefly showed me a photo. I then spent two hours looking for the bird as the fog worsened to the point that I could not see the Lighthouse behind me, and I had to admit defeat. Frustratingly, the bird was located again in the same area the following day! Even so the occasion was not without its funny side. The birder who pointed me to the bird's location was Cliff Smith. Cliff and I had been corresponding on Twitter for a while but had not met and so did not recognise each other until, that is, subsequent tweets revealed we'd met that day. Cliff is an experienced birder, famed for wearing Croc shoes, having achieved an impressive year list of 337 for Britain in 2017, according to BUBO listings. Cliff was another character I just knew I'd see more of on my travels.

May had closed and I had achieved 247 species, three short of my 250 goal. Looking online at the BUBO listings, it was not a bad total so far and certainly put me amongst their top 10 listers for the year to date, though I dare say there are keen twitchers out there who, like me, have typically not published their lists on BUBO. Even so, I was encouraged. I had made reasonable progress, though I knew now that I was not sufficiently fanatical, nor well-funded to top the BUBO chart.

JUNE

Scotland and Mull

It's well known that late May and early June, before the midge season is in full swing, is perhaps the best time to visit Scotland. This year we were about a week later than usual due to commitments but on **2nd June** Mary and I headed off at 05:30 to the Boat House Guest House in Boat of Garten. This is a superb central location for the Spey Valley, often known as "Osprey Village". It's a stop on the Strathspey Steam Railway with a delightful pub and restaurant known as The Boat. No time for that now, we were straight off to Loch Garten mid-afternoon. Stop offs in the lanes around Loch Garten reserve failed to produce Crested Tit. A visit to Nethy Bridge: again, no Crested Tit on the feeders, only Red Squirrels flipping open the feeder lids with their tiny paws. It was early days, of course, and we were tired from the long drive. Perhaps **3rd June** would be better. It was a hot day for the time of year and we certainly covered some ground, with visits again to Loch Garten, Nethy Bridge and Loch Mallachie in the morning failing again to deliver new ticks. The Findhorn valley too failed to produce the sought-after Golden Eagles, yielding only a single Peregrine Falcon and Red Kite among the many Common Buzzards, each of which we'd keenly checked out as some can at distance appear like Golden Eagles. Lochindorb produced the first trip tick with **Red Grouse** 15:40. There were many grouse here with young families, holding up vehicles as they trundled across the narrow road around the Loch. Other birders and bird groups like Heatherlea, the services of whom we had enjoyed in the past, were there too. They were no doubt watching the spectacularly summer-plumaged Black-throated Divers with two young, as the birds battled between dives to keep the marauding Common Gulls at bay. That evening saw Mary and I at Insh marshes where, after watching 2 nesting Ospreys, we waited till 00:30 to see Spotted Crake in our favoured location. No luck! Clad in shorts, Mary simply succeeded in providing a sumptuous buffet for the dense swarms of ravenous midges.

Things were looking to be a struggle, so on *4th June* I decided we'd take on Cairngorm Mountain. We knew there would be mist in the morning but that was expected to clear by 14:00. Seeing a female Ring Ouzel on the road only metres in front of us, as we pulled into the car park, reminded me of the lengths I had gone to earlier in the year to see three of these birds in Oxfordshire. Chatting during our climb up Cairngorm, Mary and I stupidly took the wrong path, unwittingly missing the preferred left fork. As we ploughed on up through the thickening mist, staying close together, our first **Ptarmigan** 12:59 shot straight across my path, then a couple more; plenty calling all round now. Then there were **Dotterel** 13:15 calling, probably 2 birds, as we mounted the top and rocks gave way to areas of short grass. They were proving difficult to see in the swirling fog, but gaps were beginning to appear, revealing some seemingly lost walkers in a precarious location. Concerned for their safety, we hoped they would see us so they could work their way back to the path, but they disappeared over a crag and out of sight. Singing Whinchats now punctured the comparative silence; a sharp-looking bird that I am always pleased to see.

Upon returning to the car park, I'd learnt from a friendly tour guide that the Coire na Ciste watch point was good for Black Grouse, at least in early spring. Mid-afternoon in June, was not likely to produce much but worth a shot. Tired from the climb, I took the opportunity for a snooze in the car, where I had an extraordinary experience: I'd been dreaming of Golden Eagles and, as I opened my eyes, I was looking at one crossing the valley! **Golden Eagle** 17:03. I was thrilled as the bird, on powerful wings, consumed distance before hovering and then eventually disappearing into the wooded valley. I wondered if my old birding companion David Perrett, whose ashes we had loosed on the Cairngorm Mountain a few years earlier, had been watching over me. Perhaps it was he who had nudged Mary and me on to take the wrong mountain path knowing I would locate the Dotterel there.

Returning to Loch Garten area that evening, I despaired at failing to see Crested Tits yet again, despite seeing Spotted Flycatchers, Coal Tits, Tree Pipits, Redstarts and Crossbills (which, sadly, were not of the Scottish variety).

6th June – back at Coire na Ciste watch point by 04:30 but this time in a chilly 8°. **Black Grouse** 04:52 flew right across the expanse before us: just a single bird, no further sightings. We were off to a good start with a full sunny day ahead. Even so, further visits to Feshiebridge, an area between the Rothiemurchus centre and Loch Morlich, and the Loch Garten reserve failed to produce Crested Tit. Eventually, at Loch Mallachie **Crested Tit** 13:00. They took their time to reluctantly reveal themselves, with Mary, as usual, being my sharp-eyed locator. In fact, we were to see two more on 6th June at Loch an Eilein along with 3 singing Wood Warblers as we hoofed around the entire loch followed by a late afternoon ice-cream. The weather had been astonishingly good.

Having added six more species in our five-night stay in the Spey valley, I was looking forward to our early drive to Oban on *7th June* where we would embark for the Isle of Mull. Mary and I had visited previously but only for a day, and that was certainly too short. This time I had the best part of three days and the listing kicked off with a **Hooded Crow** 06:25 at Fort William before we even arrived. I was surprised we had not picked up one sooner, but then again, these birds are more common towards the west coast. Four Black Guillemots greeted us in the harbour in fine summer plumage and I wondered why I'd spent those hours in Eastbourne seeing a scraggy-looking example earlier in the year when this species was pretty much a certainty here. A Minke Whale broke the sea's surface as we left the harbour as if to herald the wilderness that lay ahead. Occasional Black Guillemots and 36 Kittiwakes dotted our path to Craignure where **Rock Doves** 10:55 greeted us. The Mull birds, I understand, are still deemed to be a good example of the pure form of this species.

Despite the beauty of Mull and the exploration we planned, aided by my excellent little *Birdwatching on Mull and Iona* pocket guide by David Sexton and Philip Snow, Iona would be our first stop to find Corncrake. That is, of course, after much layby stopping and window gazing for eagles as we drove through Glen More. It was painful for me not to give this area the attention it deserved but I knew we'd be back. The priority was to catch the earliest boat to Iona, in our case 10:30. Sadly, we just missed the ferry, because of heavy traffic and an emergency vehicle that dangerously, without any warning lights, forced everyone off the road in its haste to make the ferry. We boarded the later 11:45 ferry; the short crossing had little to offer except an abundance of Shags and Kittiwakes. As we worked the areas behind the fire station and below the abbey, the heat, long drive and early starts began to take their toll. Once again, I took the opportunity for a siesta. Back to the fire station again and BINGO! **Corncrake** 16:42 calling 30m away just near where 2 Hooded Crows had been keenly watching: one of them grabbed a small chick perhaps belonging to a Corncrake. The Hoody's departure must have signalled the all clear to begin calling once again. As usual, the Corncrakes proved hard to see bobbling through the grass but from conversation with a local shop-keeper it was clear that there were numerous birds here calling at night, keeping the locals awake for hours on end with their throaty-croaky calls.

Staying in Tobermory at the Park Lodge Hotel in the north-east of

28 Keen birder (Terry Wells), stealthily pursuing Corncrake, Isle of Iona, Inner Hebrides, 7th June. (Courtesy Mary Cundick)

Mull, we decided to take the scenic west coast route around Mull from Iona. For anyone who has never tried this, the roads are tarmacked but very narrow and with limited passing places. There are a couple of sheer drops too but the most spectacular views in the evening sun. It truly gets wild here and I highly recommend it though it will take you several hours to complete the route.

8th June was to be a truly special day. I had booked us onto a trip to Staffa and the Treshnish Isles, of which Lunga is the principal island and our first point of disembarkation.

The six-hour boat trip departed Tobermory around 09:45, after a small hiccup that revealed we were not on the passenger list! **Puffins** 10:40, a single **Great Skua** 11:07 then an Arctic Skua. Birds were appearing everywhere on the sea en route to the Treshnish Isles. Eighty plus Shags floating effortlessly, 8 Eider, large numbers of Kittiwakes,

29 Puffins, Isle of Lunga, Treshnish Isles, 8th June. (Terry Wells)

Razorbills, Guillemots and Fulmars on the water. It was a birder's feast. At Lunga a further 2 Bonxies fought over a carcass below cliffs teaming with seabirds while Great Black-backed Gulls menacingly patrolled along with Ravens which, at one point, forced 250+ Puffins to leap simultaneously to the safety of the sea below. A young family of Wheatears, their young tumbling over a small rocky outcrop by the path, was an encouraging sight. Puffins, too, would waddle past you to bobble into burrows by your feet, perhaps feeling safer from aerial predators amidst the human throng. Cutely, they would utter soft nasal sounds as they passed, appearing to exhibit discernible but surprisingly varied facial expressions! Or, was that just my imagination? Shags close to the ascending path: oily, glistening olive and purple, resplendent in the midday sun. They were quick to adopt a threatening posture to over curious walkers, stretching tall, wings half open, and showing a menacing gape. Otherwise, the Shags contented themselves by delivering dead twigs to their partner with nesting young – a bonding act, perhaps, given that nest maintenance was no longer the priority.

As we traversed Lunga, up and along its narrow coastal path, we were confronted with the grand finale, a cacophony of sound, a theatrical display of all key species orderly grouped according to type. Squabbling birds would tumble from the sky, falling momentarily into the wrong species quadrant only to suffer a severe pecking. Clearly, strict rules apply here!

The Isle of Staffa produced, frankly, more of the same birds, though

30 "Shake a stick at it!" Resplendent Shags with nesting young, Isle of Lunga, 8th June. (Terry Wells)

31 "Seabird theatre!" Isle of Lunga, 8th June. (Terry Wells)

here Fingal's Cave and the basalt rock formations, evidently created by the same lava flow that led to the Giant's Causeway in Ireland, were breath taking and took centre stage, well, for an hour or so.

Cruising back to Tobermory we were promised a shot at the Sea Eagles, which, aside from the Puffins, were the main draw of this trip for me. As usual our first sighting was a speck in the distance, a huge bird battling with a Crow. **White-tailed Eagle** 15:59. The size difference was astonishing though I had seen these eagles before in Scotland. As we approached a rock stack where the birds were allegedly attempting to nest, a second bird on the cliff face came into view. Great views now – job done!

It does not matter whether you are a keen birder or not, I can highly recommend a visit to the Treshnish Isles at least once in your lifetime. It's wilderness and spectacle will raise the spirits, signalling hope for the many species successfully breeding there. It's a jewel.

32 & 33 Isle of Staffa, the cathedral-like Fingal's Cave (above) and basalt rock formations (below), 8th June. (Terry Wells)

Our trip to the Scottish Isles was over and I'd added 12 species, taking my total to 259, a couple more than I'd hoped, aided by unprecedented warm dry weather for this time of year.

A few days' recuperation back in Wiltshire saw me birding locally on *12th June*, hoping to catch up with Montagu's Harrier. It's common knowledge that these birds are struggling and my usual sites in Norfolk were not looking promising: Monte's is now one of the most protected species in Britain. Forgive me, then, if I don't provide any detail of this southerly location where the bird appeared to be nesting. Arriving around 10:30, I found three other birders scanning the horizon at what I presumed must be the best viewing point, soon to be joined by a middle-aged gentleman in a white van. Van man was clearly keeping a watchful eye, down-playing any news of the harriers in the hope we'd all simply disappear. I guessed he was a conservationist or warden of sorts. I'd been warned to expect his approach. In any case, I was thankful someone was keeping an eye on them. The other three birders soon departed but I stayed on for a while before moving to a nearby layby that better fitted the watch point details I'd received. By late afternoon a heavy heat haze had set in as a flash of a bird to my right suggested a harrier at last. Had I just witnessed a Monte's doing a food pass? I looked for the male but was not certain if that is what I was seeing gliding to a distant post in the shimmering haze. Then nothing! Five o'clock was rapidly approaching now, and a Marsh Harrier appeared casting further doubt as to the identity of the bird I'd seen earlier. Shortly afterwards, I was joined by Cliff Smith, an experienced twitcher, and, wait a minute, BINGO! Cliff had picked out the female **Montagu's Harrier** 17:02, exactly where I'd seen the first bird – Cliff had clearly visited before. Eight and half hours in the hot sun, two apples and a bottle of water…I was relieved, no, exhilarated and frankly surprised at my own ability to persevere! In fact, I was to be lucky again at a later date with a friend, Graham Lawler, seeing male and female birds encouragingly undertaking a food pass. Magic!

Looking at the prospective species I could get during summer it dawned on me that I'd hit that wall, you know, where every bird is several hundred miles away, visible best in twilight hours and/or moves as soon as it is reported. News then via my Twitter connections of a local site near Marshfield for Common Quail was most welcome but after two hours on *14th June* in the hot sun I'd given up. Perhaps my timing was off, though Quail can be notoriously tricky to even hear especially in a late afternoon breeze. I had a feeling chasing Quail was going to become something of a quest in the absence of new scarcities being reported. Visits to Salisbury Plain on *18th* and *22nd June* and *15th July* would fail to produce a single clear Quail call though Mary, my partner, would claim to hear one on the 22nd at one of the plain's reputed hotpots for Quail, while I stood just 50m away from her, looking in the wrong direction! She is rarely mistaken, so I was truly frustrated.

A visit to Acres Down watch point on *15th* and *27th June* in stifling heat produced: a few Goshawk, 2 Hobby, 2 Peregrine sightings; plenty of Common Buzzards; a brightly coloured orange Common Crossbill (presumed male); 2 Hawfinches; a nesting Woodlark, but no Honey Buzzard! I'd done plenty of homework on Honey's characteristics and jizz, but nothing seen that day came close to meeting the desired criteria. Each time I would meet someone who would exclaim "saw one a few days ago, flew right over my head" only then to silently question their siting as they went on to misidentify a bird in front of me. All I know is, I'd spent nine hours so far looking for Honeys and was beginning to think that a better location was required. Just how many reported Honey Buzzard sightings are, well, Honeys and not Common Buzzards, I wondered?

A visit to Fen Drayton Lakes on *19th June* after a 05:38 departure yielded a singing **Great Reed Warbler** 09:58 on Elney Lake. These birds can really boom out a song, being audible at distances that well surpass those of similarly located Sedge and Reed Warblers. The last Great Reed Warbler I'd heard was at Goole in the early 1980s; this one was proving very difficult to see, staying well hidden in the reeds by a small channel to my right. Bitterns here were performing superbly, too, one brazenly preening in the open as a lone Turtle Dove shot across the lake (only my second of the year) between the Common Terns softly dancing over the lake in the warming morning sun.

Yank prank

As I trundled home from Fen Drayton, Cambridgeshire, on the 19th I kept a keen eye on the RBA news just in case I could pick something up en route. The weather was fine and the daylight hours long, albeit I was tired from the early morning start. At 18:25 news broke of an American Royal Tern at Church Norton in Sussex! Wow – a British lifer for me! Perhaps this was the same bird that had been on the Channel islands a month or so earlier. I determined it was more than 100 miles from my present location, a couple of hours. It would be tight. I'd have little time to locate the bird in the fading light. I'd also be exhausted by the time I got home in Wiltshire that night. Frustratingly too, travelling down early next morning was not an option. I'd committed to taking Mary to hospital in Swindon for some medical tests. I'd let her down once before and deeply regretted it. That simply could not happen again. I concluded the bird would have to wait. I was already in danger of falling asleep at the wheel and did not want to contemplate the consequence of that. That evening, I remained restless as the bird continued to be seen. The following day, **20th June**, I headed for Church Norton after taking Mary to hospital in the morning and arriving at Pagham around 12:30. The RSPB Pagham Reserve car park was jam-packed with cars. Squeezing into a parking spot, I took time to grab a snack, given the bird had not been seen since 04:37! My chances did not look good. Taking the harbour path to Church Norton, I was greeted by the odd head-sagging birder having given up the pursuit. Hundreds of birders remained on the shingle opposite the church, many clearly fatigued but remaining hopeful of the bird's return. Yes, the good and the great were all here as I surveyed the throng, reinforcing the weight and beauty of Royal Tern. The hours passed but without sign. A gull carrying a long orange piece of plastic prompted shouts for the bird. "I'm on it!", "Flying left!", "Now right!", "It's over the small fence posts; the gate."

The cheeky impersonator was quickly caught out with the aid of a quick-snapping photographer. Still, the impersonator had woken up the living dead strewn on the shingle: all were now up and alert. Evening ground on and the sun dipped; birder numbers dwindled as aching feet, backs and rumbling tummies took their toll. Rumour spread, too, that the bird was now at Lodmoor and my RBA Pro app bleeped at 20:07 to confirm that. It was the last nail in the coffin. Too far, and too late for me. At 20:15, conversation with my determined colleagues exhausted, I left Church Norton and headed home to the jubilant Tweets of the deserving few who'd made it to Church Norton before dawn to see the bird. As I congratulated them, I cursed myself for not going that extra mile and chancing it the night before.

Late June continued to frustrate. My third visit to Salisbury Plain on *22nd June* failed to produce any Quail. Lodmoor, Ferrybridge and

34 Royal Tern twitch at Church Norton, Pagham Harbour, 20th June.
(Terry Wells)

Bowleaze Cove on **25th June** failed to produce further ticks and no more reports of the elusive American Royal Tern. A watch for Honey Buzzards on **27th June** at Acres Down 08:30–12:00 also failed to produce the required bird; only Tree Pipits, Hawfinches, Spotted Flycatchers entertained. I decided to while away an hour or two at the Farm café talking to locals, taking in a brief tour of the amazing novelty teapot collection by the kind proprietor. It all seemed a million miles away from the early, dark, cold starts of winter. My pain was further compounded when both a Pacific Golden Plover and Franklin's Gull were reported the last weekend of June at Hayle Estuary while I was due to be away in Somerset at Brympton House for my Niece's Wedding, a sumptuous affair like an event from *Vogue* magazine. The fact is that late June had been a comparative disaster: I'd failed to root out tricky breeding species and had not made enough forays to the north-east coast where pickings were consistently better. I needed to get some miles in. At this point my total was a disappointing 261 and I fully expected July to offer little solace.

JULY

During July the heatwave continued and looked set to break all records. Winds continued to prevail from the north-northeast and opportunities for further ticks were few. Following the wedding-weekend, I determined to catch up with the Pacific Golden Plover at Hayle Estuary on **2nd July**. Not knowing the area that well, I decided my first stop should be to park at Ryan's Field and check the area from the Eric Grace Memorial Hide. Nothing here, the tide was out. Scanning the large flocks of gulls on the estuary produced only a Barnacle Goose of interest. I then walked round Carnsew Pool, parking up at Asda. Whimbrel and Common Sandpiper here but no sign of either target bird. The Pacific Golden Plover was announced at St Gothian Sands, Gwithian, at lunchtime. That was just a hop down the road. Again, I could find no sign! I took the opportunity late afternoon to do a little sea watching in this breath takingly beautiful spot owned by the National Trust. Looking out across Godrevy beach towards the lighthouse I counted 127 shearwaters in a stop-watch 5-minute count! Very impressive. The silhouetted birds made species determination difficult, but most were almost certainly Manx Shearwater, possibly with the odd early Balearic. I made a mental note to organise trips to see whether I could pick up further shearwater and petrel species in the weeks to come. Late evening, I returned to Ryan's Field to see the gulls arriving to roost as expected. One gull partially fitted the description of Franklin's Gull, possessing white spots on the tips of primaries, white crescents on the eyes appearing to join behind the eye. Beyond that no further characteristics were discernible and the head was more chocolate-brown than black. I wondered if this was indeed the reported bird! Either way, I and the three other birders present remained unconvinced this was a Franklin's so, painfully, it was one that got away.

After a night's stop at my family's apartment in Looe, I returned to St Gothian Sands but again no luck, this time even the shearwaters had deserted. Only a Green Sandpiper on the pool there entertained. Still, meeting fellow birders, including one with whom I'd shared a B&B on St Mary's the previous year, was most pleasing. There is a camaraderie amongst birders: it's like an extended family you bump into, unexpectedly, and in odd locations.

On **5th July**, I decided to put right the frustration of seeing that earlier indeterminate Iberian/Common Chiffchaff at Hinksey Heights Golf Club, which had triggered so much debate. I headed to Thurstaston where an Iberian had been hanging round for some months, obliging many birders. This was a more than 400-mile round trip (about eight hours of driving). It was a measure of my desperation to repair the damage of a slow June. Still, this bird was not without its challenges to locate. After arriving around midday, I struggled to find the right spot even, first contacting friends on Twitter for better location detail, and then RBA, who kindly texted me a grid reference that placed the bird's last location inside a primary school playing field! I was confused. I called RBA to validate; they then re-directed me a little closer to the correct location. Eventually, I nailed the spot by flagging down a couple of National Trust reserve employees in a white van (thanks, guys). **Iberian Chiffchaff** 13:48 flitting through nearby trees, clearly calling repeatedly. It had taken me an hour and half to locate the correct spot but just 15 minutes then to locate the bird once there! The confusion was caused by reference on RBA to a clearing with a dry-stone wall at the back. By now, summer growth had rendered the wall invisible from the main footpath. – a simple thing. Both the three-note *"sweet, sweet, sweet"* call and the full three-part song (including a the all-important "*wheet*" note) were clearly discernible.

Reward: coffee and cake in the Benty Tea Rooms café before listening to the bird one more time followed by the long drive home, tired but feeling restored at last.

7th July saw an early start to Chelmarsh Reservoir in Shropshire for a Little Bittern. As the bird was calling almost incessantly, I had no problem locating it in the reeds by the causeway that crosses the reservoir: **Little Bittern** 11:05. Although the bird was no more than 10m away at times, it disappointingly failed to provide good views in the 28° heat but would do so later that evening and the next day for following visitors.

Failing to locate Honey Buzzards after two attempts at Acres Down in June, I had been searching for an alternative site. There seemed to be an absence of sightings at Swanton Novers, Norfolk, casting doubt as to the summer residence of the birds there. Sightings in Suffolk too were scattered, minimising chances of a successful stake-out. Therefore, on *12th July*, my new target location for this species was Wykeham Forest, Yorkshire. Here the birds seemed to be showing consistently.

Determining that the village of Sawdon was perhaps best located, I'd booked myself into The Anvil Inn to give Honey Buzzard the best part of

35 Male Little Bittern, Chelmarsh Reservoir, Shropshire,
7th July. (Courtesy Ian Bollen)

two days. (If successful on the first day, I could backfill with some coastal sea watching off one of the headlands, given I still required Roseate Tern, which was being regularly seen along the north-east coast.) After a noon arrival, I'd located my first bird over the woodland opposite the viewing point at Wykeham – **Honey Buzzard** 13:15. Even so, I needed to enjoy more of these birds. As I waited patiently, I noted a further bird continually calling in the woodland below me. Honey Buzzard calls are, to my ear at least, quite discernible in the field from most species including our own Common Buzzard. A further sighting was had a little later too in the valley just below me, the grey mantle/tones being particularly evident on this one. Apparently, up to 3 birds were reported at this site.

In all, I'd probably spent nearly 20 hours looking for Honey Buzzards and Ian's super photo is certainly better than the best of my views. On such occasions other things do, however, not go unnoticed. In common with many birders, I increasingly find myself interested in a wider diversity of species. By example, this ferocious huge Golden-ringed Dragonfly

36 Honey Buzzard, Wykeham Forest, Yorkshire, 2nd July.
(Courtesy Ian Bollen)

crashed into the grass at my feet holding a bee in its jaws! The two wrestled for some five minutes – the bee eventually escaped.

The following morning, I made my way c.20 miles to Flamborough

37 Golden-ringed Dragonfly, Wykeham Forest, Yorkshire, 7th July.
(Terry Wells)

Head on the East Coast, arriving at 07:00. This was my first visit and although Roseate Terns were not making themselves conspicuous, a pale-phase Arctic Skua and small rafts of Puffins below the cliffs were. Add in the usual array of Guillemots, Razorbills, Gannets, Manx Shearwaters and Kittiwakes in large number and you have a super highway for these birds, a regular spaghetti junction, making for spectacular viewing in the early morning sun.

My journey home saw me veer towards Titchwell for a reported Lesser Yellowlegs but, sadly, the bird disappeared early afternoon for several hours when I was near Lincoln and I decided to abort. It was a decision I would quickly regret as the bird reappeared early evening. Perhaps I would get a chance to catch up with it later.

15th July, as previously mentioned, was another failed attempt to see Quail on Salisbury Plain, spending several hours with Graham Lawler, trawling every location he knew. We were deservedly rewarded with views of Montagu's Harrier at an undisclosed southerly location, male and female food passing, but otherwise drew a blank and were left wondering, perhaps, why we had not gone for the Greater Sand Plover that had been reported at Kilnsea in Yorkshire the evening before.

On *17th July* I headed for Brandon Marsh, Warwickshire. **Pectoral Sandpiper** 14:00 from the East Hide along with 3 Little Ringed Plovers and 2 Green Sandpipers. While the pectoral band was evident on this bird, for me it was the feathering on the mantle that stood out, seeming to be "flecky/scaly" with each feather visibly distinct, reminding me somewhat of Buff-breasted Sandpiper, but without the buff breast, of course. This was my first visit to Brandon Marsh Nature Reserve. It was good to find myself in Warwickshire, a county I rarely visited for birding. Sadly, a reported flyover Black Stork at nearby Anstey did not drop into the reserve to provide some much-needed icing on the cake. As is usual for storks, the bird went AWOL and was not twitchable later that day.

20th July – I departed around 06:45 for Titchwell. It was sunny, warm but with the odd shower. An uneventful four-hour drive saw me at last scoping the previously reported **Lesser Yellowlegs** 11:19. in front of the Parrinder Hide. I have seen a number of these birds across the years and this one had been around since the 13th, I recall (what had taken me so long?). Their elegant stance, mottled mantle, and contrasting yellow legs contrive to portray a refined clean-looking bird. The Yellowlegs performed close in to a packed hide which held a rather significant number of "dudes" many of whom had an irritating habit of standing in front of my scope to get that extra special close-up snap. A moulting Spotted Redshank, 3 Curlew Sandpipers, 2 Egyptian Geese and a raft of Black-tailed Godwit, Avocet and Dunlin made for an attractive summer morning spectacle at what must be one of Britain's premier reserves for rarities.

22nd July saw me heading out at 06:10 for Oare Marshes in Kent where a White-rumped Sandpiper had been reported the previous day. I don't recall having previously visiting this local nature reserve and it was certainly many years since I 'd seen the targeted species. Successfully

38 Lesser Yellowlegs, Titchwell, Norfolk, 17th July.
(Courtesy David Carter)

securing a spot in the small (but unexpectedly free) crammed car park, I joined the straggle of birders that lined Church Road in the early morning sun to squint at the flocks of waders. Amazingly, a Temminck's Stint, Little Stint, Bonaparte's Gull and Turtle Dove were here, making an impressive cast along with several Southern Migrant Hawker dragonflies. This small reserve is an impressive gem, easy to navigate and view from the elevated encircling sea wall. Sadly, though, the White-rumped Sandpiper did not reappear that day and beyond, perhaps encouraged by the balmy weather to press northwards, examples were reported during the following weeks in Cleveland, Shetland and County Sligo, Ireland.

The prevailing heat and light winds from the north to north-east occasioned few new migrants in July and what there was continued to favour the north-east coast, presenting long journeys for me and potentially expensive overnight stays in B&Bs at high-season rates. Having completed my Wiltshire Ornithological Society quarterly submission the previous week, I decided that this week I'd focus, then, on "clean-ups", i.e. those birds I had missed to date and might be able to pick up locally.

Corresponding with a fellow birder, Paul Rich, on Twitter a week earlier, I'd been able to secure detail on a local site for Quail. Would they still be there? I'd already invested a lot of time failing to locate these birds on Salisbury Plain. On **24th July**, Mary and I headed out to Leighterton; a perfect warm sunny evening with just a light breeze. After patrolling the footpaths through Barley fields, I eventually picked out two birds calling from an inaccessible part of the crop, or perhaps just beyond the wall in the next field. It was hard to tell as the birds seemed to be moving. **Quail** 21:10. The birds (two at least) called three times but despite my listening from multiple points till the fading light, and in a strengthening breeze, they failed to show themselves. Still, for reader clarity, I am happy to tick such birds whose calls I know well, which, sadly, is as often as good as it gets for this secretive species. In fact, I did not see further reports of these birds, suggesting we must have been fortunate indeed.

The absence of Roseate Tern on my list continued to niggle me.

If they were not appearing on the north-east coast, then appearances within a 200-mile radius of my home were often fleeting, making the birds difficult to twitch. I'd deliberated on a trip to Coquet Island in Northumberland but could not see additional species in that area to justify the expense. Minsmere again was an option but still distant, and reports were far from consistent for such a well watched location. Titchfield Haven looked the better option and, given its growing reputation for good ticks, I wanted to check out the reserve. Having arrived around 07:30, I found that my first obstacle was entry as the reserve does not open until a lackadaisical 09:30! Still, it has an impressive information centre, café and facilities, and the waiting around was certainly no hardship. The rising sun gradually irradiated the Meon Head harbour boats at high tide against a clear blue sky, raising the curtain on the reedy reserve behind. It was like a Shakespearian performance about to begin. Terns screeched overhead, traversing back and forth between the seashore to the reserve pools, announcing their arrival, often with fish for their young or a nesting partner. I immediately began checking the calls of Roseate Terns. Would I be able to discern them in the throng? I followed the warden into the Meon Hide; the Roseate call was pointed out almost immediately, though this is not a bird I am happy to tick on call alone. As such, it took me a further anxious 15 minutes before locating the bird. **Roseate Tern** 09:47. It would take many sentences to expound the subtleties of this ocean-roaming wanderer. Calls aside, the overall pale colour in flight, long tail streamers and slimmer/elongated shape as compared with the nearby territorial Common Terns stood out. Pleasingly, before departure, I was able to pick out these two birds again and again as they swirled over the scrape amongst the large flocks of Common Terns and Black-tailed Godwits, occasionally spooked by a local Sparrowhawk or Lesser Black-backed Gull.

Much in the same vein of trying to remain reasonably local, *28th July* saw me at Upton Warren by 08:15, after missing the poorly signposted entrance several times. My aim was to catch up with a

Spotted Crake that had been seen on the flashes. This was the first showery day I'd encountered since May! I shivered in the hide in my tee shirt and shorts, failing to locate the crake, a species I'd already been unsuccessful with at my favoured site, Insh Marshes, Scotland!

I'd heard much of Upton Warren in my early days of birding and, despite some good habitat and hides, it seemed to me that it had been overtaken by various other NNRs around the country. Even so, the 5 Green Sandpipers present perhaps hinted at its continuing potential to attract rare and scarce waders.

That evening, I contemplated my next step. It seemed that the warm weather could be breaking and, as evidenced on Twitter, a sea watch at Porthgwarra on the 29th by one of my birding colleagues, Graham Lawler, produced: 92 Great, 36 Cory's, 42 Sooty and 12 Balearic Shearwaters; Trinidad Petrel; 56 Storm Petrels; 9 Bonxies; 2 Arctic Skuas; 2 Mediterranean and 2 Yellow-legged Gulls. I had missed a great opportunity and felt I'd not given due weight to the potential that late summer sea watches had to offer. The only other reasonable options seemed to be a Semipalmated Sandpiper, which appeared at Snettisham on the 29th and remained until the 30th, or a Marsh Sandpiper that had been visiting Rainham Marshes between 27th and 29th. I decided a Sea Watch would be a refreshing change and so headed for Devon and an overnight stay at the pristine and welcoming Chillington House, Chillington. As always, I'd picked a village proximate to my birding destinations, in this case Berry Head and Start Point, and, of course, with a good local pub/restaurant (the Bear and Blacksmith) in which to celebrate my anticipated good fortune!

Up at 06:00 on *30th July*, then, I drove to Berry Head. First bird up was a pleasing Cirl Bunting rattling above the car park. I'd seen them already at Labrador Bay but nice all the same. Then **Balearic Shearwater** 10:47, while several porpoises entertained close in to the headland. It was slow-going, to be fair, so after some lunch in the Guard House Café, I headed to the lower vantage point by the quarry, which afforded a better angle for sea watching, I gauged. Here I met Mark and Adele, a couple of keen-eyed experienced sea watchers and the day's birds began to ratchet up. I recorded: 35 Balearic and 52 Manx Shearwaters; 1 juvenile Yellow-legged Gull; 3 Whimbrel, and even what looked to be a Leather-backed Turtle! Certainly, a first for me in British waters. I felt sure my eagle-eyed companions had recorded higher counts, but it was a decent watch. By 16:30, however, the truth was I'd picked up only one new year tick, Balearic Shearwater. Perhaps tomorrow on Start Point would prove better.

That night I lay awake tormented by the loudly ticking clock in my room and, frankly, the guilt of not being beside my dying mum.

The next morning, again up at 06:00, and out the door by 06:45 with a packed breakfast, courtesy of the B&B owner, I was negotiating the tight bracken-sided lanes that lead from Chillington to Start Point. I'd always wanted to visit Start Point and on this early summer's morning the spectacle upon arrival did not disappoint. However, the lighthouse,

39 Calm seas at Start Point, 31st July. (Terry Wells)

beyond the wall of which afforded the best vantage point for sea watching, was not due to open until 11:30! I did consider contacting Trinity House, the keeper of the lighthouse, with the hope of gaining earlier entry but, given the calm sea and lack of bird movement, what was the point? I proceeded to clamber over the point and indeed traversed the headland back and forth twice viewing from various locations but there was barely a bird in sight. Too calm, too mild. After a couple of hours, I abandoned the sea watch and headed home. My total, now 269, was one short of my month's target. July, then, had been a struggle, but I was pleased at least with my efforts to pull in a few difficult ticks, despite not having laid best plans for the month.

AUGUST

My plans for August were simple: get down to the coast, avoid the crowds (as it was peak holiday season) and do some serious sea watching. That, I would most likely complement with the odd venture to the north-east coast and/or Norfolk, picking up ticks and missed birds. Entwined with that, I expected to be at my parents in Gloucester twice a week, given my mother's deteriorating condition and pending hospitalisation, and my father's need for day-to-day support to get by. So, in short, keep it simple, I thought.

High on my radar was Spotted Crake. Birds had been appearing in past weeks across the country and Titchfield Haven or Potter Heigham seemed to offer the best prospects, but Titchfield was nearer. Sadly, it was the wrong choice: while the Potter Heigham bird continued to perform over the next few days the Titchfield Haven bird was not reported after the 4th and I had arrived on *5th August*! Still, a beautiful day: 2 Wood Sandpipers, 3 Green Sandpipers were nice to see as was the sunbathing family of swans in the beach car park that ventured for a quick, en masse, dip in the sea.

6th August – I opted for a couple of days sea watching in Cornwall. I'd booked myself into the cheapest B&B I could find in Penzance, Carnson House, near the railway station. Everywhere is close to Penzance on the Cornwall peninsula, and the options for affordable accommodation and dining are plenty in Penzance. Arriving in the afternoon, I made my first stop at Pendeen. Between 15:00 and 17:00 I recorded more than

40 Swanning around, 5th August, the beach car park at Titchfield Haven, Hants. (Terry Wells)

1,000 shearwaters, with a ratio of 1 in 5 Balearic to Manx. Encouraging movements but no ticks here.

On *7th August*, I opted for Porthgwarra. I arrived about 06:30 with a take away breakfast from the B&B. The café at Porthgwarra where you pay for parking did not open till 08:30, so I placed a note on the windscreen saying I would pay later and ventured off in the morning drizzle. Sadly, despite trying several vantage points and enjoying the spectacular scenery, I drew a blank: only Balearics, Manx Shearwaters and Fulmars put in a show.

After a few hours and the ritual coffee at the local café, I ventured through the narrow lanes to Pendeen. The winds were slightly more favourable. Two Choughs and a **Sooty Shearwater** 15:23. All dark, longer winged, more purposeful flight than Manx; just the one bird. A trip to Cape Cornwall in the evening produced nothing further, aside two more Choughs and a raft of c.400 Manx Shearwaters close in. As

41 & 42 Sea watching, 7th August. Spectacular views Porthgwarra (above) and Pendeen (below), Cornwall. (Terry Wells)

the sun set and the breeze strengthened, I was forced to find what little cover there was amongst the rocks to the east side of the lookout station. It was a beautiful wild setting, but I missed not having Mary with me.

I arrived home on the 8th to the news that my 87-year-old mother was not eating and deteriorating fast and my 89-year-old father had been taken into hospital after collapsing with a water infection. Once again, I felt acute guilt at not being by their side and now needed to make that my priority.

The fact was I had struggled at sea watching. I seemed to have developed the patience for it in my latter years but perhaps my rusty technique, imbalanced scope, and less than perfect eyesight were not helping. I knew that wind direction and strength were important but, frankly, could do with more eyes on the sea. I was not done yet, though, as there were still Cory's and Great Shearwaters, Storm, Leach's and Wilson's Petrels to be had, not to mention Fea's or Desertas Petrels, which had been reported at Porthgwarra on 27th July and would again reappear on *11th August*, while I was viewing an obliging **Spotted Crake** 09:45 at Gibraltar Point NNR, Lincolnshire. Having awoken at 04:15, I'd arrived before 09:00 at Gibraltar Point, parked near the Mere Hide where the bird had last been reported. As I approached, I asked birders standing behind the hide whether the bird was showing. "It's in the hide!" a gentleman exclaimed in a strong northern accent.

"Wow, in the hide, that's a first," I replied. The early morning humour clearly whistled straight over his head. The hide was indeed packed and, as I squeezed between several equipment-laden photographers, the bird performed admirably no more than 10m away albeit for a few minutes at a time. It certainly made up for my two earlier dips of this species at Insh Marshes and Titchfield Haven.

Once in Lincolnshire I needed to make my 200-mile drive count. Just as I was leaving the reserve and checking RBA news on my mobile, report of a mega, Blue-winged Teal, surfaced at Alkborough Flats in the north of the county. While the birding destination was unfamiliar to me, the former steelworks I passed at Scunthorpe as I approached

43 Spotted Crake, Gibraltar Point NNR, Lincs., 11th August.
(Courtesy Mark Rayment)

the location was not. I had managed business with them for IBM some years back and recall the site being the subject of a series of strikes at the time, no doubt as employees fought to secure their jobs in the light of changed plant ownership. I also recall how Hen Harriers had performed on the nearby marshes as I headed home one afternoon. Unsurprisingly, at this time of year, there was unlikely to be any Hen Harriers. I pulled into the small car park nearest Prospect Hide from which the bird had been reported (I confess I guiltily had to use a disabled bay, the only one available). I shot to the hide, which was no more than a couple of hundred metres away. **Blue-winged Teal** 12:52. The consensus was it was most likely a young male in eclipse. The bird had teasingly sat on the mud in front of the hide behind a large group of Shoveler before providing those definitive views. This bird could so easily have been overlooked. The scaly-looking sides, dark through eye, dark bill and white lores were now evident. Hats off to the original finder! After 30 minutes or so I left, grateful for two year ticks (and no parking ticket), feeling the 500-mile round trip was probably justified.

My *15th August* records reveal that my mum has been taken into hospital. It seems she is rambling and of muddled mind. It breaks your heart. Time is now being taken up by more frequent 80-mile-round drives to Cheltenham Hospital: I go every couple of days to check on her and also on my father, who, unsurprisingly, is struggling to cope with her impending death and the changed circumstance that will bring. Meanwhile, I am somewhat guiltily watching much-needed birds slip by: on Tresco a Solitary Sandpiper; Wilson's Storm Petrels repeatedly seen on the ever popular Scilly Pelagics; Pacific Golden Plover in the Findhorn valley Scotland; a Baird's Sandpiper at Ardivachar in the Western Isles. An American Golden Plover on Hazelwood Common, Suffolk, closer to home arrived on the 13th but had departed by the 15th. The Aquatic Warbler ringed at Fleet flagged up yet another watch-for species at this time. And, once again, the King Eider was being reported from Ceredigion in Wales, albeit the comparatively drab female of this species.

On *19th August* I decided a 24-hr jaunt to Porthgwarra was warranted. There were too many birds left on the table and Mary, my keen-eyed partner, was eager to join despite not being a fan of sea watching. Waking at 03:00 we arrived Porthgwarra around 07:40 and, frustratingly, it was foggy! Birders were gathered in number with the same idea, amongst them Graham Lawler, who I knew was an able and experienced sea watcher already having tweeted some spectacular sightings during the past weeks from this location. As the fog cleared, we moved to a lower vantage point close to the car park. The air in the inlet here was somewhat clearer and the position sheltered from the wind. I picked out my first **Storm Petrel** 15:05. I managed about 3 of these and half a dozen Sooty Shearwaters and 8 Common Scoters but I missed a lot more as I struggled to get on the birds quickly with my unwieldy Nikon scope. Sadly, there were no Great or Cory's Shearwaters, which were what I was really hoping for. Still, it enabled me to obtain greater appreciation of Sooty Shearwater jizz. Surprisingly, Balearic Shearwaters were very few indeed on this occasion compared with recent sea watches.

By now Mary had gone for the café pasties, and after what was a long day, we arrived home around 22:00. No doubt she was left wondering why the hell she had opted for an eight-hour car ride to stand in cold fog with a bunch of dishevelled middle-aged men on her day off!

44 More eyes on the job but this time a foggy Porthgwarra,
Cornwall, 19th August. (Terry Wells)

21st August, Minsmere: **Semipalmated Sandpiper** 15:12. I'd made a leisurely trip up to Suffolk, in view of the fact that several recent early starts had left me tired. As reported, the bird obliged in front of the South Hide on the South Scrape, feeding with Spotted and Common Redshanks. At about 120m photographic opportunities were poor and there was certainly no chance of seeing those webbed feet for which the bird is so named – *palmated.* The bird appeared smaller than the Dunlin close by; breast and underside clean white, giving the bird a comparatively pale appearance. The mantle centre was dark brown, the legs black. The bill, shorter than a Dunlin's, was straight black. There was the appearance of a white line above the eye and a little grey/brown to buff on the sides of the neck. Despite noting these details, I confess that at this distance I would still struggle to separate this species from other rare sandpipers that can occasionally reach our shores, e.g. Western Sandpiper, which I'd enjoyed seeing close-up daily on the beaches of Dominican Republic alongside Semipalmated Sandpiper.

On ***24th August***, I found myself on Beachy Head. A Melodious Warbler had been reported there on RBA since the 21st and it seemed comfortable with its surroundings. After an early start, I arrived at the location around 10:00 and was soon looking at some lichen-covered bushes to the west of a hotel car park with a few other birders. After a couple of hours of checking out the odd Whitethroat and Chiffchaff, and marvelling at the antics of Peregrine, Hobby and Sparrowhawk overhead, I decided to snooze in the car with the window ajar. The recent sadness of my mum's deterioration in health and hospital visits was beginning to take its toll. I awoke to find myself staring at a large somewhat grey-lemon, slow-moving warbler with a pale orange bill, in the largest lichen-covered bush. It was the bill that struck me first and I was up and out of the car in seconds, bins raised, shouting: "It's there in the bush!" Not very helpful given there were lots of bushes. **Melodious Warbler** 12:40. The bird was paler than expected, presumably being a juvenile, the lemon breast barely visible. Viewing time was probably no more than 30 seconds before the bird hopped out of sight. Others present sadly did not manage to get on the bird and I spent the next hour trying to help them relocate it, sensing their dismay at an impending dip. A Magpie seemed to be taking a very keen interest, searching for prey in the exact same bush, so that no doubt forced the Melodious to seek cover. I did so much want to enjoy the bird too as it had been a few years since I'd last found one. Sadly, it was not to be. Thankfully, the bird reappeared the next morning for others to enjoy but was gone by the 26th.

It was the second time this year I'd picked up a tick while half asleep in the front seat of my car, the last being a Golden Eagle at Coire na Ciste car park in the Cairngorms. Perhaps I should adopt the Twitter tag of 'Snoozy Birder'!

I can't believe that on **29th August** I was back at Porthgwarra yet again. I had spent the previous day sorting out a WIFI router in my family's holiday let in Looe, Cornwall, which provided a great base from which to scoot to Porthgwarra in the early hours. The wind was blowing west to west-northwest and beginning to favour Pendeen more as the morning wore on but before doing so, I had my much-needed **Cory's Shearwater** 10:40 from the cliff tops of Porthgwarra. The bird was close in, spiralling around in the opposite direction to the main shearwater flow, its slower wing action giving away its greater size; brown mantle, dirty-sided face and neck. The occasion was marred only by the fact that I sat on the Swiss roll in my coat pocket that was to be my late breakfast/brunch!

After a quick coffee and time to consider options, I tackled the back lanes to Pendeen Lighthouse. The wind had shifted a touch and felt more north-northwest than earlier at Porthgwarra. A quick exchange with two departing birders revealed they had seen c.8 Great Shearwater and a Cory's, but that activity had now slowed. They were right: despite a continuing good breeze there was little besides a couple of Choughs, a few Manx Shearwaters and Kittiwakes. After an hour or so I began the 200-mile journey home, subconsciously wondering whether my mother would survive till the weekend.

SEPTEMBER

My mother passed away on September 2nd, sometime around six o'clock in the morning. I could not be certain of the exact time, but she was still warm when I arrived. It was a harrowing sight: so much weight lost, pain so bravely borne. It is an image I will never forget. For the following week time was taken helping my distraught father through the process of medical certification, death registration and the administration that comes with the tidying of my mother's affairs. With my sister overseas on a cruise, I bore the brunt of the work for that first week and any birding unfortunately took a firm back seat. My father and mother had been in their 65th year together and I can only imagine how my father must have wondered what was the purpose of his remaining alive.

It was **5th September** before I next managed to twitch a bird. My target was an Ortolan Bunting on Portland's High Angle Battery, which had again been sighted that morning at 07:50 according to RBA. It's the thing with birding: you get to go to the strangest, most remote locations and despite knowing Portland well I found myself staring down at a peculiar concrete structure for which the display board indicated it was used to shell ships in the Channel during the Second World War. I reflected upon how fortunate I was to be retired early and have such freedom with my time, unlike so many at the time this battery would have been in operation. Sadly, despite what was probably a fleeting view of the disturbed bird, I dipped, only to return home in the evening to see that 2 Ortolans had been seen by the path at Fancy's Farm on the other side of the track! Looked like I'd been scouting the wrong area then. Still, Ortolans were turning up all over the south coast, so I gauged I would get another shot at this tricky species – providing, that is, the French don't eat this traditional delicacy first!

At this point I calculated I was on 276 species for the year, well behind my 280 target for the end of August and a week into September. I was, frankly, worried! I felt I was perhaps off the pace to make the 300! My response had to be to dig a little deeper and go for more distant birds given that, sea watching aside, the west seemed disappointingly bereft of any birds I needed. An early departure on *7th September* saw me en route to the RSPB reserve at Frampton, Lincolnshire, where, disappointingly, the Long-billed Dowitcher did a no show, despite giving consistently decent views since 28th August. In fact it reappeared over the next few days, favouring a creek with Snipe by the sea wall. For

45 High Angle Battery, Portland Bill, Dorset, 5th September. (Terry Wells)

heaven's sake, why did I not check the sea wall? I cursed myself for being lazy or perhaps I was partly pre-occupied with the loss of my mum. My only consolation was a very sharp-looking adult **Ruddy Shelduck** 16:00 that landed in front of the information centre. These birds crop up all over the country but have a habit of roving, i.e. not staying in one place long, making them a risky twitch, or at best a chance encounter. The downside is that while Ruddy Shelduck is on the BOU list, it's a category B Species, i.e. birds that have been recorded in an apparently natural state at least once between 1st January 1800 and 31st December 1949 but have not been recorded subsequently. I am not certain I entirely agree with this categorisation, but rules are rules, so we cannot count it. Still, Frampton is certainly a super reserve and the 2,000 Black-tailed Godwits on the main scrape provided a spectacular backdrop for a single Spoonbill, Whooper Swan, multiple Spotted Redshanks, Grey and Golden Plovers and a Wood Sandpiper, several of which had been inhabiting the reserve of late.

Something happened on that long seven-hour round trip to Frampton. I'd reminded myself why I loved the open spaces and unique insights that birding had given me. I knew I'd be back, and I knew that I had the stamina and good steel to complete my quest of reaching 300 birds, if only to be able to dedicate this book to my recently departed mother.

11th September – Frampton RSPB Reserve. I was back! **Long-billed Dowitcher** 13:28 in the creek just before the see wall. A ruddy underside, eye stripe, mottled flanks. The bird seemed relaxed in the company of Common Snipe and Black-tailed Godwit – it was similar in size to the snipe, which had a very similar feeding action, but was a lot smaller than the godwit. A Little Stint at the 360 Hide, Curlew Sandpiper at the Reedbed Hide, Yellow Wagtail in front of the information centre, and 2 Marsh Harriers patrolling the reserve and mud flats beyond the sea wall complemented. Small flocks of Reed Bunting peppered the reserve and a larger Goldfinch flock of some 100+ birds

46 Sunset, Frampton RSPB Reserve, Lincs., 11th September.
(Terry Wells)

47 Long-billed Dowitcher feeding near Common Snipe, Frampton
RSPB Reserve, Lincs., 20th September.
(Courtesy Chris Grimshaw)

179

suddenly landed on the path and thistles all around me while I was making my way back to the car, as if trying to convey some hidden message. As the sun lowered but still warmed the reserve following the earlier unpleasant mizzle, I knew at that moment my mum was smiling down at me and I felt great comfort in the isolation and beauty of this unique place.

Despite my resolve to recover lost ground, things did not immediately get any easier. My father was requiring quite a lot of support after his bereavement and needed company. A trip to Braunton near Barnstaple, Devon on *13th September* brought little solace, dipping on a Woodchat Shrike that had been frequenting the coastal dunes. Despite an extensive search of the area in the hot sun all I could manage was a single Whinchat and Wheatear. In addition, the traffic en route had been a nightmare: the M5 was suddenly closed due to an accident and I'd been forced onto minor roads amid the precipitating chaos as everybody's Satnav, like mine, was frantically searching for an alternative. Indeed, my Satnav did not save me from receiving a £30 fine in the coming days for entering a bus lane! A brief attempt to locate the Rose-coloured Starling at Northam Burrows Country Park in the afternoon had been aborted, too, largely due to my frustration that every British coastal location sought an opportunity to fleece visitors with extortionate parking fees! (I am probably unfair in this instance as at least it is a reserve.) Either way, I'd finally lost patience and found myself staring across the River Torridge estuary at Appledore with a flask of coffee simply sucking in the panoramic views. I could not understand why I'd not visited this area before (traffic jams aside), nor did I see many bird sightings on RBA from this location despite some very special coastal habitat.

From mid-September an unprecedented number of Grey Phalaropes began to push into mainland Britain and conveniently on *15th September* I was able, with a little help from colleagues on Twitter, to locate an early bird at Cheddar. **Grey Phalarope** 08:30 on the muddy

48 First-winter Grey Phalarope, Cheddar Reservoir, Somerset, 16th September. (Courtesy Bri Thompson)

edge between the Axbridge entrance and the boat club. This was a first-winter bird, grey sides to mantle, white above the eye, buff neck with dark down the back, pale legs, straight dark medium-length bill. The bird seemed clumsy, waddling across the mud as compared with the agile antics most phalarope species are capable of once on water.

Buoyed by my early morning success, I decided the Ortolan Bunting that had been showing well these past days at Cosham, Hampshire, represented a good opportunity to make up for the earlier bird dipped on Portland Bill. The turnout of birders reflected the difficulty many twitchers were having catching up with this species, which always seem to be reported as "last seen flying towards" or "heard only" comments. Indeed, on this occasion birders had decided the bird, suspected of hiding in the corner of the field, needed some encouragement to reveal itself. As half a dozen of them walked forward in a line, sure enough a bird appeared, twice uttering a call reminiscent of Ortolan but then it shot across the road only to disappear into an adjacent scrubby field! Birders rushed down the lane to gain new vantage points but despite early claims the bird was not relocated until half an hour later when it reappeared back in its favourite Hawthorn bush. **Ortolan Bunting** 14:40.

Okay, so the day was going well when a call came out for 5 White Storks disappearing over the horizon! My immediate response was to question the sighting: "You sure they weren't Spoonbills?"

"No, Storks!" came the taut reply. Within a minute the birds spiralled back into visibility, eventually passing overhead. I felt a twinge of guilt having questioned the finder's powers of identification, but five birds together were certainly more than I had seen reported in Britain. **White Stork** 14:45. I didn't know which way to look: the Ortolan Bunting was posing for attention in the Hawthorn while the Storks whirled above. Amazing! One stork clearly had a badly damaged wing,

49 Ortolan Bunting, Portsdown Hill, Cosham, Hants., 15th September. (Courtesy Lee Fuller)

which looked to have been the result of a shooting. As the other four birds spiralled ever higher, gaining much-needed altitude, perhaps for a Channel crossing, the injured bird struggled to follow, and my heart ached at its sad plight. One of the four birds seemed deliberately to slip lower down as if offering encouragement to the injured bird. I can't help but wonder what became of it and was momentarily reminded of Chris Packham's gallant efforts to thwart the killing of such migrants in Malta where shooting tragically remains rife.

Whichever way you cut it, this was one of those birding days you don't forget – three difficult year ticks, all giving great views in decent weather. There was of course one looming question: "Can we be sure these White Storks were wild in origin?" More than a dozen migrating birds are normally reported in the UK each year, of which no doubt some have originated from the handful of countries across Europe that have successfully reintroduced this species. Indeed, the Sussex-headquartered *Knepp Wildland Project,* which supports the reintroduction of British wildlife, was also reported in the *Telegraph* in July 2018 to have released 6 White Storks into the wild! The truth is it's not possible for me to be sure. To my knowledge there were no further reports of the collective "famous five", which soared to several thousand feet heading south-east over the Channel before my departure. All I know is it was a most uplifting sight…more of this, please!

I was now on 280 species for the year and probably the most upbeat I'd been since my mother's passing. Her funeral was scheduled for 20th September and I knew that pending circumstances would prevent me from being in the field for the best part of a week, given funeral preparations. On **21st September** I took the opportunity to head for Therfield in Hertfordshire to locate a Pallid Harrier that had been there from the 18th. It was drizzling when I arrived. Birders were grouped at two vantage points, one low in the valley; me and others on the hill top, which afforded more panoramic views of the surrounding countryside. It took three hours but finally the bird suddenly emerged above a brow a hundred metres or so away. **Pallid Harrier** 14:50. What happened next was completely unexpected. As the harrier seemed to take keen interest in the Skylarks that it flushed ahead of it, a Merlin on the ground was spooked and shot up into the air, at first appearing to chase the much larger Harrier! Within seconds the Merlin had overtaken the Harrier, barrel rolled and plucked a Skylark from the air. It was breath-taking. It then headed off with fast straight flight with the Harrier in hot pursuit. The Harrier somewhat expectedly lost out to the faster more agile Merlin, and the Skylark sadly became lunch.

Feeling extremely satisfied but with the wind and rain strengthening I headed for the car only to be confronted by a rather angry lady holding a baby. "And whose car is this?"

"It's mine!" I replied. For the next few minutes the lady proceeded to give me a dressing down. She had clearly been lying in ambush and had left a hand-written note on my windscreen. The note she left gives an idea as to her talent for colourful language:

50 Juvenile Pallid Harrier and Merlin battle for a Skylark lunch, 21st September, Therfield, Herts. (Courtesy Owen Crawshaw)

To the complete moron who owns this car. My husband has motor
neurone disease and I am looking after my 1 yr. old grandson.
Can you tell me how the f---k I am supposed to get out of the house
or move my car? F---k off you a---hole. I am contacting the police.

A touch disappointing but on the bright side I couldn't see any spelling mistakes! It was true, though, I had parked rather close to the rear of the lady's car to avoid blocking a nearby private drive and, indeed, she was now blocked in. Frustrating for me was that I had very considerately stepped out of my car twice to check she had plenty of space to exit before I headed off for the Pallid Harrier. There was almost two-thirds car-length space the other side, so no problem. Sadly, with the coming and going of cars (birders I dare say) some half-wit had inadvertently occupied the remaining gap and she'd decided I must be the guilty party worthy of her broadside.

It just goes to show that sometimes when birders do try to park sensibly, they can get it wrong. I do, of course, apologise for my part in any inconvenience suffered by the lady and I sympathise with her circumstance but perhaps she should reflect on the rude vocabulary she had just equipped her one-year-old grandson with!

22nd September saw me attempting to pick up a Leach's Petrel at Burnham on Sea, Somerset, where two had been seen the previous day and a number flying past Stert Point. After an hour or so in a steady downpour, and with the tide now half way out, I abandoned the sea watch to contemplate whether I should have gone to Shetland for the week where a White-throated Sparrow was showing on Foula, a Citrine Wagtail and Common Rosefinch on Unst (and one on Fetlar too) and a Yellow-breasted Bunting showing on Whalsay, Shetland! What's more, I knew this was just a taste of what Shetland could deliver in the coming weeks.

One bird that year-on-year I'd struggled with when year listing was Buff-breasted Sandpiper. I knew Davidstow Airport in Cornwall was a good location, but the birds had not been seen there since June and there was still a chance I might pick them up on the way to the Scillies in the autumn. I could not take that chance. Eventually, On *24th September* I opted for three birds that had been reported at the Royal Naval Air Station (RNAS) in Dale, Pembrokeshire. The forecast was still, sunny, the gen reasonable and with the aid of Google maps I'd worked out where to park and the correct entry gate to RNAS. Homework is key for long twitches and airfields are not inconsiderable in size. After pacing around to ascertain where exactly the birds were last seen, and what looked to be the best habitat, I decided to cut round the edge of a field just below the entry gate where I'd parked. Other birders were starting to arrive. To my delight I flushed three wary birds and, after following them for a few minutes in the long grass to secure privileged views, I alerted others to come and enjoy the spectacle. **Buff-breasted Sandpiper** 11:20. Given the lack of wing bar on one bird, I suspected at least one of the three was a juvenile bird.

51 Buff-breasted Sandpiper, Dale RNAS, Pembs., 24th September.
(Courtesy Thomas Winstone)

With more than half a day left, I was determined to make the most of my time in Wales. The nearest opportunity was a juvenile Woodchat Shrike at Ynyslas, Borth in Ceredigion, where in fact a female Eider had previously been reported, though not for some weeks. It was a long drive, but I had time and light enough. After struggling to find the right location, I flagged down a birder on the main road who by chance had been watching the bird only minutes earlier. He quickly scoped it and, yes, a distant **Woodchat Shrike** 15:37 at the back of Searivers Caravan Park. Being a big fan of shrikes I was determined to get closer views. Nervously parking inside the holiday park, fearing clampers, I approached what looked to be the bushes in which the bird was perched, only to step squarely in a large pile of dog poo! Nice. After a short delay, and a lot of boot cleaning, I eventually spied the bird from the road by the holiday park. It revealed its pale throat and underside, limited brown to the head and faint barring on the wings. Although, sadly, not a spectacular adult, this bird was at least happy to remain perched in full view for long periods on mature brambles bordering the holiday park.

With light fast fading, and not having eaten breakfast, lunch or dinner, I pulled off into a layby for long-overdue coffee and cake. Contented with my day's exploits, I opted not to conduct a thorough search of the estuary for the female King Eider in the dwindling light and headed home through the winding roads of mid-Wales, enjoying the sunset and unusually clear blue skies. I arrived home before 10 p.m. to read that the King Eider had been spotted at Ynyslas that evening! Once again, self-flagellation was warranted for not pushing hard enough to make the most of the location and opportunity.

Two days later on *26th September* I am back at Borth, and yes, dipped again, this time after flogging the Dyfi estuary from 1–7.20 p.m., I sought to console myself with a medium Mr Whippy with flake and found myself confronted with the world's largest ice cream, much to the amusement of onlookers parked up on the beach! Bloated, disappointed,

I set off home with a dysfunctional Satnav, arriving late in the night after many unwanted detours on Welsh back roads. Once again, the bird was sighted the very next day exactly where I had been walking. Oh, despair! Forget the self-flagellation, I'll try banging my head on the wall. Still, watching a car full of chavs get stuck in the estuary sands with the rising tide had afforded me some entertainment. They seemed to dream up Baldrick-style cunning plans between them by which to free the vehicle. It was a blast, but no doubt the locals had seen it all before.

October was nearly upon us and at 283 birds I was in reasonable shape but the Borth experience had left me wondering just how many long-haul dips I would endure in order to secure the 16 or more birds I needed. A last-minute decision saw me booking the Scillonian, Scilly Parking, and Crebinick guest house on St Mary's. Yes, I would be on the Scillies for an extra week from **29th September** ahead of my week there with Mary later in October. A dream start saw me picking up a **Pomarine Skua** 10:00 and **Great Shearwater** 11:00 from the Scillonian along with 5 Bonxies, Arctic Skua, Grey Phalarope and 2 Sooty Shearwaters – a good haul. A **Yellow-browed Warbler** 14:44 at Newford Duck Pond on St Mary's in the afternoon completed my hat trick for the day. The Great Shearwater had been particularly welcome given my failure to pick one up on the many sea watches in Cornwall. The Pom. too enabled me to put behind me that "nearly-bird" at Portland Bill earlier in the year. My only disappointment was dipping a Lapland Bunting on St Mary's golf course in the afternoon by about 200m after hot-footing it from Peninnis Head where an Ortolan Bunting had been giving birders breathtaking views just after my departure. Still, in the fading light a brief stop at the somewhat dilapidated Hilda Quick Hide on Lower Moors produced very close views of the golden-braced bobber (a Jack Snipe), one of my favourite birds seen earlier in the year at Slimbridge. September was not done yet. The best bird in town was the Tawny Pipit, which I'd last seen in May 2017. The next morning, **30th September**, I took myself to Bryher and with about a dozen birders began sweeping the area to the paths at the back of Great Popplestone beach where the bird had last been seen. It took about an hour to be in the right place at the right time but at last this tall, upright sandy-looking bird appeared, straining as if to see us while skitting along the sandy path. **Tawny Pipit** 11:45. During the next hour a reported Rosefinch in nearby scrub failed to reveal itself despite an extensive search, which unearthed a Pied Flycatcher, 2 or 3 Spotted Flycatchers, Redstart and Whinchat, and a few Blackcaps. Clearly there were plenty of migrants here, just not the Rosefinch. The return to St Mary's yielded a lone Spoonbill on the rocks. It always fascinates me how spotting the same bird on the rocks, seen several times already, became a daily game during island hopping. I'd ended the month on 287 species, and I was pleased I'd made the last-minute decision to be here. At the log that night only 22 souls made it into the backroom of the Scillonian for the second log call of the

52 Tawny Pipit, Great Popplestone, Bryher, Isles of Scilly, 2nd October. (Courtesy John Judge)

season, and six of those were late! It was a far cry from the heady 1980s. I picked up the excellent *ISBG Bird and Natural History Review 2017* to add to my growing collection. As usual this annual publication did not disappoint: great facts, photos from top birders, many of whom I had known for years.

Yes, the Scilly season was just ramping up and I was ready for the feast, but I could not help wondering how the local inhabitants (plus the regular rowdy football watchers of the Scillonian Club's large indoor projection screen) would feel about being invaded yet again by the green-clad army.

OCTOBER

If you are a birder that has had the great fortune to regularly attend the Scilly Isles in October there can be no doubting that this is the top birding month of the year. Only the increasingly popular Shetland Islands can rival its reputation for producing year on year scarcities and major rarities. The keenest twitchers will often visit the latter in late September to make the most of both island groups. What perhaps sets Scillies apart is its extra mild climate at this time of year, the close cluster of islands with excellent bus-like boat services, numerous pubs, restaurants and, of course, the nightly ISBG (Isles of Scilly Bird Group) log in the Scillonian Club. The log itself can foster camaraderie, providing great entertainment as quick quips, retorts and rivalries play out. Regular characters, some having attended for 30–40 years, have become knowledge-soaked antiques of a by-gone age, when quality binoculars were a luxury, cheap ex-army clothing was the norm, and birders patrolled the islands in their thousands. Many are just fatter, baggier and balder than before (or is that just my reflection) but with the same burning passion and glint in their eyes, recalling events as though emanating from a rum-breathed pirate revealing secret treasure. Priceless! For those guest birders who, on occasion, are invited to conduct the log, it must, then, feel like entry to some divine order, a secret society amongst whom sightings of the rarest birds are first shared only in the strictest of confidence. Although I have travelled to the islands a dozen or more times since my first visit in 1984,

I still feel humbled and privileged to be part of the occasion.

As a part of the Scilly birding furniture, then, I decided **1st October** would see me on my first Scillies Pelagic. Yes, that's right, I am embarrassed to reveal, my first! Scilly Pelagics are run each year by the likes of Joe Pender, a well-known local character. These trips are legendary for yielding close-up views of those difficult species that usually appear as dots on a cold early morning sea watch. In the past I had avoided these excursions despite high accolade for Joe's outings, in part for fear of missing a new bird on the islands and, to be brutally honest, because I was keen to avoid the embarrassment of being sea-sick! While I am not a particularly poor sea traveller, being ill on a trawler off Cornwall in a force 7 or 8 in my school years had exposed an underlying vulnerability. While I do take the Scillonian boat each year to and from the Scillies without once having been sick, heading off island in a small boat in wilder waters to see shearwaters, skuas and rare gulls is a different matter. Even professional fishermen have been seen traipsing back past the town's Co-op looking somewhat pale and queasy and not daring to speak after such trips for fear of revisiting their breakfast. So, with that in mind I bravely clambered aboard. Five hours later I had counted: nearly 200 Great, 20–30 Sooty and up to 10 Balearic Shearwaters; 5 Bonxies; 12 Purple Sandpipers; 1 Grey Phalarope; 2 Puffins and 1 (probable juvenile) Yellow-legged Gull following the boat as food was thrown from the back. Dolphin numbers were astounding, probably 150, sidling up to the low-sided boat, and surfacing to eyeball its occupants. Clearly, they were on a Dolphin *let's-spot-a-Human* holiday and had been promised some exceptional close-ups! The views all round were superb, affording good comparison of species as we moved from one distant spiralling flock of Gannets to another, given these flocks usually signalled a feeding frenzy. On the downside, I did not see any new year ticks, e.g. the hoped-for Sabine's Gull, and it was getting late in the season for petrels (Leach's aside, perhaps) but it was an unforgettable experience, nonetheless. Importantly, I'd managed to keep my breakfast down, which could not be said of all the craft's occupants some of whom made good use of the onboard shared toilet.

Returning to St Mary's late afternoon, I found that the Lapland Bunting had again been reported and, this time, the skulking bird was not to escape me. It was located next to a stone wall near the second tee on the golf course. **Lapland Bunting** 17:08. Despite momentarily being hemmed in by a small huddle of birders and photographers, this bird seemed undaunted, affording superb views and walking towards its observers rather than taking the path of least resistance. After seeing it well, I was keen to get off the golf course where routinely, year on year, birders are warned: "Don't walk on the fairways!" Though I'd been careful, other birders arriving seemed a tad less mindful in their haste to tick the bird.

2nd October was spent on Tresco where the target bird was Red-breasted Flycatcher. Indeed, there were 2 birds reported to be between the two hides on Great Pool. The birds were to prove very elusive but, even as many gave up hope, a couple of us heard a call that sounded very much like our bird. We decided to wait it out. We had

53 Lapland Bunting, Golf Course, St Mary's, Isle of Scilly, 1st October. (Courtesy Cliff Smith)

arrived on the island around 11:00 and it was gone 15:00 before the bird showed itself. **Red-breasted Flycatcher** 15:05. As usual, there was not much red to be seen but a rather plump-looking, grey-brown bird, contrasting white underside, large dark eye ringed with a little white. As the bird flicked among the undergrowth, occasionally making visible its white tail patches, we became familiar with its favoured perching points to obtain well-earned views before catching the last afternoon boat back to St Mary's.

3rd October proved to be something of a disappointment. Cool grey skies, mizzle and no new birds for me despite a trip to St Agnes where I failed to re-locate the reported Rosefinch near Great Pool. *4th October* saw me on the morning boat to St Martin's. Unless a rarity is reported there, St Martin's is perhaps the least visited island by birders because, in the past at least, one could often find oneself out of range of the Walkie Talkies and so miss breaking news of a mega. On this occasion there was a small handful of birders who, like me, hoped to pick up Rose-coloured Starling. But first, 7 Sandwich Terns, uncommon on Scillies this late in the season, posed on yellow buoys off St Mary's quay. As we disembarked on St Martin's I headed to Lower Town where the juvenile Rosy had last been reported, below the Seven Stones Inn on the coast path, eating berries from bushes near a small tin shed. Fortune prevailed as 10 minutes after my arrival at the site a Peregrine flew through, putting everything to flight. As I followed the Starling flock wheeling before me it was immediately evident that there was a particularly grey bird among them and, importantly, it had a pale rump and contrasting darker wings! I followed the flock to eventually secure good views of the bird feeding on Blackberry bushes 50m ahead of me. **Rose-coloured Starling** 11:21. I was pleased I'd done my homework. Juveniles of Rose-coloured Starling can, to an uninformed, appear grey much like juvenile Common Starling but are differently marked and not that hard to distinguish in flight. Having put the bird out on the newly formed Scilly What's App group and RBA, I enjoyed a coffee at the Seven Stones Inn before being entertained by a House Sparrow perched on my boot as I sat cross-legged at Lower Town quay awaiting the 14:30 boat. Why was I the only one here? Was everyone twitching a mega? As unease spread over me as it dawned that I might be at the wrong quay! 14:30 came and went, still no people and no boat. I stopped by the Karma Hotel reception and my fears were confirmed, but at least I had time to walk to Higher Town quay at the other end of the island to catch the later boat. As luck would have it, I was rewarded with my second Rose-coloured Starling in scrub to the back of the toilet block at Higher Town!

Rose-coloured Starling was my 290th bird of the year and made up for the one I'd missed earlier at Portland. I'd already hit my week's target for my first week on Scillies with a couple of days to spare. It's fair to say I was now beginning to feel confident of making 300 given I had yet another week in Scillies planned for mid-October.

The remainder of the day was uneventful except for two things: 1) it was announced that my boat home to Penzance on Saturday was cancelled and I'd now be departing Sunday; 2) Dogs! Yes, Dogs. They are everywhere – on beaches, on the ferry boats. "What's the problem?" you may well ask. Too many! Certainly, several fold more than in previous years. St Martin's, by example, is renowned for its Sanderling flocks on what is one of best beaches in the country. All I could see now was dog walkers with dogs. And again, on the ferries, yelping, whimpering. Some owners seemed oblivious to the fact that wet dog lolloping all over passengers was not everyone's idea of fun. Now, don't get me wrong: I have nothing against dog owners and dogs in general. We regularly have dogs staying at my partner's farm and my partner is a keen former dog owner. The Scilly authorities do put signs up insisting dogs must be kept on a lead while on the beach at certain times of the year. And yes, if I were a dog owner I'd want to let the dog off the lead and some small part of me might even be hoping he'd poo while I was not looking so that I wouldn't have to carry the smelly deposit home with me. Either way, we need to find a harmonious solution here if we are to preserve the nature on these unique islands. Pets *must not* take precedence over the wild inhabitants...OK, rant over.

I spent **5th October** on St Mary's generally birding and enjoying the island's remote and pretty spots. Whimbrel, Spotted Flycatcher, Bar-tailed Godwit, Whinchat, Grey Wagtail; a Buff-breasted Sandpiper on the airfield (I can't think why I drove all the way to Pembrokeshire for one) and a Merlin in Buzza Quarry devouring what looked to be a House Sparrow at impressively close quarters. I had been enjoying the last of the day's sun on Penninis when the call went out for the putative Wilson's Snipe at the Hilda Quick Hide! Just enough time to hoof it. It was a squeeze but there was just enough space in the hide and, by chance, I was in the right place to see the bird. The Wilson's was with a couple of Common Snipe and was remaining well tucked into nearby reeds. **Wilson's Snipe** 18:45. The bird fitted the bill nicely according to published criteria. I'd seen this species previously on St Mary's and, given the number of records for the islands, it seems to be becoming something of a regular autumn visitor.

To be honest, Scillies was comparatively quiet but, as more of the regular autumn birders arrived, the Walkie Talkies buzzed with fresh banter; familiar voices announcing themselves. Mental images appeared before me as I warmly recalled each like old friends gathering in anticipation before a Christmas party. Old hands like Dick Filby, using his super-powered handset (the clarity and power of which no one else could match), was always adept at clarifying crackly reports of some new migrant, like the control tower master at Heathrow. In crisp tones his "copy that" announcements were somehow legendary as if shooting a starter pistol at which we might all tear-off after some new rarity. Some reports were indeed downright funny: "A large heron has been reported somewhere or other." Doesn't exactly narrow things down, does it? A Tri-coloured perhaps!

Right now, there were only two birds of interest to me on the islands: Common Rosefinch and Wryneck, which had been seen on St Agnes; and again, a single Common Rosefinch on Bryher on the 5th. Perhaps there was still time. The forecast high winds and heavy rain on **6th October** had postponed my departure from the islands and so I'd gained an extra day on St Mary's, birding. A report of a Wryneck at Carn Gwaval in the late afternoon was not rewarded with success, just another soaking. As I was about done for the day, aching from head to foot and looking forward to escaping my sodden waterproofs, a call came out: "Barred Warbler showing at Porthellic Pool!" Why do they always have to be at the other end of the island? For the second day in a row I found myself hot-footing it across the island in the last hour of light, and once again with well-deserved success! **Barred Warbler** 17:44 in the bushes, beach side of Porthellic Pool. The bird, large, grey and surprisingly ungainly for a warbler, bobbled about in the last sunlight of the day.

Amazing that somehow the walk back to the B&B from a successful twitch is just, well, not tiring. Surprising too was that I'd taken only 10 seconds to glance at a Cattle Egret sat in a horse field on the way to the Barred Warbler. It was my first ever for Scillies, perhaps unsurprising as these birds previously did not arrive in Britain in anything like the numbers they do today. Even so, could I be getting a touch blasé?

October, then, was off to a great start and the extra week on Scillies had paid off with nine further species, bringing my total to 292 and in one week's time I'd be back for more. Or at least that's what I thought. Once again, weather continued to frustrate and the Scillonian boat to St Mary's from Penzance was cancelled on the 13th so Mary and I could not get onto the islands until the 15th, losing a couple of days. To smooth the journey, we decided to drive down to Penzance on **14th October** and conveniently take in an **Isabelline Shrike (probably Daurian)** 15:53 that was performing on the coastal side of a golf course at Thurlestone, Devon. This was a rather grey-looking first-winter bird, as so many of the shrikes we see in Britain are, with a rufous tail and

54 First-winter Isabelline Shrike (probably Daurian), Thurlestone, Devon, 13th October. (Courtesy Pete Aley)

shadowy mask. Markings on its pale buff breast indicative of an immature bird were barely evident. After watching the bird hawking insects for some 30 minutes, we took in a brief stop at All Saints' Church, which dates back to 1230, I believe, to admire the stained-glass windows before heading off to Hope Cottage, our B&B for the night in Crowlas.

The Scillonian voyage to St Mary's the next day, **15th October**, was, by comparison with my earlier trip, somewhat uneventful. No skuas, but there were shouts for several Grey Phalaropes, Sooty Shearwater, Puffin and, oddly, a Merlin far from land that did give me a momentary start as it imitated perhaps a rare petrel. I also struggled to convert any of the juvenile Kittiwakes into Sabine's Gulls, though I later learnt that one had indeed been reported on the crossing. After a quick check-in at the now very familiar Anjeric B&B that we'd booked most years on St Mary's, it was as though I had never left the islands. First, the nearby lifeboat station rocks looked a good check-for location and we were immediately rewarded with an obliging, superbly plumaged male Black Redstart. Then we found ourselves on the path that runs alongside the dump staring at a flock of House Sparrows in a small weedy field, only one wasn't; was it? As the birds alighted into neighbouring bushes Mary homed in on an individual that had also caught my eye. **Common Rosefinch** 14:02 – at last! Aside from the fact she is my lovely partner, I was immediately reminded what an asset Mary is on these trips: sharp-eyed, patient and usually binocular-free. Her capacity to see detail that, for most of us is visible only with binoculars, is frankly astonishing and always leaves me wondering just how much my eyesight must have deteriorated. We ambled up the island towards the riding stables where a Wryneck had been reported but without luck, only Black Redstarts and White Wagtails seemed abundant amongst the horses here. Then a shout came over the Walkie Talkie: "Bobolink at Trenoweth Farm!" courtesy of Kris Webb! At first, I thought I'd misheard: "A Bobolink"! A mega I'd missed in my early birding days, a life tick I had yet to catch up with. We smartly padded off to the farm, imitating a walk of calm composure where thirty or so birders eagerly waited on a nearby track, hoping to be given access to private land in the now fast-fading light. Sadly, the bird could not be located, and so access was not granted. The Bobolink simply disappeared without further report.

"Meow" – cat in the bag

While you might have expected the Bobolink to be the focus of attention at the evening's log, it wasn't. News broke that a "Grey Catbird" had been found on Land's End near Treeve Moor House! Now to put this in perspective, if accepted by the British Birds Rarities Committee (BBRC), this North American Vagrant would be only the second of its kind to be accepted in Britain. Other records relate to Jersey, Channel Islands 1975 and Co. Cork, Ireland 1986. One bird apparently arrived at Portsmouth in style on the QE II in October 1998 and so was deemed ship assisted and so not counted. Shrewd bird, though! Aside from those the only accepted record was for a single bird in Anglesey in 2001. In Birder lingo, then, this was a "serious mega" though not the rarest bird for me, which remains to this day Little Whimbrel, a first for Britain in Mid Glamorgan in 1982! In those giddy heydays birders twitched in their thousands and I recall to this day looking across a barren field upon arrival only to see a couple of hundred scopes looking back at me and my fellow birders. No, the hubbub in the log was about what planes birders could catch the next day to go see the bird? Who had left already? Would it still be there? It was literally a case of who would blink first in an OK Corral shoot out. Personally, I found it a somewhat unwelcome intrusion. On the one hand, here I was with Mary trying to soak up the best the Scillies had to offer, on the other hand I was contemplating whether the short return day flight to Cornwall and taxis for £250+ was worth it. I guess such hesitation is what separates me from the frenetic few who boast a British life list of 500+. Mary made a call the next morning, *16th October*, to check on available flights/costs and we quickly established there were still two seats available. Despite that, I coolly opted to stay on the islands and go find the **Eastern Yellow Wagtail** 10:55 that was frequenting the airfield. Perhaps I felt comfort in remaining close to the airfield or simply wanted to check who was flying out! The Eastern Yellow at least was a rather smart bird compared to the one I'd seen on St Mary's in October 2016, and a Yellow Wagtail was on hand too, affording a good comparison. As usual, while the majority accepted this was indeed an Eastern, the debate was raging over which race the bird was and other candidates began to surface on the Scilly WhatsApp that, by comparison, did not look the part. Either way, this bird received the thumbs up from the majority and so would go on the list subject of course to final BBRC acceptance. The day completed with a typically grey-looking juvenile Red-backed Shrike near Toll's Island (which at least I had the pleasure of re-finding and pointing out to one of the several and increasingly popular bird tour groups on the island) and a couple of Whimbrel on Porthellic beach.

17th and *18th October* brought little further consolation as more and more birders hopped away to tick off the Cornwall Catbird. In truth, the only game in town in Scilly was the Grey-cheeked Thrush inhabiting Covean Cove on St Agnes. It had been reported late afternoon on the 17th after I'd spent a day on Tresco where I was in trundle mode watching Merlin, Black Redstarts, Red-throated Diver and a pleasing young Surf Scoter from the Block House. The early boat on *18th October* laid on for Agnes saw most birders, like me, dip the Grey-cheeked Thrush despite many hours staring at the same bushes. God knows how Mary remained so patient. It was not without some frustration, too, as I located a preening bird atop a tall bush that seemed to fit the bill just as a shout went up from behind of "that's it!" Having seen Grey-cheeked Thrush before, I was not wholly convinced and knew I'd just have to let it go, though I think the other birder was most probably correct. Aside from the usual Ring Ouzel, Merlin, Peregrine, Sparrowhawk, another Red-backed Shrike and several Black Redstarts on Horse Point, Agnes seemed to disappoint. Perhaps I'd been spoilt by recent successes? Even the Yellow-browed Warbler and flycatchers at the parsonage were not co-operating. The only surprise was a female Bullfinch at Covean (which Mary saw, and I didn't), which became the talk of the day amongst old-guard birders keen to add this Scilly scarcity to their islands' list. Yes, there are lists for everything. It would not surprise me if there are listers for one of the bigger rocks in the Tresco channel too, like Green Island!

One of the great things about Scilly is that just as things seem to go flat, up pops a rarity. With the Catbird still meowing in my ear from Cornwall and another trip to St Agnes on the morning of *19th October* to dip the Grey-cheeked Thrush once again, the shout came for Red-eyed Vireo on Bryher! A boat was laid on from St Mary's at 15:30 and we were on it with about 50 top twitchers, most swivelling on the boat's long bench seats to view the Great Northern, Red-throated Diver and Shelduck (a scarcity here) on the way. Adding to the occasion Dick Filby, (founder of RBA) and a familiar face on the islands in autumn, had taken an elevated position on the boat from which to update us on the Vireo's whereabouts and where we needed to head for. It reminded me of a WWII night commando raid with the commander giving the final speech: *Now, men, when you hit the beach, stay low… Use the natural cover and make your way to the rendezvous point.* Atmospheric. As usual circumstance and characters came to the fore to make for good theatre. A quick hoof across the island, we surrounded the tall hedge by Great Pool. Patience, and…yes, **Red-eyed Vireo** 16:02. Whether it is a combination of the name and the bird's sharp plumage (and, let's face it, we don't see too many vireos in the UK) Red-eyed Vireo is one species that never fails to excite birders, and this was no exception. The happy throng swept from one vantage point to another following the bird's every move before eventually it shot across the road, disappearing in a much larger scrub area.

55 Red-eyed Vireo, Bryher, Isles of Scilly, 22nd October.
(Courtesy Simon Slade)

Returning on the boat to St Mary's from Bryher, I could not help but feel that inner warmth you get from a day out in the elements that eventually pays off. Had I been in Cornwall watching the Grey Catbird, I might have missed the Vireo. A quick search round the back of Porth Mellon in the fading light failed to produce Little Bunting but so what? It had been a successful day and, tomorrow morning, I could explore the small scrubby fields behind the beach where the Little Bunting was last seen. A Kingfisher flying southward down Telegraph Road seemed to be pointing the way back to the B&B, or was it the Scillonian Club for a much-needed pint of Betty Stogs award winning bitter.

While the Grey Catbird continued to perform in Penzance before a continuous stream of visitors, I was leaving the islands today, **20th October**, and so by now had made up my mind that a B&B in Penzance and a visit the following morning was the most sensible option. Meanwhile on St Mary's the Little Bunting was again seen behind Porth Mellon. As I greeted a few old friends, I was encouraged to learn the bird had been showing through a narrow gap in the hedge just minutes before my arrival. The shout came out: "There it is; that's it!" I found myself staring at a Bunting that indeed looked to be a Little. **Little Bunting** 12:40. Then suddenly there were two! Then they were gone. As I walked away from the location, I saw a report of two female Reed Buntings on WhatsApp in the same field! Doubts began to grow. I just had to go back. Sure enough, there were indeed female Reed Buntings here but this time I was standing next to a Heatherlea Guide when again our real candidate re-appeared and, yes, there were surprisingly not one but two Little Buntings! All relevant features were confirmed as the birds perched obligingly in the tallest bush in the hedgerow and I felt pleased I'd made the effort to eliminate any nagging doubt: after all, the list is sacrosanct.

The afternoon crossing back to Penzance was sunny, calm and, frankly, uneventful. All I could think of was where exactly was the Grey Catbird? Would it still be there in the morning and would I be thwarted by fog as once before while sea watching from nearby Porthgwarra? Finding our B&B in Morrab Place was the first challenge as the Korean Satnav decided that alleyways were fair game for my car. No matter how we tried, the best we could do was circle the general area that surrounded the drop-pin on the map. To add to the misery, the key safe located in the B&B porch had jammed, making entry difficult and we were then confronted with five flights of narrow stairs with heavy bags before collapsing on our concrete-hard bed. Oh, and the shared bathroom was on a separate floor. Why did I book an attic room when I knew we'd have heavy suitcases? Even so, it was a pleasant room, great location from which to enjoy food and drink in Penzance, and the proprietor was most welcoming.

22nd October – **Grey Catbird** 09:50. Even on the day of sighting we'd played it cool, taken a leisurely breakfast before driving up to the area near Treeve Moor House, where the bird had last been seen. We were confronted by a field full of cars and familiar faces from the Scillies, including Michael, a gentleman that regularly visited the isles and stayed at the Anjeric B&B with us. I felt a twinge of guilt as Michael, now with walking frame, had the day before been angling for a lift from Penzance

56 Grey Catbird, second for Britain, Trevescan, Cornwall, 20th October. (Courtesy James Packer)

204

to the site of the Catbird. I had not volunteered to help, largely due to our uncertain day plan and the need for me to remain flexible. We picked a spot amongst the throng of birders now numbering a hundred or more on two sides of the field; it did not take long for our feathered guest from the US to appear. Seemingly larger than a Song Thrush, the bird first appeared to my right, affording frankly average views but then after a few circuits of the area, interspersed with momentary disappearance amongst extensive brambles, the Catbird dropped into the ditch 5 or 6m in front of me and, amazingly, began meowing! It produced a rather screechy sound rather like the tones of a Jay, I thought. Just fantastic! The bird did not disappoint with its sharp black cap atop a smooth medium-grey body, gorging on the nearby berries to the machine-gun-like shutter action of cameras on either side of my head. As if somewhat put out, a Short-eared Owl roosting in the bushes behind nonchalantly looked on as though pondering what all the fuss was about. Yes, Britain's second Grey Catbird ever was in the bag…at last!

If you are anywhere near Land's End and there are lots of top birders about it's odds-on another rarity will be found. Just as we were leaving the Catbird to continue to amuse the constant flow of birders still arriving, including one family who'd parked up without even knowing what was going on, news broke of a Dusky Warbler at Porthgwarra. I knew this could be a very tricky bird, skulking in the bracken and scrub that covered the valley of this top birding spot. Sure enough, when Mary and I arrived the bird had scarpered up and over the bracken to the back of the lighthouse. With only five of us looking it was going to be a needle in a haystack job. My sense was that the bird would head into the small valley below, perfect for such warblers. Sure enough, with a wave and a shout from a fellow birder I was hot-footing it down the hill the way we'd come and into the secluded valley.

Now, I confess I am no expert on Dusky Warbler calls, but others assured me the "clicks" I was hearing did indeed belong to a Dusky. With that marvel of technology (the mobile phone), I too began to tune into the call, which was not entirely unlike Blackcap. Having put the bird out again on RBA to entice a few more pairs of eyes to join the pursuit, we spent the next couple of hours following every glimpse and leaf-flick in the bushes. Suddenly, a bird shot up vertically no more than 2m, either to take an insect or check whether we were still watching. No one else seemed to have noticed it but I knew immediately from the jizz that this was almost certainly our Dusky and so I held my station some 50m right of the group, hoping it would reappear. I simply could not call it…yet. Then after 10 more minutes thankfully the bird circled round, calling, 10m to my right and headed over the narrow road to the car park. Got him! **Dusky Warbler** 13:38. It had been a test of patience and after a few more brief views I left the remaining birders to play cat and mouse with the little fellow.

I vowed that next October when back on Scillies I would make more of the days either side of my vacation with Mary to unlock the hidden gems of this famed Cornwall peninsula.

Now, I had originally thought Dusky Warbler was special. Subject to any BBRC approvals/rejections in the future that may affect the total, this surely was my 300th species of the year – I had achieved a key milestone in my birder's journey and all before October was out. As I alerted fellow birders on Twitter to my achievement, it was pleasing to receive so many congratulatory replies from acquaintances new and old. But I knew this was not the end game, merely a benchmark attained. I was determined to press on and see what total I could reach within my reasonable means. I was still loving every moment, a joy ride I did not want to end, continually meeting new people, encountering familiar faces, and discovering the hidden beauty Britain has to offer. It was like a permanent holiday. I'd learnt I was most at peace roaming the shores and footpaths absorbing nature, seeing things differently and delighting at the strange behaviours and habits of the creatures around me; and not just birds. I was learning how to look, honing my senses, knowledge and anticipation. Just as a Scientist achieving my Doctor of

Philosophy through the discovery of some scientific minutiae, chasing 300+ birds had provided a new platform from which to philosophise, a veritable spring from which flowed a greater personal understanding of self. Perhaps that is the true value of such hobbies.

(Back to earth: A later recount revealed that I was in fact on 299, having mistakenly counted Ruddy Shelduck on my bird tracker despite knowing this was a B category bird as described earlier! While, in the interests of the reader all totals from the date of that sighting, 9th September, have of course been corrected so as to be accurate in this publication, I wanted you to savour the moment just as I did. In any case were the Italian Sparrow deemed to be acceptable by the BBRC, then Dusky Warbler would indeed have been my 300th bird but I'd decided to discount the Sparrow for the time being pending DNA test results and BBRC ratification. Still, I had enjoyed the delusion and momentary walk-on-water.)

24th October and following Twitter exchanges with some fellow local birders, a small wood in Wiltshire in the Marlborough/Hungerford area was thought to be a good spot for Willow Tit. This species has struggled for decades now and I was desperate to find a new, local hotspot. I traipsed round the wood, confident I could identify the bird by its distinct nasal call "*tchaa, tchaa, tchaa*" or sometimes "*tseu, tseu, tseu*" call and that I was searching for the right habitat, e.g. Hazel or Birch. I had been reminded, too, not to stray from the footpaths and encounter the keeper who, I was guessing, had something of a temper. Fortunately, there seemed to be sufficient access, and large flocks of birds – mainly Chaffinch; Brambling; Coal, Great, Long-tailed and Blue Tits – were swarming through the area. After an hour or two walking, I located a crossroads in the paths and noticed the area around me supported an abundance of Hazel. The place was buzzing with birds and, sure enough, after no more than 30 minutes a couple of Willow Tits could be heard uttering both call types two or three times. But where were they? On the second pass through of this enormous tit flock I managed to catch one bird in a line of trees bordering a fresh-cut woodland on the opposite side of the intersection. Small, stocky, bull head, elongated cap and – there it is – the wing panel, all viewed with the bird calling. **Willow Tit** 12:42. Very nice, an underrated bird. So often an annual bogey bird for me along with Lesser Spotted Woodpecker, which has similarly struggled to hold territory in the UK. After watching the birds two or three times during the next 30 minutes as the tit flock danced from one side of the path to the other, I decided to exit…just in case I was on a path I should not have been!

So, at last I'd achieved my minimum benchmark of 300 with a couple of months to spare but remaining on 300 is too close for comfort given the vagaries of BBRC rulings and, in any case, what might I achieve if I push on?

Buoyed by the morning's success with Willow Tit, a report around lunchtime of a Baird's Sandpiper at Goldcliff Pools, Newport, was my next stop. Despite being no more than an hour away from the location, thanks to the fast M4 corridor, it took me closer to two hours before I was stood looking at the pools! I always seemed to go wrong finding this poorly signposted reserve. On this occasion, it may have cost me dear. The bird had last been seen around 14.30. I cursed myself but all the same tried to persuade myself that, had I not got lost, I would still have missed the bird by 15 minutes. I explored the estuary onto which the bird was deemed to have flown but the tide was out and the light faltering. With a Peregrine sat on an island and a female Sparrowhawk patrolling, I decided just to soak up the ambience of a beautiful sunset.

26th October – **Baird's Sandpiper** 10:10. Yes, that's right, I was back at Goldcliff's Avocet Hide, the bird having shown repeatedly on the 25th. Even so, upon my arrival I found the Peregrine to be still sat on the same island, same spot, and the small wader flocks were definitely uncomfortable. I'd noticed that tucked in with a circling group of Lapwings was one wader that the Lapwings had once or twice tried to shun. It was small and particularly long-winged. I pointed it out to the couple of other birders in the hide. Could that be our bird? The flock frustratingly disappeared over the estuary behind the hide. An hour or so then passed before we eventually located the Baird's to our left on the near shore almost by accident. How had we not seen it fly in? No sooner had we put it out on Twitter and RBA than birders began to arrive after the long trudge to the hide only to learn it had given us the slip. I empathised with their frustration. Despite that setback, the Baird's did continue to entertain at Goldcliff well into the first week of November, affording many the chance to return and get to grips with what is a tricky species to identify in the field, in common with many rare peeps and stints.

October was not done yet and, as usual, Norfolk was providing its fair share of rarities. From *29th* to *31st October* I'd booked myself into Stable Court in Langham again and immediately questioned my decision as I saw that the 30th was going to be a complete washout with heavy rain forecast all day! My first target bird was an Eastern Stonechat presumed to be Stejneger's, a claim which subsequent scientific analysis of the bird's droppings would appear to support. Crikey, were birders now required to carry swabs and Petri dishes for sample collection and analysis in order to tick a bird? I had neither Stejneger's nor Siberian (the other possibility) on my year list so it would be a good bird to see not least because Stejneger's is a rare visitor to these shores and as such a UK life tick for me too. Conveniently, Stonechats tend to be rather conspicuous, perching to give good visibility in the scrubby areas they prefer to inhabit. This bird proved to be just that, and within minutes of my arrival, and despite occasional drizzle, the bird obliged. **Stejneger's Stonechat** 12:41. So casual had my twitch been the bird had been present since the 19th and I hadn't even risen early to go see it. The bird worked between a couple of set perches, making an easy subject for the photographers too. From the front the bird could be confused with perhaps a first-winter female Stonechat with paler underside and more extensive white to the throat sides. From the back its plumage and tone recalled Whinchat but, noticeably, there was no streaking on the rump. There were of course many more plumage subtleties and extensive debate online as to the bird's identity but given that the BOU recognises both Stejneger's and Siberian as distinct species either would do nicely, thank you.

Sadly, the rest of the day did not deliver. At Warham Greens, a hot spot for Hen Harrier, I could find only a couple of Marsh Harriers and a few Grey Plover despite a couple of miles of walking the coastal wall dodging showers. Again, the light began to defeat me as I arrived at Titchwell shortly after 16:00 only to dip the Red-flanked Bluetail that had turned up that lunchtime. Curse my poor mobile signal on those mud flats! It was probably the same bird that had been seen in recent days at Holkham. Five Marsh Harriers floating into roost with the backdrop of a moody sunset seemed to predict the next day's unwelcome storm.

My visit to Titchwell was not without some amusement. As I ventured to use the toilets in the late afternoon darkness it was evident that to remain seated and stationary for the whole performance was

57 Stejneger's Stonechat, Meadow Lane, Salthouse, Norfolk, 25th October. (Courtesy Rich Bonser)

impossible with a five-second timer that would switch off all lights unless you moved. From the outside of the building it must have looked like a disco!

30th October – the heavens opened. Part of my reason for being in Norfolk was not just the Eastern Stonechat but a King Eider: yes, the species I'd painfully dipped twice at Ynyslas, Ceredigion. This bird was reported to be an eclipse drake as opposed to the comparatively drab adult female at Ynyslas, so a tad more interesting. Even so, this bird would not prove easy in the wild seas and pouring rain forcing all birders to seek cover in the shelters that adorn the promenade at Sheringham. There were Common Eider here too! "There it is!", "Beyond the green and yellow buoy." "No, it's down again." "Lost it!" "It's by the red buoy… now." "No, it's over here; that one's an Eider, our bird flew left."

It was confusing but suffice to say I'd been watching a bird that looked to be the real McCoy. After a few more confirmatory views and at one point being rudely shouted at by some guy who said that I was in his way (and after he'd declined to let me peek through his scope, too!) I decided it was job done – **King Eider** 14:23. In fact, I went back the next day, ***31st October***, and located the bird again much closer in and in better light. This time even the orange-red bill colouration was evident. I felt pleased: my earlier homework and diligence had paid off.

Before departing from Norfolk, I checked in at Titchwell (no not to re-enact the disco) just in case a Bluetail reappeared, and to grab a bacon butty, hot chocolate and Eccles cake (obviously not dieting). As I inspected the bird log in the information centre, I could not help but overhear the conversation between a lady visitor and the female RSPB representative on duty.

Visitor: "Yes, but what will I see?" After a brief explanation from the RSPB representative she then pressed harder. "Yes, but if I pay to come in will I see lots of birds?"

Lady RSPB rep: "You come in and let me know what you've seen when you get back!"

Most diplomatic, I thought, given the visitor seemed to imply that she did not want to pay an entrance fee unless she was guaranteed to see a minimum number of birds. If only nature was so dependable. Obviously, she must be employed in a contracts department, or perhaps no one told her birds can and do fly away!

My Norfolk jaunt yielded no other ticks. I did blink a petrel species twice at Sheringham on the 30th between the waves and my scope's drip-covered objective lens in the pouring rain. These were deemed to be a Leach's Petrel but after some deliberation I just felt I could not tick the bird. All I had was dark shape and jizz and, frankly, little else by way of key features in the soaking rain. Looking back, I am not certain what else it could have been but by now I may simply be going down with a desperate case of *tick grabbers virus*! By contrast Arctic Skua, Bonxie, Little Gulls and Common Eiders were proving somewhat easier to pick out at Sheringham and Cley.

I calculated that October had ended with some 303 species bagged, of which a dozen alone were from the Scillies! It just serves to indicate how the Scilly Isles remain such a vital location to visit for birders taking on the challenge of big year listing.

NOVEMBER

My plans for November were very simple. I expected to spend more time in Cheshire/Wirral and the north-east coast, and to visit Norfolk yet again – probably more than once – to pick off what I could when and wherever it arrived, balancing risk/cost of long-haul twitches. Importantly, I'd decided to rule out making special trips to Scotland to catch up with say Black Scoter and to limit overnight stays where possible. My annual budget had, frankly, taken a hammering. After all, I was not striving for a record of some sort, merely trying to see what was possible for the average birder through a sustained but measured approach to year listing. Well, that's the theory…honest! With that in mind, my next endeavour, on *3rd November*, was to act local and scour Salisbury Plain in search of Hen Harriers. There are two advantages to doing this in the winter: 1) your car does not get filled with that infernal dust from the plain every time you open the window and 2) the Harriers, if present, will return to regular roost sites, in which case it should be a doddle to see them in the hours before dark, right? Wrong! I spent a whole day till dark and dipped having traversed miles of the permitted and restricted byways using gen from top local birders. A beautiful male Merlin in the east section of the plain, its blue mantle shockingly vivid in the morning sun, did at least brighten my day. Hen Harriers would just have to wait a little longer. Reports of them at Parkgate, Cheshire, were becoming daily now but that's a 400-mile round trip! I'd need more of a reason to do that drive in a day, e.g. like a mega close by!

Since 2nd November, reports had been appearing of a possible White-billed Diver in Kent, near Ramsgate and then Margate. For some reason it had taken me until **5th November** to wake up and realise this was the best game in town, given the bird, though mobile, was being seen every day, and it was in summer plumage! Perhaps I was just not eager to repeat those rain-soaked, wind-swept days sea watching in Norfolk for the King Eider. By 06:45 I was off to Margate, a 350-mile round trip. First task: spot the spotters. I collared a couple of birders returning to their car to get some gen. The bird was reported to be moving along Margate sea front and sure enough, after a few stop-offs and jump-outs from the car, I properly scoped the bird in all its glory near Margate's pumping station. **White-billed Diver** 10:42. Peter Alan Coe's spectacular picture below says it all.

I had struggled with a winter-plumaged Pacific Diver back in February off Pendower Beach and then again off Penzance harbour, so this White-billed Diver, by comparison, was a gift. Its white bill stood out like a peeled banana, contrasting with its black face and neck and discernible red eye.

58 Adult White-billed Diver, Margate, Kent, 4th November.
(Courtesy Peter Alan Coe)

The combination of coastal currents and the diver's ability to swim under water at speed for several minutes amazed me as I needed to jog along the sea front just to keep the bird in sight. Truly an Olympian amongst divers!

Having nailed the White-billed Diver, what next? Disappointingly, there was little else in Kent I needed, though a Waxwing would be reported in Ramsgate later that day. My best option was to take a shot at the Pallas's Warbler at Beachy Head that had been reported late morning in the old trapping area. It would make my round journey home closer to 400 miles but, hey, something else might just turn up late afternoon on the south coast as well. I knew Beachy Head well, too, having recently visited for the Melodious Warbler, but I simply had no clue at all of the whereabouts of the "old trapping area" in which the bird was apparently skulking. As I passed a sharp bend in Beachy Head Road, I spotted a few birders exiting their cars. I parked up and hastily joined the dozen or more birders now looking down at a sheltered area of scrub c.80x80m square. This should not be too difficult, I thought, as a very obliging Firecrest kept us entertained. After 20 minutes I decided that I needed to take a better look at the habitat as I was not convinced the hopeful birders were in the best spot. Indeed, I'd spotted one baseball-capped birder lurking in scrub at the back. Clearly there was a hidden access point and I ventured to join him. Within minutes a small warbler alighted from sallows to my left, flew vertically upward, hovered and fluttered to display a yellowish rump! The guy next to me shouted: "that's it!" I agreed – we had our bird – **Pallas's Warbler** 15:17. As the bird perched low in some brambles affording better views, my first impression was of a rich olive-green, short-bodied, heavily striped warbler. The yellowish supercilium and larger of the two wing bars were particularly prominent. I could easily make out the head stripe too. I had seen several Pallas's before, and it is one of my favourite warblers. Given that someone, possibly mistakenly, had put out a Yellow-browed Warbler for the same location that morning, I wanted to be 100% certain. We watched the bird for no more than a couple of minutes as it shuffled in and out of the dark recesses of the low bramble merely 5m from me. While I spent another hour or so hoping to enjoy further views, the best I could get was a couple of short flicks before light faded. Most birders had departed: few had seen it. I congratulated myself in following my intuition. Had I not ventured to the back of the scrubby area I most certainly would have dipped.

What a great day! Two birds in one day was unexpected at this juncture and took me to a flattering 305 species for the year and I was still just as motivated as that very first outing to Plock Court, Gloucester, to see Penduline Tit on a frosty 1st January.

The theme of getting two birds in a day was to continue on **8th November** with only my second trip of the year to the north-west, my first being to see the Iberian Chiffchaff at Thurstaton, Merseyside. As such I was pleased to be back and to explore what the region had to offer. From my experiences in the 1980s I knew, too, that there are many very experienced birders in the north-west, many still active but now probably retired like me. I was therefore surprised I was not seeing more rarity reports from this region on RBA. Perhaps they were more reliant on free social media (Twitter, Facebook) to share breaking bird news. The bird in my sights was a Pied Wheatear at Dove Point, Meols in Cheshire, which had first been reported on the 6th November and seemed to be showing well both on and by the sea wall. My first Pied Wheatear was a few decades ago on 23rd November, 1985 after a 03:45 start from my digs in London. I recall it was dark when I'd parked up at Sheringham and, after tramping the stony shoreline for a quarter of a mile, I'd been the one to re-find the bird against the cliff-face, resulting in a stampede of birders along the shingle. By contrast, this time I'd taken the luxury of a lie-in till 06:00 before setting off for Meols, where I was greeted by a large circle of some 60–70 birders, most trying to photograph the Pied Wheatear on the sea wall. Dried mealworms scattered the pavement to entice the bird ever closer for the eager photographers. It had to be the easiest tick of the year. First-winter male **Pied Wheatear** 10:36.

Momentarily the bird would drop out of sight behind the sea wall and, with the tide full in, must have clung to just inches of land/weed there, if indeed not to the base of the sea-wall itself. Somewhat humorously, this did not stop photographers lying on the wall and hanging over with their hefty lenses to get that unique shot. Mercilessly, I think a small part of me was hoping for a big splash to add to the entertainment!

Providing I'd been lucky enough to tick the Pied Wheatear in the morning my backup plan was to visit the marshes that connect Parkgate, Neston and Burton where Hen Harriers were now a regular feature. After I had pulled up along the road at Parkgate, Hen Harrier was literally the first bird I saw, a female **Hen Harrier** 12:00. Two ticks up for the day and I hadn't even had lunch! Parkgate in fact is a superb location, with ample parking and affording great views of some of the most extensive marshland in the country. As I pleasantly chatted with fellow birders, they seemed intent on comparing the remains of their

59 First-winter male Pied Wheatear, Dove Point, Meols, Merseyside, 9th November. (Courtesy Oli Mockridge)

lunch boxes. It was clear that despite any north–south divide we all shared one thing in common...the fruit was the last to be eaten and the biscuits never go soft...because, of course, they are all eaten first! So much for a birder's healthy lunchbox. Once again, local dialect and banter were making my visit entertaining. Before departure I enjoyed further views of both male and female Hen Harrier, 2 Peregrines on a dead tree, several Marsh Harriers, Pink-footed Geese nestling in the marshes and Snipe in panicky flight as the Harriers scoured the marshes for prey. The four to five-hour drive home through 50-mile limit bollard-lined M6/M5 was a painful reminder of why I did not visit this part of the country more often.

I was essentially grounded from 10th to 12th November. My father was coming to stay for a couple of days and, at the age of 89, food, warmth, and family were his priority. As I kept watch on RBA and Twitter, Pallid Swifts were continuing to make their presence felt along the east coast along with Rough-legged Buzzards and Waxwings, all of which I still needed! In addition, beginning to show themselves again in Norfolk were Parrot Crossbills, a species I'd dipped twice earlier in the year and warranted a further shot if only because they are such charismatic little fellows. Tundra Bean Goose, too, a bird I'd certainly expected to bump into last winter, was beginning to be reported at Horsey then Titchwell, Norfolk. The biggest news by far was a Little Swift that made an appearance at Hartlepool from 11th. I wrestled with myself as to whether I should go for the Swift on the 13th when I became free but I decided not to risk it...which turned out to be the right decision: the bird disappeared around midday on the 12th. The only other candidate of interest was a Hooded Merganser that appeared at Blythburgh, Suffolk, on the 12th and was seen again in the following days but, as expected, was quickly labelled an escape. All things considered then my best option was beginning to look like a return visit to Norfolk but then a Franklin's Gull, a bird I had somewhat painfully dipped along with a Pacific Golden Plover at Hayle, came on the radar on the 12th. At Hayle I had indeed spied a Franklin's-like Gull, but it did not possess all the crucial features that serve to designate this species. Bill, head colouration, size, mirrors, legs all looked good, but the eyelids were not as pronounced as they should have been, and the grey colouration of the mantle was lighter than usual. A species cross, perhaps. After some deliberation I had discounted the bird. I had now been given a second chance!

On **13th November** I set off for Radipole and the Weymouth/Portland area. I had studied gull movements for this area in the past, e.g. in light of the Ross's Gull seen earlier this year. My plan then was to stake out the Radipole car park from late morning to mid-afternoon and keep an eye on the water and posts in front of the RSPB Radipole information centre. As I watched the gull count build, I kept busy counting the Mediterranean Gulls in the flock – 34, now 47 – numbers were steadily rising. I decided to check each new gull that arrived, and for the moment, ignore those on the deck. What's this? A small dark-backed gull tumbled to the car park floor. There aren't many small gull species with a dark back that inhabit our shores. Got it! There was no doubting this sharp-looking specimen was the Franklin's, even when seen initially through the distortion of the car windscreen. I leapt out of the car to get a better view, and those birders that had not been paying attention were no doubt alerted by my sudden action that something must be afoot. It was a second-winter **Franklin's Gull** 15:39. By 16:01 the bird had flown but about 15 minutes later news came out that it was now showing near the Sea Life Tower in Weymouth bay. That was a relief as I'd alerted fellow birders on Twitter as to the Gull's arrival and knew several were en route. I wanted to be sure they did not have a wasted journey. It's the thing with birding: while there is a little healthy competition you get great joy at helping fellow birders rejoice in their successes with a little help from yourself.

I calculated I was now on 308 species for the year and felt duly-pleased with myself as I pondered what new target I should shoot for: 315, or 320 perhaps? I needed to get onto the north-east coast but,

60 Second-winter Franklin's Gull, Radipole car park, Weymouth, Dorset, 13th November. (Courtesy Graham Jaggard)

conveniently, a Pallid Swift was reported to be frequenting the Chesil Cover area of Portland Bill from the 15th and surprised me when it was still there late afternoon of the 16th. Given most sightings of Pallid Swift to date had been 200+ miles away on the east coast, I felt compelled to twitch this closer bird. Sadly, and after a 06:00 start on a cold, breezy morning of *17th November*, I dipped! I'd arrived an hour or two too late. The bird did not reappear either that day or beyond. The cool breeze, too, made birding somewhat uncomfortable in this coastal location as I lazily explored familiar spots around Weymouth and the bill to see what else I might discover. A Lesser Yellowlegs (while not a new year tick) from the west path at Lodmoor put on a good show in bright mid-afternoon sunlight, leaving watchers in no doubt as to why it was named Yellowlegs! At that point a fellow birder, Cliff Smith, arrived not wearing his signature Crocs, but a pair of wellies. I'd shared many enjoyable hours birding with Cliff in the Scillies this year, but I almost had to do a double-take to be sure that, in the absence of his Crocs, it was indeed him. I pondered how birders might recognise me:

big nose, ridiculously baggy woolly hat and a black coat with a pretty naff fur-lined hood. Cliff reminded me that one of his colleagues, Geoff Keen, was on an impressive 320 birds for the year (which I knew as his list was posted on BUBO as the highest to date for 2018). Impressive. Geoff had been mopping up everything seemingly without hesitation and I saw that he had recorded an even-more-impressive 329 species in Britain in 2017 and so was no stranger to big listing. While my endeavour was not to see the most birds, I confess I was using BUBO as a crude gauge by which to judge personal progress, though I had yet to upload my year list. If BUBO rankings were to be believed I was lying third at this stage behind Graham Jepson on 315, (he had recorded a jaw-dropping 340 in 2017), with Jim Swalwell trailing in fourth on 301, having recorded 308 in 2017. These guys were regulars. I surmised there must be others whose lists were not up-to-date or, like me, had yet to put their year list on BUBO, so I was almost certainly flattering myself. Even so, it was reassuring to know I looked to be keeping pace with the best. I knew only too well how much those extra birds must have cost these guys in miles travelled, boat rides, airfares – not to mention the deep frustration of then dipping in the cold and rain at some remote location. Hats off to them! As I looked at the gaps in my list as compared with theirs, it was clear my total largely reflected key choices made, principally the one to avoid single twitches of >250 miles in any one direction from my Wiltshire home (Scottish vacation aside).

As the Yellowlegs disappeared behind the reeds at Lodmoor I reflected on the astonishing number of rarities this single patch had offered up. It must be one of the best couple of hundred metres of track in the country for twitching, if you discount reserve hides and sea watch points of course, and there is free on-road parking nearby too!

A brief stop at Radipole car park to perhaps catch a further glimpse of the Franklin's Gull amongst the faithful gull flock drew a blank. Despite no ticks for the day, the glorious sunset once again reminded me why I just had to be in the field. Nectar indeed!

For some weeks now, I'd been tracking Rough-legged Buzzard (RLB) movements. It was a bird I particularly wanted to see and one that had eluded me for some years. My first was on St Mary's, Isles of Scilly, where I viewed a bird (most likely a juvenile) on rocks in mid-October in sleety conditions. That bird had not given a spectacular performance but nonetheless it had strangely left its mark, perhaps owing to circumstance described earlier in this book. So, when a John Gould *Birds of Britain* c.1862 original Lithograph came up for sale some years back, I snapped it up. Now, though, what I needed was the real thing and RBA Pro fabulously allowed me to look back and see where most records of this species had been over these past weeks. Horsey Mere – quite a long way – an overnight stay possibly, but wait, more recently Holme Fen and Great Fen were repeatedly yielding sightings! An RLB must be bedded down in that area perhaps with a view to overwintering. Location details were vague but a check on Twitter revealed that one of my contacts, Ian Bollen, had not only been there the day before but also taken some cracking photos. With Ian's help I'd got a drop pin on the location. Upon arrival, *20th November*, two fellow birders had parked on a grass pull-off close by the track I was intending to take. They announced they'd just had distant views of the bird. Encouraged, I set off down the exposed track, at the same time desperately wishing there was just one bush behind which I could relieve myself out of binocular view. After 400m down the desolate track a Red Kite to my right invoked a little scepticism. "I do hope the two birders had not been mistaken in their distant identification?" I put the thought out of my head as I surmised they were both competent. In fact, upon arrival I'd noted there were quite a few Red Kites in the area. Yet another kite; now a buzzard species – very pale and, as it quartered and banked with hovering so typical of RLB, the definitive key features began to reveal themselves: stand-out white rump, pale head and chest, contrasting with dark belly signifying this to be a juvenile bird as expected. The dark trailing edge to the wings, dark wing tips and joints were particularly noticeable too. The jizz was somehow different from Buzzard: a little more angle to the wings and heaviness perhaps as it flopped 20m from the shadowing Red Kite, which I suspected was waiting to ambush the RLB once it had caught its prey. **Rough-legged Buzzard** 10:45. I watched the two birds at c.100m before a second Red Kite seemed to tell the RLB it was time to move. The cool wind and threatening drizzle told me to do similar and enjoy a coffee from the flask in my car.

61 & 62 Juvenile Rough-legged Buzzard, Tower Farm, Holme Fen, Cambs., 19th November. (Courtesy Ian Bollen)

As I left the location, I was reminded that my earlier conversation with the birder had revealed there was a Great Grey Shrike no more than a mile from where I stood! As I approached the location, I saw a couple of birders alighting from the car but I judged that between now and the impending rain I probably had no more than a couple of hours if I was to catch up with a Tundra Bean Goose reported at Welney. As such I shot past, wondering how I could bring myself to pass up the chance of watching this magnificent supersized shrike. The truth is I was in twitching mode. Welney was no more than 30 miles east and, sure enough, upon my arrival the rain was pushing in. The feeders were covered with male Tree Sparrows as I entered the plush WWT reception centre to learn that in fact no fewer than 3 Bean Geese had been seen earlier that day! The odds looked good. Sadly, despite venturing to most hides between the showers, I could not locate even a Pink-footed Goose, with which the bird might be confused in the long grass, let alone a Bean. A single Barnacle Goose amongst the vast flocks of commoner wildfowl was the only curiosity. Patrolling Marsh Harriers entertained pleasingly, so characteristic of British marshes these days. As I left the last hide a pleasant elderly lady with whom I'd been conversing said: "Good luck in finding your beans!" Given the lady's age I assumed this was not meant as sexual innuendo: still it brought a chuckle to my sordid mind.

Unless some mega rarities were to show up unexpectedly, like the reported Bufflehead in County Cork, I reckoned that realistically remaining target birds were Long-eared Owl, Tundra and Taiga Bean Goose, Waxwing, Little Auk, and perhaps Parrot Crossbill. In short, very few indeed. Records showed that in November and December the north-east coast and Norfolk were likely to offer the best opportunities and with that in mind I'd booked two nights at Easington, Spurn, in Yorkshire. Looking back, I perhaps should have booked the Observatory at Kilnsea, which was advertising rooms at £16 when I arrived, considerably less than I was paying for the Marquis of Granby pub, and I might have picked up some invaluable gen there too.

I set out for Spurn around 07:00 on *26th November.* First up, then, was a Taiga Bean Goose that had been reported in fields behind Easington Cemetery with 6 Pink-foot. On my phone I could see two cemeteries in the area, but which one was it? I decided to head towards Spurn, guessing that the straight piece of road between Easington and Kilnsea on the map must be Easington Straight as mentioned in the RBA report for the Taiga. Sure enough, from here I could clearly see a church, cemetery and extensive open grassland to the rear highly suited to wintering geese flocks. As I pulled the car to one side under grey rain-filled skies, I immediately spied a promising small flock of geese. At first sight there looked to be only 6 Pink-footed Geese. Given that the Taiga had been reported with 6 Pink-foot my sense was one of foreboding. Had the Taiga flown? With the aid of a tuna sandwich and flask of coffee I decided to dig in, stake out the flock for a few minutes as it seemed to be momentarily disappearing in the field's undulations/ditches. There could be more geese here. Sure enough, to the left of the small flock another goose appeared. Yes: orange legs, a little larger, more buff-brown lacking the grey colouration of its companion Pink-footed Geese and occasionally being shunned by them too. The all-important orange colouration covering 80% of the bill was clearly visible now revealing a well-defined black tip. *Taiga in the grass.* **Taiga Bean Goose** 13:47. I couldn't believe my luck. The bird had been an easy tick and somewhat unexpectedly I'd seen it before Tundra Bean Goose, by far the more frequent visitor to our shores. With only a couple of hours of daylight remaining and, armed with the knowledge that 2 Long-eared Owls (LEOs) had been ringed in Church Field behind the Spurn Observatory, I decided to wander around Kilnsea Wetlands. Flocks of Whoopers mingled with Mute Swans in the sodden fields, 150 Tree Sparrows with a few Reed Buntings and Yellowhammers swarmed from hedge to stubble while a Barn Owl floated past against the only glimmer of setting sun for the day. Sadly, no LEOs calling or showing.

27th November – after an excellent cooked breakfast at the Marquis of Granby, the weather dictated that a bout of sea watching from the aptly named "Seawatch Hide" at the Warren was my best option. (Aren't hides normally named after some usually unknown rich benefactor/local hero?) Several regular locals in the hide immediately provided a reminder of the choppy Yorkshire dialect with shouts of: "Gilet", "Red-throat, north, past right-hand-5", interspersed of course with the occasional raucous belch as though to reinforce gritty working-class credentials. Guillemots/razorbills, Common Scoter, Wigeon and Teal flocks shot past while predominantly Red-throated Divers and a probable Great Northern Diver flew in front of the wind turbines. The turbines were in rows of fours with a row of five at the centre and ones and twos to the outside, and intelligently being used as marker points for the passing auks, divers and ducks as we attempted to scope and identify each bird. After a couple of hours of identifying specks in poor light, and with no Little Auks, I decided to walk along the shoreline from Sammy's Point in the hope of flushing an owl from the scrub in the doubtful, breezy, cold grey light. I was fortunate to disturb what was almost certainly a Short-eared Owl uttering its rasping barking (alarm) call but the bird did not show. I visited again later that afternoon before the rain was due to set in, but once more nothing.

28th November – the weather was worse. In the light rain and strengthening wind I took the morning to explore the back of the Old Church and the garden of Rose Cottage, where the LEOs might have chosen to roost. In fact, it was in the mid-1980s I'd seen my first LEO in Rose Cottage garden, sleeping in full view in a fruit tree in the spring afternoon sun. This time only an alert adult Roe Deer was lying on the cottage lawn in full view. Sea watching from the Seawatch Hide proved disappointing too; even the wind farm was no longer visible and only commoner duck species provided close flybys.

I was beginning to feel I might be in the wrong place and I should look to what else was twitchable within the county. The previous day's sighting of Waxwings on the north-east coast at Cleethorpes had presented one tempting option. Cleethorpes was about an hour-and-a-half drive from Spurn, but I had judged there was too little remaining light to twitch the birds that afternoon, given I had not intercepted the report until 14:00. I had felt too there was much left to explore at Spurn and was loath to give up on the magnificent LEOs particularly as I did not have a reliable alternative site for this species. Could those Waxwing still be at Cleethorpes today perhaps? I was struggling to get a signal on my mobile to check. Following much traipsing and poking around Spurn's bushes and trees in the pouring rain, the tables had turned. Waxwing numbers on the north-east coast were continuing to build and pressing further south. Suddenly, and once again with mobile signal, news broke of some 9 birds in trees between Sainsbury's and Aldi car parks in Hessle. Hold on, that's only 30 miles away! The birds were no doubt trying to work out which retail outlet was offering the best deal. I shot off to the location immediately, thwarted at every turn by temporary traffic lights and 30 mph village speed limits. I pulled up in Sainsbury's first. Promising-looking trees, no birders or birds, just a large flock of Goldfinches. Then I pulled into Aldi. There, a single birder with camera and tripod waited patiently. Perhaps he had some gen. As I swung the car into a nearby parking bay, I immediately spotted the Waxwings from my side window in the very trees I'd been looking at minutes earlier. The birder was looking in the wrong direction! I fought my seat belt as I hastily tried to leap from the car to set my bins on them. Yes, nine in all, cigar-shaped bodies aligned in the strong breeze in a swaying Sycamore. You could so easily have mistaken them for a few remaining autumn leaves. **Waxwing** 11:40. The birder, Tony Platten, was in fact clearly aware of their presence and informed me that they would regularly drop into a nearby Rowan tree in the Aldi car park, affording much better views. He was waiting for that unique photograph opportunity. True to form within minutes they did settle in the Rowan, making the most of the berries, at one point being only 5m above the head of a shopper loading her car with purchases, seemingly completely oblivious to the spectacle. The Waxwings would flock tightly and were reluctant to split for more than a few seconds. After no more than half an hour I departed,

63 Waxwing, Aldi car park, Hessle, Yorkshire, 28th November.
(Courtesy Tony Platten)

a car horn having startled the flock to a location beyond sight.

The 240-mile drive home did not seem much of a burden after this success: I had bagged something of a bogey bird for me. Waxwings are special – a combination of stunning looks and an almost mystical presence created by their ability to turn up in urban locations and vanish just as quickly, never to be seen again. In short, you must be quick off the mark to twitch Waxwings or just get lucky by being in the right place at the right time. So when your partner next says, "let's go to the supermarket or the retail park" in November, take your bins!

As I dawdled home, bravely opting for the Korean Satnav's scenic route, a check on my RBA Pro revealed a Tundra Bean Goose at Adwick upon Dearne! Could I bag a second bird for the day? I checked the map and saw I'd travelled some 30–40 miles past the location in torrential rain and dwindling light. I had only an hour and half of light at best. Curse these short daylight hours! I decided the Tundra would just have to wait.

DECEMBER

Looking back, November was a solid month and had put me on 311 species. I'd caught up with several hoped-for birds: Hen Harrier; Rough-legged Buzzard; Pallas's Warbler; Waxwing. And I'd had a few I did not expect: White-billed Diver; Pied Wheatear; Franklin's Gull; Taiga Bean Goose. The last few days of the month had been spent on family chores and catching up with writing commitments. The prevailing mild weather too was offering up few new birds of note. By example, rarities like Lesser Yellowlegs, Italian Sparrow, Bonaparte's Gull, Little Bittern, Lesser Scaup, King Eider and Dusky Warbler were still about but already on my list. So what next? I knew I was looking at probably no more than 6 more birds at best between now and the end of December based on previous big year lister efforts on BUBO. Tundra Bean Goose looked to be my best bet, but records revealed that visitors to the south-west usually favoured spring rather than December, so travel north-east and/or east was essential. Two birds at Hanningfield Reservoir since 25th November represented a good opportunity. They had been seen repeatedly from the causeway there.

3rd December – I set off around 06:45 for Hanningfield. I thought I knew the location from previous visits to Essex but quickly realised I was confusing it with Abberton Reservoir (old age, I guess). After a few detours I found myself on the right causeway working through several hundred Greylag and Canada Geese on two exposed mud spits. I immediately picked out two birds on the closest spit that looked good prospects for Bean Geese but almost as soon as I'd noted the bill colouration (a key diagnostic of this species) the birds, which were sitting, snuggled down, hiding their bills from view. The bill alone pointed towards Bean or Pink-footed Geese, but I could not see the full complement of definitive features nor get a decent size comparison with nearby standing geese. I knew only too well the need for caution. I walked over to nearby birders, who I'd hoped might be on the same birds, to get their opinion, but they were oblivious to the teasing twosome. Frustratingly, I could not relocate the two birds now, either, so as to get more eyes on the target. Had they departed? I walked to the far end of the causeway where a further, rather well-spoken birder, informed me somewhat directly: "Couldn't have been the Bean Geese, I have them in my scope! Been here for hours."

"Perhaps they were just Pink-footed then," I replied, "I couldn't be sure as the birds were sat partially obscured and with legs hidden."

"No, don't get those here." It was his local patch and he claimed to be a bird recorder of sorts, as if to quell any argument. I dare say he was indeed knowledgeable, but he did rather seem to be dismissing my ability to identify the species. His two birds were on the farthest spit and, despite his help, I was having trouble locating them in his scope let alone mine.

"You can see the white tertials," he bleated repeatedly, but in truth I was not even certain I was looking at the right two birds. As the Greylags and Canadas took flight to feed in a nearby field, his two geese raised their heads and stood up. Got them! **Tundra Bean Goose** 11:00. I was relieved. Legs, bills, size and colouration as expected. Good views were then had of the two birds flying and then feeding in a nearby field during the only five minutes of sun for the day. I still, couldn't believe these were the same two birds I'd seen upon arrival. How could they have given me the slip and moved spits? Just then a message came through on the birder's pager. "Essex 4 Bean Geese reported yesterday

Hanningfield reservoir!" I was pleased to gain a little redemption.

As the days began to tick by, there were few opportunities for new birds. A Dusky Thrush was reported on Isle of Whalsay, Shetland Islands. I'd ruled that out as a step too far for my budget. More promising was the Red-rumped Swallow that was repeatedly being seen at Cley. To my surprise the bird had persisted since 5th December and by the 8th I had made up my mind to give it a shot, despite that in my experience this species proved to be somewhat flighty. Enter the disruptor: *on the 8th a White-rumped Sandpiper is reported at Pulborough Brooks RSPB in Sussex and is still present late afternoon.* I changed tack and on **9th December** headed for Pulborough but only once the bird had been re-seen that very morning.

RSPB Pulborough was packed with birders, many of whom were making their way to the Winpenny Hide where the Sandpiper had been showing. After a quick check-in at the RSPB information centre, just in case the bird's location had changed, I quickly stepped to the hide just in time to grab a seat. I squeezed between the many scopes present, arriving just ahead of a following group of six birders. The bird was distant, the weather grey. Frankly, I would have struggled to pick out the White-rumped were it not for helpful birders on hand who allowed me to view the bird through their scope first then directed me to the bird in what was a somewhat featureless landscape. **White-rumped Sandpiper** 11:45. The bird was barely moving on a tiny marsh grass covered island no more than 2m across, giving rise to speculation that it might not be in the best of health. First impressions were of a small Dunlin-sized wader, greyish mantle, with contrasting white underside, medium decurved bill and conspicuous white eyeline. My congratulations to the finder/identifier. I can only assume he/she had better views than I had. No other waders were present. The bird in fact persisted at the location until 13th December, an unexpected addition to my list. As expected, there were many southern accents here; conversations in the hide swirled around the value of investing in the most expensive optics and, with every flinch of the bird, speculation as to what it would do next. It was like a betting syndicate weighing up the odds. Not half as amusing as my exploits in the Sea Watching Hide at Spurn NNR! As I too waited for the bird to move and display its white rump, I checked my mobile to see that my alternative target for the day, the Red-rumped Swallow at Cley, had relocated to Gorleston-on-sea down the coast (assuming this was the same bird, of course) but, sadly, by the 10th it had gone.

The next few days presented a source of major frustration. Family matters and personal business were proving challenging, and I had commitments to keep, particularly with respect to the handling of my recently deceased mother's estate. As news of an American Royal Tern at Anglesey broke on 10th December, I was acutely aware how circumstances had previously contrived to my missing this species at Pagham. This time, I was committed to help my father compile his application for probate. To add to my angst, I received reports throughout the day that the bird was at Traeth, Lligwy, and showing well. I vowed to go the next day but cautiously waited for an early morning announcement that the bird was still present before setting off. Nothing came through! You guessed it, the bird had flown and was not re-found. I knew I had missed yet another major opportunity, but upon reflection felt I had made the right choice. My father's needs were greater and at least I had not made the long 500-mile round trip in vain.

Aside from the Royal Tern I'd also become aware of a Red-rumped Swallow that was frequenting Torpoint, Cornwall, so, despite the east coast birds having seemingly disappeared, I now had a shot at a bird less than 150 miles away. On *13th December* an 06:00 start saw me on the M5 to Torpoint with flask, mince pies and enough layers to make an Eskimo proud. The Satnav seemed to direct me into the sea, so I was relieved to find myself in the ferry queue despite not even realising I needed to take one to Torpoint! The short 5-minute hop cost just £1.50 and I found myself parked just off Salamanca Street, where the bird was last seen. A few other birders were wandering round, some in camouflage with large camera lenses, looking a touch comic in this urban setting of terraced houses and alley ways. Only one birder, Andrew Jordan, claimed to have seen the Red-rumped Swallow, flying very low down Salamanca Street that morning, but none of us were able to relocate the bird, despite hours of searching neighbouring streets, the nearby coast, high street and monument areas where the bird had frequented. Around 14:00 I gave up the hunt. Even so, it had felt good to be in the field again. Fewer and fewer opportunities would present themselves and so I expected my ratio of dips to ticks would rise massively at this point.

Once again, the following week or so was taking up with family and personal business affairs. As I watched RBA, many of the rare bird species I'd worked hard to see earlier in the year reappeared around the country, giving others the chance to catch up or better my total: Ferruginous Duck; Lesser Yellowlegs; King Eider; Dusky Warbler; Lesser Scaup; White-billed Diver; Coues's Arctic Redpoll; Long-billed Dowitcher; Pacific Diver; Penduline Tit. My best option could have been to go look for a Black-throated Thrush near Swindon, no more than a dozen miles or so from home. A female had been reported on RBA 13th December at 19:52 with the added words "no sign today". So, it was last seen on the 12th and the first chance other birders would get to look for the bird was the 14th! My first thoughts were: "Why had it taken more than a full day to put out word of the bird?" In hindsight, I guess caution was the best policy, especially if the finder was a touch unsure/inexperienced. Despite a handful of top birders scouring the location, there was no further sign of the Black-throated Thrush.

The remaining pickings were now sparse. I could travel to St Agnes for the consistently performing Desert Wheatear or take a shot at the Black Scoter in Northumberland or, venture farther afield to Shetland for the Pied-billed Grebe. Another Royal Tern sighting was made on Tresco on the 22nd but the bird did not stay. I'll be honest – I discounted these largely based on distance/budget and probability of success. Besides, aside from Black Scoter these birds were not even life ticks. Perhaps

I'd be better off looking closer to home for the Golden Pheasants at Wolferton Triangle. Others I noted from BUBO had successfully seen them in the first quarter of the year. Why had I not done this sooner? Something of an oversight.

The reality was my next opportunity to be in the field was *31st December*, New Year's Eve. I philosophically decided to end my year where I began: at Slimbridge WWT. No mega had been reported there but Slimbridge was the first proper bird reserve I ever visited in the UK, and essentially represented the pinnacle of my early birding days before I learnt to drive. The place had expanded massively since then and, given it was holiday season, it was rammed with families, many parents sporting expensive cameras of which I suspect not many knew much about beyond the Auto button. Still, they were sucking up nature and who could say that one amongst their youngsters would not be the next David Attenborough? Perhaps it would be the young man aged six or seven who approached me and asked, "Are you shooting a film for the BBC?"

"No," I replied, "I am writing a book, but these are telescope and binoculars, not cameras."

The boy put his hands on his hips and said, "Well, I am a very good tourist indeed; I may have need of you later!" Off he trotted. Perhaps even more humorous was that this took place in the gent's toilet, which his father and I were making use of at the time. His directness certainly brought a chuckle.

Slimbridge sadly did not yield that chance mega, that last hurrah! In truth I never expected it to. Aside from 3 Cranes sporting a mix of Red, Yellow and Blue bands, locating the Dark-bellied Brent Goose (reported in the WWT log) amongst a distant large Canada flock afforded the best entertainment in that cool grey afternoon. As I pointed out a Water Rail from one of the hides near the Holden Tower, I was reminded that for many this was a difficult species to see, perhaps a first even. There is nothing more pleasurable than introducing the hitherto unseen to new birders/photographers at the start of what might be an as fulfilling a journey for them as birding has been for me. As I looked around, I could still taste that first day's birding on 1st January, which began with an early morning Penduline Tit at Plock Court, Gloucester, before ending at Slimbridge. Had it really been 365 days? A small part of me could not help but feel that while Slimbridge WWT was certainly attracting the masses it was in danger of becoming like a theme park. Even the stylised map on their website seemed to portray this. Perhaps, then, I should begin a campaign to put the wild back into WWT! After all, it's not a challenge is it if you don't get wet, muddy and hungry before you see that distant, skulking, indefinable blob that just might be your first mega!

As I left the reserve for coffee and cake at my father's home in Gloucester, my sense of achievement at reaching my goal was tinged with sadness at the thought that this phase of my journey was at an end, and that my mother was not here to witness it?

State-of-the-Game Technology – Friend or Foe?

Have a conversation with a birder formerly active in the 1980s or 90s and he/she will reminisce and tell of how there were more birders around then. Certainly, it seemed that way if you visited the Scilly Isles where numbers reached several thousand, and not the few hundred we see today. In short, birding back then was booming, a hobby for the masses and a new profession for the few best-known characters, artists and authors. Indeed, many birders in the 1980s were of a younger age group than today, like me, just in their twenties. By contrast today there is a greater proportion of post 50-year-olds approaching, if not already, retired, and many more, I am pleased to say, female birders. In short, the demographics of birding have changed dramatically, and birders are blessed too with far more reserves and conservation bodies than ever before. That at least is encouraging given the pressure on our wild open spaces through population growth and relentless building development. Increased too are the numbers of tour companies offering birding holidays in Britain. Norfolk in May, by example, is now dominated by tour groups. While the benefits are clear for some, for others it undermines that feeling of space, discovery, wilderness, and represents perhaps a shift back towards a packaged-holiday mentality.

One area that has changed the very nature of birding dramatically is the application of technology. Now, through electronic tagging birds are tracked on their migratory path from one continent to another; digital infra-red cameras make it possible to film the activities of nocturnal birds in the dark; websites like xeno-canto provide infinite recordings of bird songs and calls available in the field at the touch of a smart-phone button, or astonishing bird photos and videos captured with high-powered digital cameras can be shared with the masses instantly through social media. In addition, web access via mobile devices has enabled birders to quickly receive the latest details on a mega, including: a picture of the very bird e.g. exposing age/eclipse plumage; pin dropped on a map; route of navigation to the location; and to update details instantly for colleagues known to be en route. Is it becoming all too easy?

All this should be good news: who does not want to see a great picture of a twitched rarity for which the complete features may not have been obvious through your scope and/or bins due to impaired eyesight or poor viewing conditions? Who does not want instant updates on a bird's whereabouts, so you can switch route/destination in good time? And how handy it is to hear a recording of the bird exactly when you need it through headphones, so you can compare it with what you are hearing real-time in the field. The benefits are immeasurable and I for one enjoy them. Many folk, too, have been brought into birding through this growing technology. Arguably, none has been more potent than digital photography enabling the rapid and detailed capture far beyond that which can normally be discerned with the naked eye or through tried and trusted binoculars, but at what price?

For me the thrill of birding from the outset was its capacity to revitalise the hunter instinct in me; to sharpen my senses through practice in the field backed by an improved knowledge of nature so I could predict a bird's whereabouts and find what other ordinary folk might overlook. In short, we can genuinely change what we are able to see through what we learn. After all, it's not just sight but a mental computation that registers, checks and confirms back to us what we are seeing. Re-educate and re-equip that computation capability through experience and learning and, put simply, you will see more. It was never about collection of tangible objects, or about gaining evidence of a sighting as proof to others.

It was rather about personal confidence that I had found and correctly identified my target bird without negative interference to it or its environment. That search has taken me to new places, to reach new horizons and meet new characters, to enjoy more dawns and sunsets than any dowdy city office could afford me. In short, birding has remained that essential vehicle by which to embark on a voyage of self-discovery as well as of exploration of the unique natural world we inhabit. With that in mind my hope is that the next generation will be able to embrace technology to fulfil greater ambition but will not underuse/sanitise the capabilities we as humans inherently possess but which may simply have been rendered stale through under use in the new world we created.

Technology, then, does introduce new risks. For sure, bird recordings can be used to entice birds out from safe cover in the field; photographers can and do often get too close when striving for that stand-out photo; spotting birds can be reduced to bland rapid-fire photography of wader flocks, the pictures to be viewed subsequently to identify birds; and information of bird whereabouts can equally alert egg collectors to the location of a threatened species e.g. a Montagu's Harrier or Golden Oriole.

Given the pace of technological evolution and accelerated rate of uptake by birders there can be few clear answers other than it is incumbent upon us all to work together with good conscience and consensus to ensure we can continue to enjoy this pastime without detriment to our feathered friends. With that in mind, I have only to look behind me in my office to see just how far we have come. There hangs a lithograph by John Gould, one of the foremost ornithologists and artists of his age, of a Red-necked Goatsucker from the late 1860s/early '70s from *Birds of Great Britain*. The accompanying text begins with "An undoubted specimen of this fine Nightjar having been killed in England, it becomes necessary to give it a place among *The Birds of Great Britain*". Reference is made to a specimen having been "shot at Killingworth near Newcastle". Sadly, back then shooting was the preferred means to achieve detailed identification of a species, given the absence of today's technology. I think it's fair to say we have moved on…a little.

The Impossible Round-Up

In writing this book it has been my hope that others will come to recognise and reflect on what could be their vehicle for a new journey. For me it has clearly been birds (birding), an interest since childhood, that led me to this point of taking on the challenge of seeing 300+ birds in Britain in 2018. That quest saw me travel some 39,000 miles by car, book into 11 B&B's, and take 20 short boat trips during the year. It certainly wasn't cheap, but upon reflection I genuinely feel it provided me with one of the best years of my life.

As I look at the present BOU British Bird List I'm reminded that there are 619 species in total for the all-important categories A–C that make up the accepted British list and some of these may not have been seen since the 1800s! To have seen more than half of these in one year is, I feel, an achievement though there are a few who did better and indeed have managed to step up to the challenge again and again. My 314 species was the fourth highest list recorded on BUBO for 2018 and surpassed my hope of scraping into the top ten. Indeed, had I achieved the same total for 2015, 2016 and 2017 I noted that I would have finished third, fifth and sixth respectively so making the top 10 for the past three years. "All well and good," you may say, "give that man a medal!" However, to a large extent position and total have limited relevance here. The point is that through the lens of the big 300+ challenge you (like me) can meet like-minded people that will inspire, teach and coach you, welcome and laugh with you. You will visit places you never knew of and may never have a chance to visit again. You will remember those magnificent dawns, sunsets, breath taking vistas, lush woodlands, beaches, extensive marshlands, biting cold mountains and the freedom of open space. The deeper you look, the more questions will arise; the more you search for answers, the better equipped you will become to seek and find. Beyond bird identification nature will reveal its beauty and astonish you revealing new interdependencies, habits and habitats. Butterflies, dragonflies, plants, mammals, reptiles, weather and even tidal patterns get more interesting. (You might even enjoy the shipping forecast, heaven help us!) You will come to know yourself a little better too; perhaps find sanctuary amidst grief as I did with the loss of my mother, or relief from the stress of everyday family/work life. And, finally, you may just help to build the next generation of enthusiasts who will inspire us all in our dotage by discovering unforeseen bird peculiarities.

For me Journey to the Big 300+ is, then, "a journey of personal fulfilment", and I feel fulfilled. Go begin your own special journey... today!

Big 300+ Tracker Worksheet

British (English) vernacular name	IOC World Bird List international English name	Scientific name	Category
Brent Goose	Brant Goose	*Branta bernicla*	AE
Canada Goose		*Branta canadensis*	AC2E*
Barnacle Goose		*Branta leucopsis*	AC2E*
Greylag Goose		*Anser anser*	AC2C4E*
Taiga Bean Goose		*Anser fabalis*	AE*
Pink-footed Goose		*Anser brachyrhynchus*	AE*
Tundra Bean Goose		*Anser serrirostris*	AE
White-fronted Goose	Greater White-fronted Goose	*Anser albifrons*	AE*
Mute Swan		*Cygnus olor*	AC2
Bewick's Swan	Tundra Swan	*Cygnus columbianus*	AE
Whooper Swan		*Cygnus cygnus*	AE*
Egyptian Goose		*Alopochen aegyptiaca*	C1E*
Shelduck	Common Shelduck	*Tadorna tadorna*	A
Mandarin Duck		*Aix galericulata*	C1E*
Garganey		*Spatula querquedula*	A
Blue-winged Teal		*Spatula discors*	AE*
Shoveler	Northern Shoveler	*Spatula clypeata*	A
Gadwall		*Mareca strepera*	AC2E*
Wigeon	Eurasian Wigeon	*Mareca penelope*	AE*
American Wigeon		*Mareca americana*	AE
Mallard		*Anas platyrhynchos*	AC2C4E*
Pintail	Northern Pintail	*Anas acuta*	AE

Date Seen	Time	Number	Location	County	Page
Jan 6th	1230	44	Ferrybridge, Portland	Dorset	71
Jan 1st	1000	>20	Ashleworth Ham, Gloucestershire Wildlife Trust	Gloucestershire	229
Jan 11th	1000	1	Snettisham, over The Wash	Norfolk	76
Jan 1st	1000	>20	Ashleworth Ham, Gloucestershire Wildlife Trust	Gloucestershire	229
Nov 26th	1347	1	Easingston Straight, Kilnsea	Yorkshire	225
Jan 11th	904	>100	Snettisham	Norfolk	76
Dec 3rd	1100	2	Hanningfield Reservoir	Essex	230
Jan 1st	1420	>20	Slimbridge WWT	Gloucestershire	
Jan 1st	1000	<10	Ashleworth Ham, GWT	Gloucestershire	168
Jan 1st	1400	>20	Slimbridge WWT	Gloucestershire	67
Jan 1st	1215	1	Frampton Court Lake	Gloucestershire	67
Jan 9th	1026	2	Fields near Burnham Market	Norfolk	72
Jan 1st	1000	>10	Ashleworth Ham, GWT	Gloucestershire	201
Jan 19th	1325	5	Cannop ponds, Forest of Dean	Gloucestershire	78
Mar 11th	950	1	Farlington Marshes Nature Reserve	Hampshire	103
Aug 11th	1252	1	Alkborough Flats	Lincolnshire	172
Jan 1st	1015	>10	Ashleworth Ham, GWT	Gloucestershire	172
Jan 1st	1200	>10	Frampton Court Lake	Gloucestershire	
Jan 1st	1015	>20	Ashleworth Ham, GWT	Gloucestershire	77
Jan 15th	1238	1	Matford Marsh RSPB, Exeter	Devonshire	77
Jan 1st	1015	>20	Ashleworth Ham, GWT	Gloucestershire	38
Jan 1st	1400	>10	Slimbridge WWT	Gloucestershire	

243

Teal	Eurasian Teal	*Anas crecca*	A
Green-winged Teal		*Anas carolinensis*	A
Red-crested Pochard		*Netta rufina*	AC2E*
Pochard	Common Pochard	*Aythya ferina*	AE*
Ferruginous Duck		*Aythya nyroca*	AE
Ring-necked Duck		*Aythya collaris*	AE
Tufted Duck		*Aythya fuligula*	A
Scaup	Greater Scaup	*Aythya marila*	A
Lesser Scaup		*Aythya affinis*	A
King Eider		*Somateria spectabilis*	A
Eider	Common Eider	*Somateria mollissima*	A
Surf Scoter		*Melanitta perspicillata*	A
Velvet Scoter		*Melanitta fusca*	A
Common Scoter		*Melanitta nigra*	A
Long-tailed Duck		*Clangula hyemalis*	A
Goldeneye	Common Goldeneye	*Bucephala clangula*	AE*
Smew		*Mergellus albellus*	A
Goosander	Common Merganser	*Mergus merganser*	A
Red-breasted Merganser		*Mergus serrator*	A
Black Grouse		*Lyrurus tetrix*	AE
Ptarmigan	Rock Ptarmigan	*Lagopus muta*	A
Red Grouse	Willow Ptarmigan	*Lagopus lagopus*	A
Red-legged Partridge		*Alectoris rufa*	C1E*
Grey Partridge		*Perdix perdix*	AC2E*
Quail	Common Quail	*Coturnix coturnix*	AE*
Pheasant	Common Pheasant	*Phasianus colchicus*	C1E*
Red-throated Diver	Red-throated Loon	*Gavia stellata*	A

Jan 1st	1015	>20	Ashleworth Ham, GWT	Gloucestershire	77
Jan 15th	1020	1	Greylake RSPB reserve	Somerset	77
Jan 21st	1020	26	Cotswold Water Park	Gloucestershire	78
Jan 1st	1400	>5	Slimbridge WWT	Gloucestershire	38
Jan 29th	945	1	Walton Heath Hide, Ham Wall RSPB Reserve	Somerset	81
Jan 4th	1239	1	Noah's Lake, Shapwick Heath	Somerset	70
Jan 1st	1200	>20	Frampton Court Lake	Gloucestershire	38
Jan 2nd	1230	4	Moreton Hide, Chew Lake	Somerset	69
Jan 2nd	1305	1	Moreton Hide, Chew Lake	Somerset	69
Oct 30th	1423	1	Sheringham	Norfolk	211
Feb 18th	1455	1	Pagham Harbour RSPB	Sussex	92
Feb 6th	1200	2	Porthpean	Cornwall	86
Feb 6th	1200	1	Porthpean	Cornwall	86
Feb 4th	1650	5	Pendower beach	Cornwall	84
Jan 2nd	1420	1	Barrow, Tank no.3	Somerset	69
Jan 2nd	1100	>10	Moreton Hide, Chew Lake	Somerset	69
Jan 29th	1525	1	Pit 28, Cotswold Water Park	Gloucestershire	81
Jan 2nd	1100	2	Moreton Hide, Chew Lake	Somerset	69
Jan 6th	925	11	Portland harbour	Dorset	70
June 5th	452	1	Coire na Criste view point, Cairngorm Mountain	Scotland	143
Jun 4th	1259	1	Cairngorm Mountain	Scotland	142
Jun 3rd	1540	>12	Lochindorb	Scotland	141
Jan 11th	1215	8	Holkham gap	Norfolk	76
Feb 3rd	840	3	Cirencester to Harnhill rd., Harnhill	Gloucestershire	83
Jul 24th	2110	2	Leighterton	Gloucestershire	162
Jan 1st	745	1	From car	Wiltshire	23
Jan 17th	1330	1	Coastguard lookout, Dawlish Warren	Devonshire	77

Black-throated Diver	Black-throated Loon	*Gavia arctica*	A
Pacific Diver	Pacific Loon	*Gavia pacifica*	A
Great Northern Diver	Common Loon	*Gavia immer*	A
White-billed Diver	Yellow-billed Loon	*Gavia adamsii*	A
Storm Petrel	European Storm Petrel	*Hydrobates pelagicus*	A
Fulmar	Northern Fulmar	*Fulmarus glacialis*	A
Cory's Shearwater		*Calonectris borealis*	A
Sooty Shearwater		*Ardenna grisea*	A
Great Shearwater		*Ardenna gravis*	A
Manx Shearwater		*Puffinus puffinus*	A
Balearic Shearwater		*Puffinus mauretanicus*	A
Little Grebe		*Tachybaptus ruficollis*	A
Red-necked Grebe		*Podiceps grisegena*	A
Great Crested Grebe		*Podiceps cristatus*	A
Slavonian Grebe	Horned Grebe	*Podiceps auritus*	A
Black-necked Grebe		*Podiceps nigricollis*	A
White Stork		*Ciconia ciconia*	AE
Glossy Ibis		*Plegadis falcinellus*	AE
Spoonbill	Eurasian Spoonbill	*Platalea leucorodia*	AE
Bittern	Eurasian Bittern	*Botaurus stellaris*	A
American Bittern		*Botaurus lentiginosus*	A
Little Bittern		*Ixobrychus minutus*	A
Green Heron		*Butorides virescens*	A

246

Feb 4th	1615	6	Pendower beach	Cornwall	84
Feb 4th	1700	1	Pendower beach	Cornwall	84
Jan 1st	1120	1	Life boat station pool, Sharpness	Gloucestershire	66
Nov 5th	1042	1	Pumping Station, Margate	Kent	214
Aug 19th	1505	3	Porthgwarra	Cornwall	173
Jan 6th	1112	1	Portland Bill	Dorset	70
Aug 29th	1040	1	Porthgwarra	Cornwall	175
Aug 7th	1523	1	Pendeen Lighthouse	Cornwall	168
Sep 29th	1100	1	Scillonian III, Penzance to St Mary's	Cornwall	188
Apr 15th	1045	1	Portland Bill	Sussex	114
Jul 30th	1047	35	Berry Head NNR	Devonshire	164
Jan 1st	1230	1	Frampton Court Lake	Gloucestershire	38
Feb 4th	1639	2	Pendower beach	Cornwall	84
Jan 1st	1200	<10	Frampton Court lake	Gloucestershire	38
Jan 17th	1340	1	Estuary, Dawlish Warren NNR	Devonshire	77
Jan 6th	925	2	Portland harbour	Dorset	70
Sep 15th	1440	5	Portsdown Hill, Cosham	Hampshire	182
Jan 29th	940	1	Platform 1, Ham Wall RSPB reserve	Somerset	81
Jan 22nd	1250	1	Stanpit Marsh, Christchurch	Dorset	79
Jan 4th	1010	1	Noah's Lake, Shapwick Heath	Somerset	120
Apr 18th	1656	1	Carlton & Oulton Marshes Nature Reserve, SWT, Lowestoft	Suffolk	117
Jul 7th	1105	1	Chelmarsh Reservoir	Shropshire	157
Apr 29th	1154	1	Llan Mill, Narbeth	Pembrokeshire	123

Cattle Egret	Western Cattle Egret	*Bubulcus ibis*	AE
Grey Heron		*Ardea cinerea*	A
Purple Heron		*Ardea purpurea*	A
Great White Egret	Great Egret	*Ardea alba*	A
Little Egret		*Egretta garzetta*	A
Gannet	Northern Gannet	*Morus bassanus*	A
Shag	European Shag	*Phalacrocorax aristotelis*	A
Cormorant	Great Cormorant	*Phalacrocorax carbo*	A
Osprey	Western Osprey	*Pandion haliaetus*	AE*
Honey-buzzard	European Honey Buzzard	*Pernis apivorus*	A
Golden Eagle		*Aquila chrysaetos*	AE
Sparrowhawk	Eurasian Sparrowhawk	*Accipiter nisus*	A
Goshawk	Northern Goshawk	*Accipiter gentilis*	AC3E*
Marsh Harrier	Western Marsh Harrier	*Circus aeruginosus*	A
Hen Harrier		*Circus cyaneus*	A
Pallid Harrier		*Circus macrourus*	A
Montagu's Harrier		*Circus pygargus*	A
Red Kite		*Milvus milvus*	AC3E*
White-tailed Eagle		*Haliaeetus albicilla*	AC3E*
Rough-legged Buzzard		*Buteo lagopus*	AE
Buzzard	Common Buzzard	*Buteo buteo*	AE*
Water Rail		*Rallus aquaticus*	A
Corncrake	Corn Crake	*Crex crex*	AE*
Spotted Crake		*Porzana porzana*	A
Moorhen	Common Moorhen	*Gallinula chloropus*	A
Coot	Eurasian Coot	*Fulica atra*	A

Jan 29th	1220	20	Road from Westhay to Burtle	Somerset	81
Jan 1st	1400	1	Slimbridge WWT	Gloucestershire	39
May 15th	1610	1	Noah's Hide, Shapwick Heath NNR	Somerset	131
Jan 4th	1000	2	Noah's lake, Shapwick Heath NNR	Somerset	70
Jan 4th	1700	11	Field Near Blagdon Lake	Somerset	39
Jan 6th	1100	>20	Portland Bill	Dorset	85
Jan 6th	915	>10	Portland harbour	Dorset	147
Jan 1st	845	2	Plock Court, Gloucester	Gloucestershire	39
Apr 2nd	1916	1	Blagdon lake, east end	Somerset	109
Jul 12th	1315	2	Wykeham Forest	Yorkshire	158
Jun 4th	1703	1	Coire na Ciste view point, Cairngorm Mountain	Scotland	143
Jan 2nd	1200	1	Between Moreton and Stratford hide, Chew Lake	Somerset	163
Feb 15th	1000	2	New Fancy, Forest of Dean	Gloucestershire	91
Jan 4th	1040	4	Shapwick Heath NNR	Somerset	70
Nov 8th	1140	1	Dee Estuary Nature Reserve RSPB, Parkgate	Cheshire	217
Sep 21st	1450	1	Therfield	Hertfordshire	184
Jun 12th	1702	1	Undisclosed	Wiltshire	150
Jan 26th	1224	1	Windmill Hill, Avebury Trusloe	Wiltshire	80
Jun 8th	1559	2	Isle of Mull	Scotland	148
Nov 13th	1045	1	Northern Loop, Great Fen	Cambridgeshire	223
Jan 1st	NR	1	From car	Gloucestershire	20
Jan 15th	1045	1	Greylake RSPB	Somerset	77
Jun 7th	1642	1	Iona	Scotland	144
Aug 11th	945	1	Mere Hide, Gibralter Point NNR	Lincolnshire	170
Jan 1st	1200	<5	Frampton Court Lake	Gloucestershire	39
Jan 1st	1000	>10	Ashleworth Ham, GWT	Gloucestershire	39

Crane	Common Crane	*Grus grus*	AE*
Stone-curlew	Eurasian Stone-curlew	*Burhinus oedicnemus*	A
Oystercatcher	Eurasian Oystercatcher	*Haematopus ostralegus*	A
Black-winged Stilt		*Himantopus himantopus*	A
Avocet	Pied Avocet	*Recurvirostra avosetta*	AE
Lapwing	Northern Lapwing	*Vanellus vanellus*	A
Golden Plover	European Golden Plover	*Pluvialis apricaria*	A
Grey Plover		*Pluvialis squatarola*	A
Ringed Plover	Common Ringed Plover	*Charadrius hiaticula*	A
Little Ringed Plover		*Charadrius dubius*	A
Dotterel	Eurasian Dotterel	*Charadrius morinellus*	A
Whimbrel		*Numenius phaeopus*	A
Curlew	Eurasian Curlew	*Numenius arquata*	A
Bar-tailed Godwit		*Limosa lapponica*	A
Black-tailed Godwit		*Limosa limosa*	A
Turnstone	Ruddy Turnstone	*Arenaria interpres*	A
Knot	Red Knot	*Calidris canutus*	A
Ruff		*Calidris pugnax*	A
Stilt Sandpiper		*Calidris himantopus*	A
Curlew Sandpiper		*Calidris ferruginea*	A
Temminck's Stint		*Calidris temminckii*	A
Sanderling		*Calidris alba*	A
Dunlin		*Calidris alpina*	A
Purple Sandpiper		*Calidris maritima*	A
Baird's Sandpiper		*Calidris bairdii*	A
Little Stint		*Calidris minuta*	A

Jan 1st	1420	3	Zeiss Hide, Slimbridge WWT	Gloucestershire	68
Apr 20th	1032	3	Weeting Heath NNR	Norfolk	119
Jan 1st	1345	<5	South Lake hide, Slimbridge WWT	Gloucestershire	
Apr 9th	1236	2	Rye Harbour Farm	Sussex	112
Jan 21st	1230	1	South Lake hide, Slimbridge WWT	Gloucestershire	121
Jan 1st	1345	>1000	Slimbridge WWT	Gloucestershire	81
Jan 1st	1345	>1000	Slimbridge WWT	Gloucestershire	178
Jan 11th	930	1	Snettisham RSPB	Norfolk	76
Jan 10th	1100	1	Titchwell RSPB	Norfolk	40
Mar 26th	1242	3	Cotswold Water Park, field east of pit 305	Wiltshire	107
Jun 6th	1315	2	Cairngorm Mountain	Scotland	142
Jan 10th	1104	1	Titchwell RSPB	Norfolk	75
Jan 1st	1345	>20	Slimbridge WWT	Gloucestershire	40
Jan 10th	1011	1	Titchwell RSPB	Norfolk	74
Jan 1st	1345	>20	Slimbridge WWT	Gloucestershire	99
Jan 6th	1109	1	Portland bill	Dorset	40
Feb 18th	1410	4	Pagham Harbour RSPB	Sussex	92
Jan 1st	1400	<10	Slimbridge WWT	Gloucestershire	72
Feb 11th	1105	1	Stanpit Marsh, Christchurch	Dorset	88
May 13th	1715	1	Pennington Marshes, Lymington	Hampshire	130
Feb 18th	1020	1	West Mead hide, Pulborough Brooks RSPB	Sussex	92
Jan 10th	1110	1	Titchwell RSPB	Norfolk	75
Jan 1st	1400	>100	Slimbridge WWT	Gloucestershire	72
Jan 6th	1109	6	Pulpit Rock, Portland Bill	Dorset	70
Oct 26th	1010	1	Goldcliff pools, Newport	Monmouthshire	208
Jan 21st	1138	1	Rushy Pen, Slimbridge WWT	Gloucestershire	78

White-rumped Sandpiper		*Calidris fuscicollis*	A
Buff-breasted Sandpiper		*Calidris subruficollis*	A
Pectoral Sandpiper		*Calidris melanotos*	A
Semipalmated Sandpiper		*Calidris pusilla*	A
Long-billed Dowitcher		*Limnodromus scolopaceus*	A
Woodcock	Eurasian Woodcock	*Scolopax rusticola*	A
Jack Snipe		*Lymnocryptes minimus*	A
Snipe	Common Snipe	*Gallinago gallinago*	A
Wilson's Snipe		*Gallinago delicata*	A
Terek Sandpiper		*Xenus cinereus*	A
Red-necked Phalarope		*Phalaropus lobatus*	A
Grey Phalarope	Red Phalarope	*Phalaropus fulicarius*	A
Common Sandpiper		*Actitis hypoleucos*	A
Spotted Sandpiper		*Actitis macularius*	A
Green Sandpiper		*Tringa ochropus*	A
Lesser Yellowlegs		*Tringa flavipes*	A
Redshank	Common Redshank	*Tringa totanus*	A
Wood Sandpiper		*Tringa glareola*	A
Spotted Redshank		*Tringa erythropus*	A
Greenshank	Common Greenshank	*Tringa nebularia*	A
Kittiwake	Black-legged Kittiwake	*Rissa tridactyla*	A
Bonaparte's Gull		*Chroicocephalus philadelphia*	A

Dec 8th	1154	1	Winpenny hide, Pulborough Brooks	Sussex	231
Sep 24th	1120	3	Royal Naval Air Station, Dale	Pembrokeshire	186
Jul 17th	1400	1	Brandon Marsh SSSI	Warwickshire	160
Aug 28th	1512	1	Minsmere RSPB	Suffolk	174
Sep 11th	1328	1	Frampton RSPB	Lincolnshire	178
Mar 14th	1510	5	Townlease Farm	Wiltshire	104
Mar 27th	952	1	Slimbridge WWT	Gloucestershire	107
Jan 1st	1430	1	South Lake Hide, Slimbridge WWT	Gloucestershire	72
Oct 5th	1845	1	Hilda Quick Hide, Lower Moors, St Mary's	Cornwall	196
May 19th	1232	1	Rye Harbour Nature Reserve	Sussex	132
May 28th	1325	1	Slimbridge WWT	Gloucestershire	138
Sep 15th	830	1	between Axbridge entrance to boat club, Cheddar Reservoir	Somerset	180
Feb 6th	1153	1	Porthpean	Cornwall	86
May 11th	1823	1	Portbury Wharf Nature Reserve, North Pool Hide	Somerset	129
Jan 2nd	1000	1	Chew Lake, Moreton Hide	Somerset	69
Jul 20th	1119	1	Parrinder South Hide, Titchwell RSPB	Norfolk	161
Jan 1st	1400	<20	Slimbridge WWT	Gloucestershire	79
May 5th	1150	2	Coombe Hill Meadows, Grundon Hide, GWT	Gloucestershire	126
Jan 10th	930	1	Staithe Lane, Thornham old harbour	Norfolk	74
Jan 17th	1530	2	Dawlish Warren NNR, Estuary	Devonshire	78
Apr 9th	1838	>800	Splash Point, Seaford	Sussex	112
Feb 25th	1330	1	Spit, Teignmouth	Devonshire	97

Black-headed Gull		Chroicocephalus ridibundus	A
Little Gull		Hydrocoloeus minutus	A
Ross's Gull		Rhodostethia rosea	A
Franklin's Gull		Leucophaeus pipixcan	A
Mediterranean Gull		Ichthyaetus melanocephalus	A
Common Gull	Mew Gull	Larus canus	A
Ring-billed Gull		Larus delawarensis	A
Great Black-backed Gull		Larus marinus	A
Glaucous Gull		Larus hyperboreus	A
Iceland Gull		Larus glaucoides	A
Herring Gull	European Herring Gull	Larus argentatus	A
Caspian Gull		Larus cachinnans	A
Yellow-legged Gull		Larus michahellis	A
Lesser Black-backed Gull		Larus fuscus	A
Sandwich Tern		Thalasseus sandvicensis	A
Little Tern		Sternula albifrons	A
Roseate Tern		Sterna dougallii	A
Common Tern		Sterna hirundo	A
Arctic Tern		Sterna paradisaea	A
White-winged Black Tern	White-winged Tern	Chlidonias leucopterus	A
Black Tern		Chlidonias niger	A
Great Skua		Stercorarius skua	A
Pomarine Skua	Pomarine Jaeger	Stercorarius pomarinus	A

Jan 1st	NR	1	From car	Wiltshire	97
Mar 19th	1511	1	The Patch Hide, Dungeness	Kent	106
Feb 28th	1527	1	Radipole RSPB, Weymouth	Dorset	99
Nov 13th	1539	1	Radipole RSPB, Weymouth	Dorset	219
Jan 6th	1300	30	Ferry Bridge, Portland	Dorset	71
Jan 1st	845	<10	Plock Court football pitch, Gloucester	Gloucestershire	142
Jan 22nd	1500	1	Ibsley Water, Blashford Lakes Nature Reserve	Hampshire	79
Jan 6th	1230	1	Ferry Bridge, Portland	Dorset	146
Feb 5th	1130	1	Newlyn Harbour	Cornwall	85
Jan 10th	1335	1	Royal Cromer Golf Club, course	Norfolk	75
Jan 1st	NR	1	From car	Wiltshire	89
Feb 11th	1435	1	Pig Farm, Tidpit	Hampshire	89
Jan 22nd	1500	12	Ibsley Water, Blashford Lakes Nature Reserve	Hampshire	79
Jan 1st	NR	1	From car	Wiltshire	163
Mar 20th	1100	>100	John Gooders Hide, Rye Harbour Nature Reserve	Sussex	106
May 2nd	1747	7	Ferry Bridge, Portland	Dorset	125
Jul 25th	947	2	Titchfield Haven NNR, South Scrape, Meon Shore Hide	Hampshire	163
Apr 19th	1100	2	North Wall, Minsmere RSPB	Suffolk	118
Apr 26th	1739	2	Pontoon at Frampton Sailing Club	Gloucestershire	121
May 22nd	1415	2	Eyebrook Reservoir	Rutland	133
May 21st	1405	6	Pit 74, Cotswold Water Park	Wiltshire	132
Jun 8th	1107	1	Boat to Lunga	Scotland	145
Sep 29th	1000	1	Scillonian III, Penzance to St Mary's	Cornwall	188

Arctic Skua	Parasitic Jaeger	*Stercorarius parasiticus*	A
Common Guillemot	Common Murre	*Uria aalge*	A
Razorbill		*Alca torda*	A
Black Guillemot		*Cepphus grylle*	A
Puffin	Atlantic Puffin	*Fratercula arctica*	A
Rock Dove		*Columba livia*	AC4E*
Stock Dove		*Columba oenas*	A
Woodpigeon	Common Wood Pigeon	*Columba palumbus*	A
Turtle Dove	European Turtle Dove	*Streptopelia turtur*	A
Collared Dove	Eurasian Collared Dove	*Streptopelia decaocto*	A
Cuckoo	Common Cuckoo	*Cuculus canorus*	A
Barn Owl	Western Barn Owl	*Tyto alba*	AE*
Snowy Owl		*Bubo scandiacus*	AE
Tawny Owl		*Strix aluco*	A
Little Owl		*Athene noctua*	C1E*
Short-eared Owl		*Asio flammeus*	A
Nightjar	European Nightjar	*Caprimulgus europaeus*	A
Swift	Common Swift	*Apus apus*	A
Kingfisher	Common Kingfisher	*Alcedo atthis*	A
Hoopoe	Eurasian Hoopoe	*Upupa epops*	AE
Lesser Spotted Woodpecker		*Dryobates minor*	A
Great Spotted Woodpecker		*Dendrocopos major*	A
Green Woodpecker	European Green Woodpecker	*Picus viridis*	A
Kestrel	Common Kestrel	*Falco tinnunculus*	A

May 13th	715	4	Portland Bill	Dorset	129
Jan 6th	1109	>100	Portland Bill	Dorset	85
Jan 6th	1445	2	Old Castle, Portland Bill	Dorset	71
Mar 20th	1500	1	Sovereign Harbour, Eastbourne	Sussex	106
Jun 8th	1040	>250	Boat to Lunga	Scotland	145
Jun 7th	1055	>20	Isle of Mull	Scotland	144
Jan 18th	NR	1	From car	Wiltshire	41
Jan 1st	NR	1	From car	Wiltshire	41
May 7th	1248	1	Otmoor RSPB Reserve	Oxfordshire	126
Jan 1st	NR	1	From car	Wiltshire	41
Apr 18th	2001	1	Island Mere Hide, Minsmere RSPB	Suffolk	118
Jan 7th	1809	1	Townlease Farm, Hullavington	Wiltshire	72
Apr 6th	940	1	North side Carn Lidli, St David's Head	Pembrokeshire	111
Jan 1st	1145	1	Frampton Court Lake	Gloucestershire	67
Feb 2nd	1900	2	Townlease Farm, Hullavington	Wiltshire	83
Jan 24th	1419	3	Aust Wharf, Bristol	Gloucestershire	79
May 22nd	2112	1	Kelling Heath	Norfolk	134
Apr 24th	1629	1	Lodmoor, Weymouth	Dorset	120
Jan 1st	1230	1	Frampton Court lake	Gloucestershire	67
Apr 15th	925	1	Portland Bill, Observatory garden	Sussex	114
Apr 1st	1245	1	Savernake forest	Wiltshire	108
Jan 1st	1230	1	Frampton Court Lake	Gloucestershire	101
Jan 2nd	1300	1	Between Moreton and Stratford hide, Chew Lake	Somerset	69
Jan 1st	NR	1	From car	Wiltshire	42

Red-footed Falcon		*Falco vespertinus*	A
Merlin		*Falco columbarius*	A
Hobby	Eurasian Hobby	*Falco subbuteo*	A
Peregrine	Peregrine Falcon	*Falco peregrinus*	AE
Ring-necked Parakeet	Rose-ringed Parakeet	*Psittacula krameri*	C1E*
Red-backed Shrike		*Lanius collurio*	A
Daurian Shrike	Isabelline Shrike	*Lanius isabellinus*	A
Great Grey Shrike		*Lanius excubitor*	A
Woodchat Shrike		*Lanius senator*	A
Red-eyed Vireo		*Vireo olivaceus*	A
Golden Oriole	Eurasian Golden Oriole	*Oriolus oriolus*	A
Jay	Eurasian Jay	*Garrulus glandarius*	A
Magpie	Eurasian Magpie	*Pica pica*	A
Chough	Red-billed Chough	*Pyrrhocorax pyrrhocorax*	AE*
Jackdaw	Western Jackdaw	*Coloeus monedula*	A
Rook		*Corvus frugilegus*	A
Carrion Crow		*Corvus corone*	A
Hooded Crow		*Corvus cornix*	A
Raven	Northern Raven	*Corvus corax*	A
Waxwing	Bohemian Waxwing	*Bombycilla garrulus*	AE
Coal Tit		*Periparus ater*	A
Crested Tit	European Crested Tit	*Lophophanes cristatus*	A
Marsh Tit		*Poecile palustris*	A
Willow Tit		*Poecile montanus*	A
Blue Tit	Eurasian Blue Tit	*Cyanistes caeruleus*	A
Great Tit		*Parus major*	A
Penduline Tit	Eurasian Penduline Tit	*Remiz pendulinus*	A

May 30th	1325	1	Isle Brewers	Somerset	138
Feb 5th	1430	1	Cott Valley	Cornwall	85
Apr 26th	1110	4	Tor View Hide, Ham Wall RSPB	Somerset	120
Jan 27th	1635	1	Slimbridge WWT	Gloucestershire	81
Feb 12th	1550	1	St Anne's Church, Oldand Common, Bristol	Gloucestershire	90
May 8th	1533	1	Dawlish Warren NNR	Devonshire	128
Oct 14th	1553	1	Beach path, Thurlestone Golf Club	Devonshire	197
Jan 19th	1206	1	Crabtree Hill, Forest of Dean	Gloucestershire	78
Sep 24th	1537	1	Sea Rivers Caravan site, Ynyslas	Ceredigion	187
Oct 19th	1602	1	Bryher	Cornwall	202
May 2nd	1400	1	Portland Bill	Sussex	125
Jan 2nd	1300	1	Between Moreton and Stratford hide, Chew Lake	Somerset	69
Jan 1st	NR	1	From car	Wiltshire	175
Feb 5th	1420	2	Cott Valley	Cornwall	85
Jan 1st	845	1	Plock Court, Gloucester	Gloucestershire	42
Jan 1st	NR	1	From car	Wiltshire	18
Jan 1st	NR	1	From car	Wiltshire	18
Jun 7th	625	1	Fort William, on route to Oban	Scotland	143
Jan 7th	1300	2	Corsham Court churchyard	Wiltshire	85
Nov 28th	1140	9	Aldi car park, Hessle, York	Yorkshire	227
Jan 1st	1130	1	Frampton Court Estate	Gloucestershire	23
Jun 5th	1300	1	Loch Mallachie	Scotland	143
Jan 19th	1012	1	Highnam Woods RSPB	Gloucestershire	78
Oct 24th	1242	2	Undisclosed	Wiltshire	208
Jan 1st	1130	1	Frampton Court Estate	Gloucestershire	20
Jan 1st	1130	1	Frampton Court Estate	Gloucestershire	23
Jan 1st	830	1	Plock Court, Gloucester	Gloucestershire	66

Bearded Tit	Bearded Reedling	*Panurus biarmicus*	A
Woodlark		*Lullula arborea*	A
Skylark	Eurasian Skylark	*Alauda arvensis*	A
Shore Lark	Horned Lark	*Eremophila alpestris*	A
Sand Martin		*Riparia riparia*	A
Swallow	Barn Swallow	*Hirundo rustica*	AE
House Martin	Common House Martin	*Delichon urbicum*	A
Cetti's Warbler		*Cettia cetti*	A
Long-tailed Tit		*Aegithalos caudatus*	A
Willow Warbler		*Phylloscopus trochilus*	A
Chiffchaff	Common Chiffchaff	*Phylloscopus collybita*	A
Iberian Chiffchaff		*Phylloscopus ibericus*	A
Wood Warbler		*Phylloscopus sibilatrix*	A
Dusky Warbler		*Phylloscopus fuscatus*	A
Pallas's Warbler	Pallas's Leaf Warbler	*Phylloscopus proregulus*	A
Yellow-browed Warbler		*Phylloscopus inornatus*	A
Hume's Warbler	Hume's Leaf Warbler	*Phylloscopus humei*	A
Greenish Warbler		*Phylloscopus trochiloides*	A
Great Reed Warbler		*Acrocephalus arundinaceus*	A
Sedge Warbler		*Acrocephalus schoenobaenus*	A
Reed Warbler	Eurasian Reed Warbler	*Acrocephalus scirpaceus*	A
Melodious Warbler		*Hippolais polyglotta*	A

Feb 23rd	1214	2	Lodmoor RSPB	Dorset	95
Apr 18th	1640	2	Westleton Heath NNR	Suffolk	118
Jan 6th	1300	7	Ferry Bridge, Portland	Dorset	71
Jan 9th	1450	1	Field south of light-house, Happisburgh	Norfolk	74
Mar 28th	1656	3	Kent End Quarry, Cotswold Water Park	Gloucestershire	107
Apr 4th	1410	1	Hungerford Marsh Nature Reserve	Berkshire	109
Apr 9th	1559	3	West Rise Marsh, Eastbourne	Sussex	112
Jan 1st	1500	1	Slimbridge WWT	Gloucestershire	127
Jan 1st	850	2	Plock Court, Gloucester	Gloucestershire	207
Apr 5th	1115	1	Home garden, Sutton Benger	Wiltshire	110
Mar 11th	1544	2	Selsey Bill,	Sussex	103
Jul 5th	1348	1	Thurstaston	Merseyside	156
May 1st	1600	1	Nagshead RSPB, Forest of Dean	Gloucestershire	124
Oct 21st	1338	1	Porthgwarra	Cornwall	206
Nov 5th	1517	1	Beachy Head	Sussex	215
Sep 29th	1444	1	Newford Duck Pond, St Mary's	Cornwall	188
Jan 9th	1335	1	Shangri-la Chalet, Waxham	Norfolk	73
May 24th	848	1	Titchwell, Norfolk	Norfolk	135
Jun 16th	958	1	Elney Lake, Fen Drayton RSPB	Cambridgeshire	151
Apr 9th	1220	7	Rye Harbour Nature Reserve	Sussex	112
Apr 9th	1530	1	West Rise Marsh, Eastbourne	Sussex	112
Aug 21st	1240	1	Beachy Head	Sussex	174

Grasshopper Warbler	Common Grasshopper Warbler	*Locustella naevia*	A
Savi's Warbler		*Locustella luscinioides*	A
Blackcap	Eurasian Blackcap	*Sylvia atricapilla*	A
Garden Warbler		*Sylvia borin*	A
Barred Warbler		*Sylvia nisoria*	A
Lesser Whitethroat		*Sylvia curruca*	A
Whitethroat	Common Whitethroat	*Sylvia communis*	A
Dartford Warbler		*Sylvia undata*	A
Firecrest	Common Firecrest	*Regulus ignicapilla*	A
Goldcrest		*Regulus regulus*	A
Wren	Eurasian Wren	*Troglodytes troglodytes*	A
Nuthatch	Eurasian Nuthatch	*Sitta europaea*	A
Treecreeper	Eurasian Treecreeper	*Certhia familiaris*	A
Grey Catbird		*Dumetella carolinensis*	A
Rose-coloured Starling	Rosy Starling	*Pastor roseus*	AE
Starling	Common Starling	*Sturnus vulgaris*	A
Ring Ouzel		*Turdus torquatus*	A
Blackbird	Common Blackbird	*Turdus merula*	A
Fieldfare		*Turdus pilaris*	A
Redwing		*Turdus iliacus*	A
Song Thrush		*Turdus philomelos*	A
Mistle Thrush		*Turdus viscivorus*	A
Spotted Flycatcher		*Muscicapa striata*	A
Robin	European Robin	*Erithacus rubecula*	A
Bluethroat		*Luscinia svecica*	A

Apr 18th	1813	1	Carlton & Oulton Marshes Nature Reserve, Lowestoft	Suffolk	117
Apr 19th	957	1	Island Mere Hide, Minsmere RSPB	Suffolk	118
Apr 11th	1506	4	Kingsgate Park, Yate	Gloucestershire	113
Apr 26th	1107	1	Ham Wall RSPB	Somerset	120
Oct 6th	1744	1	Porthellic, St Mary's	Cornwall	197
Apr 18th	1625	1	Minsmere RSPB	Suffolk	118
Apr 26th	1120	1	Ham Wall RSPB	Somerset	120
Feb 21st	940	2	Slufters Enclosure, New Forest National Park	Hampshire	93
Mar 19th	1154	4	Denge Marsh rd., Dungeness	Kent	105
Jan 2nd	1230	1	Moreton Hide, Chew Lake	Somerset	119
Jan 1st	1130		Plock Court, Gloucester	Gloucestershire	44
Jan 1st	1140		Frampton Court Lake	Gloucestershire	
Jan 9th	1030	1	Santon Warren	Norfolk	72
Oct 21st	950	1	Treeve Moor House, Land's End	Cornwall	204
Oct 4th	1121	1	Lower Town, St Martins	Cornwall	194
Jan 1st	NR	1	From car	Wiltshire	194
Apr 4th	1715	3	Linkey Down, Ashton Rowant	Oxfordshire	110
Jan 1st	1140	1	Frampton	Gloucestershire	44
Jan 7th	900	1	Townlease Farm, Hullavington	Wiltshire	
Jan 1st	900	<10	Plock Court, Gloucester	Gloucestershire	
Jan 1st	740	1	Home garden, Sutton Benger	Wiltshire	205
Jan 7th	1500	2	Pinchin's Mill, Box	Wiltshire	
May 27th	1630	3	Nagshead RSPB	Gloucestershire	137
Jan 1st	730	1	Home garden, Sutton Benger	Wiltshire	57
Mar 19th	1208	4	Denge Marsh rd., Dungeness	Kent	105

Nightingale	Common Nightingale	*Luscinia megarhynchos*	A
Pied Flycatcher	European Pied Flycatcher	*Ficedula hypoleuca*	A
Red-breasted Flycatcher		*Ficedula parva*	A
Black Redstart		*Phoenicurus ochruros*	A
Redstart	Common Redstart	*Phoenicurus phoenicurus*	A
Whinchat		*Saxicola rubetra*	A
Stonechat	European Stonechat	*Saxicola rubicola*	A
Stejneger's Stonechat		*Saxicola stejnegeri*	A
Wheatear	Northern Wheatear	*Oenanthe oenanthe*	A
Pied Wheatear		*Oenanthe pleschanka*	A
Dipper	White-throated Dipper	*Cinclus cinclus*	A
House Sparrow		*Passer domesticus*	A
Tree Sparrow	Eurasian Tree Sparrow	*Passer montanus*	A
Dunnock		*Prunella modularis*	A
Yellow Wagtail	Western Yellow Wagtail	*Motacilla flava*	A
Eastern Yellow Wagtail		*Motacilla tschutschensis*	A
Grey Wagtail		*Motacilla cinerea*	A
Pied Wagtail	White Wagtail	*Motacilla alba*	A
Richard's Pipit		*Anthus richardi*	A
Tawny Pipit		*Anthus campestris*	A
Meadow Pipit		*Anthus pratensis*	A
Tree Pipit		*Anthus trivialis*	A
Water Pipit		*Anthus spinoletta*	A
Rock Pipit	Eurasian Rock Pipit	*Anthus petrosus*	A
Chaffinch	Common Chaffinch	*Fringilla coelebs*	AE

Apr 18th	1900	1	Westleton Heath	Suffolk	118
Apr 12th	1115	1	Kingsgate Park, Yate	Gloucestershire	113
Oct 2nd	1505	1	Pool Road, Tresco	Cornwall	194
Jan 1st	1100	1	Dock Road, Sharpness	Gloucestershire	66
Apr 4th	1656	1	Linkey Down, Ashton Rowant	Oxfordshire	110
May 4th	1510	2	Chipping Sodbury Common	Gloucestershire	126
Jan 6th	1110	1	Portland Bill	Dorset	209
Oct 29th	1241	1	Meadow Lane, Salthouse	Norfolk	209
Mar 24th	1409	3	Portland Bill	Dorset	107
Nov 8th	1036	1	Dove Point sea wall, Meols	Merseyside	216
Feb 15th	1530	1	Great Berry Quarry, Lydbrook, Forest Dean	Gloucestershire	91
Jan 1st	845	>10	Plock Court, Gloucester	Gloucestershire	96
Jan 26th	1118	>100	Avebury Trusloe	Wiltshire	80
Jan 1st	845	1	Plock Court, Gloucester	Gloucestershire	
Apr 9th	1627	3	West Rise Marsh, Eastbourne	Sussex	112
Oct 16th	1055	1	Airfield terminal, St Mary's	Cornwall	200
Jan 1st	845	1	Plock Court, Gloucester	Gloucestershire	196
Jan 1st	1300	1	Slimbridge WWT	Gloucestershire	
Jan 13th	1100	1	Fields by river, Arlingham	Gloucestershire	76
Sep 30th	1145	1	Great Popplestone, Bryher	Cornwall	189
Jan 6th	1230	1	Ferrybridge, Portland	Dorset	109
Apr 2nd	1400	1	Sand Point, Middle Hope National Trust	Somerset	109
Feb 7th	1320	8	Chapel Amble	Cornwall	87
Jan 6th	1105	<5	Portland Bill	Dorset	86
Jan 1st	1130	1	Frampton	Gloucestershire	93

Brambling		*Fringilla montifringilla*	A
Hawfinch		*Coccothraustes coccothraustes*	A
Bullfinch	Eurasian Bullfinch	*Pyrrhula pyrrhula*	A
Common Rosefinch		*Carpodacus erythrinus*	A
Greenfinch	European Greenfinch	*Chloris chloris*	AE
Twite		*Linaria flavirostris*	A
Linnet	Common Linnet	*Linaria cannabina*	A
Common Redpoll		*Acanthis flammea*	A
Lesser Redpoll		*Acanthis cabaret*	A
Arctic Redpoll		*Acanthis hornemanni*	A
Crossbill	Red Crossbill	*Loxia curvirostra*	A
Goldfinch	European Goldfinch	*Carduelis carduelis*	A
Siskin	Eurasian Siskin	*Spinus spinus*	A
Corn Bunting		*Emberiza calandra*	A
Yellowhammer		*Emberiza citrinella*	A
Ortolan Bunting		*Emberiza hortulana*	AE
Cirl Bunting		*Emberiza cirlus*	A
Little Bunting		*Emberiza pusilla*	A
Reed Bunting	Common Reed Bunting	*Emberiza schoeniclus*	A
Lapland Bunting	Lapland Longspur	*Calcarius lapponicus*	A
Snow Bunting		*Plectrophenax nivalis*	A
Total			313

Feb 21st	1230	20	Mark Ash Wood, New Forest	Hampshire	93
Jan 7th	1315	4	Corsham Court church-yard, Corsham	Wiltshire	72
Jan 1st	NR	1	From car	Wiltshire	201
Oct 15th	1402	1	Recycling centre, St. Mary's	Cornwall	199
Jan 10th	1200	<5	Titchwell RSPB	Norfolk	45
Jan 10th	905	17	Old Harbour, Thornham	Norfolk	74
Jan 6th	1100	20	Portland bill	Dorset	101
Jan 10th	1400	15	Cromer	Norfolk	76
Jan 4th	1005	1	Noah's Lake, Shapwick Heath NNR	Somerset	70
Jan 10th	1400	2	Cromer	Norfolk	75
Jan 19th	1200	1	Crabtree Hill, Forest of Dean	Gloucestershire	78
Jan 1st	NR	1	From car	Wiltshire	92
Mar 15th	1455	1	Nagshead RSPB	Gloucestershire	104
Jan 26th	1130	30	Windmill Hill, Avebury Trusloe	Wiltshire	80
Jan 26th	1124	50	Windmill Hill, Avebury Trusloe	Wiltshire	80
Sep 15th	1405	1	Portsdown Hill, Cosham	Hampshire	182
Mar 8th	1029	2	Labrador Bay RSPB	Devonshire	102
Oct 20th	1240	1	Porth Mellon, St Mary's, Scilly Isles	Cornwall	203
Jan 10th	1012	2	Titchwell RSPB	Norfolk	101
Oct 1st	1708	1	Golf Course, St Mary's	Cornwall	193
Jan 9th	1420	31	Field south of light-house, Happisburgh	Norfolk	74

Other birds			
Red-breasted Goose		*Branta ruficollis*	AE*
Ruddy Shelduck		*Tadorna ferruginea*	BDE*

Variants e.g. Races/ Subspecies/hybrids			
Horned Lark		*Alpestris/hyoti/ praticola*	
White Wagtail		*Motacilla alba*	
Thayer's Gull		*Larus glaucoides thayeri*	
Italian Sparrow/hybrid?		*Passer italiae*	
Channel Wagtail		*M.f.flava x flavissima?*	

British Ornithological Union (BOU) Classification Guidelines, 1st February, 2019: www.bou.org.uk

Species in Categories A, B or C form the British List

Species in Category A have been recorded in an apparently natural state at least once since 1 January 1950.

Species in Category B have been recorded in an apparently natural state at least once between 1 January 1800 and 31 December 1949, but have not been recorded subsequently.

Species in Category C, although introduced, now derive from the resulting self-sustaining populations. View Category C sub-categories.

Species in Category D would otherwise appear in Category A, except that there is reasonable doubt that they have occurred in Britain in a natural state. Species placed only in Category D form no part of the British List, and are not included in the species totals.

Category E comprises those species that have been recorded as introductions, human-assisted transportees or escapees from captivity, whose breeding populations (if any) are thought not to be self-sustaining. Species in Category E that have bred in the wild in Britain are designated as E*.

Jan 1st	1420	1	ESCAPE, Slimbridge, Holden Tower	Gloucestershire	68
Sep 9th	1600	1	B CATEGORY, RSPB Frampton Marsh	Lincolnshire	178
Jan 31st	1230	1	Staines Reservoir	Surrey	82
Feb 1st	1000	2	New Passage, by the Pill	Gloucestershire	199
Feb 11th	1620	1	Pig Farm, Tidpit	Hampshire	89
Feb 25th	1100	1	Included in BUBO 2018 list. East Budleigh	Devonshire	96
Apr 27th	1600	1	Northwick Warth	Gloucestershire	121

British List Interpretations and Discrepancies

- For overseas birds I have adhered to the naming convention used by the IOC.
- The British list has been recorded using the British Ornithological Union (BOU) listing publicly available at the time of writing: 313 species recorded.
- Species seen have been entered on online with BUBO: 314 species recorded (includes Italian Sparrow "pending" but current understanding is DNA analysis has yet to be concluded for this bird).
- **Red-breasted Goose**, 1st January, at Slimbridge, Gloucester. Deemed likely escape.
- **Ruddy Shelduck**, 9th September, Frampton RSPB, Lincolnshire. While it appears on the BOU British list it is a 'B category' bird. According to the BOU definition: "Species in Category B are those which have been recorded in an apparently natural state at least once between 1st January 1800 and 31st December 1949 but have not been recorded subsequently. For this reason Ruddy Shelduck does not count towards the annual total of wild bird species recorded."

Acknowledgements

In producing this book there have been many selfless contributions. First, there are plenty of terrific birders, twitchers and conservationists out there who have supplied vital information on bird whereabouts, prospective locations through social media and face-to-face conversation. So often a tiny shred of information makes the difference between success and failure, or sometimes it is just sound advice, positive words of support or help with field identification. Many have become good contacts and new friends with whom I share a passion and some have even afforded a fresh perspective on how I might continue to develop my hobby during retirement years. Then there are the photographers without whose patience, talent behind the camera, and generosity I would not have been able to show so many great pictures. My only regret is that due to the usual print limitations it is impossible to reproduce the excellent image clarity that most of us enjoy on our computer screens. As an author it is one thing to find a pretty picture for your readers, but another to be able to use a photo of the actual bird seen, in the same location, and often on the very same day to keep it real. In short, they have placed trust in me not to misrepresent them, so I do hope this book goes a little way perhaps to showcasing their achievements and offering my thanks. I'd like to thank the BOU for enabling me to make use of their published British List and for guidance on selective species status interpretation; the RSPB, WWT and the many NNRs for information and reserve access. I'd like to thank RBA (Rare Bird Alert). You may argue that if you are paying for a service like RBA why the special thanks? When members of their staff take time to tweet back and take calls from you to help you locate a bird in the field, that is going beyond the expected. Great service, thank you! Finally, I would like to thank SilverWood Books for helping bring this book to successful publication, and Sylvia Sullivan for her careful editing of the text.

Abbreviations and Terms

Abbreviations

BOU	British Ornithological Union. The body aims to encourage the study of birds (ornithology) in Britain in order to understand their biology and aid their conservation.
BUBO	A free, flexible and widely used site for the comparison of birding lists. Used by top twitchers and beginners alike to post lists of birds seen each year, by country, during their lifetime, or self-found. For Britain it adopts the BOU bird species list.
CWP	Cotswold Water Park
DIC	Diploma of Imperial College
IOC	International Ornithological Congress. An open access resource of the international community of ornithologists that provides a World Bird List that has now been adopted by the BOU.
ISBG	Isles of Scilly Bird Group
LEO	Long-eared Owl
LSW	Lesser Spotted Woodpecker
PhD	Doctor of Philosophy
RBA	Rare Bird Alert. Established in 1991 and based in Norwich, Rare Bird Alert is a long-running instant bird news service
RLB	Rough-legged Buzzard
RSPB	Royal Society for the Protection of Birds

SWAT	(Special Weapons and Tactics) team is a USA law enforcement unit which uses specialized or military equipment and tactics
WOS	Wiltshire Ornithological Society
WWT	Wildfowl & Wetlands Trust

Terms

Bins	Binoculars
Birder	Someone who studies, identifies, records (lists) birds.
Dip	To travel but fail to see a bird you wanted to see.
Dude	A posh birder, who doesn't really know all that much about birds.
Egging	A term often used to describe the hobby of unlawful egg collecting. (sometimes also known as nesting) back in the 1960s and early 1970s.
Gen	Information on the rare bird, e.g. species, description, location, habit.
Jizz	The overall impression or appearance of a bird garnered from such features as shape, posture, flying style or other habitual movements, size and colouration combined with voice, habitat and location.
Mega	A very rare bird indeed to tick, e.g. one perhaps recorded only a handful of times in the UK previously.
Scope	Telescope
Tick	The tick put alongside a species when you see it.
Twitcher	Someone who is obsessed with ticks, races around the country chasing and frantically collecting (ticking) rare birds.

An excellent source and more extensive explanation of the peculiar terms and language adopted by twitchers and birders is Bill Oddie's *Little Black Bird Book*, first published in 1980 by Eyre Methuen Ltd.